THE CHUM STORY

THE CHUM STORY

From the Charts to Your Hearts

ALLEN FARRELL

Published in 2001 by
Stoddart Publishing Co. Limited
895 Don Mills Road, 400-2 Park Centre,
Toronto, Canada M3C 1W3

www.stoddartpub.com

To order Stoddart books please contact General Distribution Services
Tel. (416) 213-1919   Fax (416) 213-1917
Email cservice@genpub.com

10 9 8 7 6 5 4 3 2 1

NATIONAL LIBRARY OF CANADA CATALOGUING IN PUBLICATION DATA
Farrell, Allen
The CHUM story: from the charts to your hearts
ISBN 0-7737-6263-9
1. 1050 CHUM (Radio station: Toronto, Ont.) — History. I. Title.
PN1991.3.C3F37 2001   384.54'06'5713541   C2001-901989-0

Credits for cover photographs where source known: photos of CHUM-a-Go-Go float, Bob Laine, the CHUM satellite station, the CHUM studio, Jay Nelson, Mike Darow and Jane Morgan, and Dick Clark by Neil Newton Photography; photo of Elvis Presley by Rick Shaban Promotions; photos of Al Boliska and Millie Moriak by Graphic Artists Photographers. Every reasonable effort has been made to obtain reprint permissions. The publisher will gladly receive any information that will help to rectify, in subsequent editions, any inadvertent errors or omissions.

Cover and Text Design: Bill Douglas at The Bang

THE CANADA COUNCIL | LE CONSEIL DES ARTS
FOR THE ARTS | DU CANADA
SINCE 1957 | DEPUIS 1957

We acknowledge for their financial support of our publishing program the Canada Council for the Arts, the Ontario Arts Council, and the Government of Canada through the Book Publishing Industry Development Program (BPIDP).

Printed and bound in Canada

This book is dedicated to the CHUM listeners. I have always suspected that they were almost as crazy as we were.

And to Allan Waters. Since his innate modesty won't permit him to take the credit for CHUM's success, I'll allow him to take the blame. Gotcha!

Contents

PREFACE

This book follows CHUM Radio from its inception in 1945 until 1967, perhaps the most colourful years of a very colourful history. During this period, CHUM first survived, then went from strength to strength as one of North America's most explosive stations. By '67, CHUM was well-poised to harness the hope and promise of Canada's Centennial, and manage the challenges and opportunities of the tumultuous, change-driven final third of the 20th century.

To tell the CHUM story, I have focused on the remarkable people who lived this true-life adventure. I feel confident you'll like them. They are a fun-loving, unpredictable, talented lot.

From the beginning of this project, I have worried about being misunderstood. (So did Nixon, and look what happened to him. He's dead.) A generation or two ago, I was involved with most of the wild, weird, and questionable promotions of CHUM during a dynamic growth period. My fear — let me lay it on you — is that by mentioning myself in a number of events in this book, you'll think that I think my contribution was more important than those of my gifted and highly productive associates at CHUM. This is patently not true: not true that it was, and not true that I think it was.

When I outlined this fear to my wife, CHUM personnel, friends, unfrocked clergy, and sherry-breathed strangers, they all expressed some version of this piece of sagacity: "Quit your whining and kvetching and just bloody write the book!"

Tough love, but good advice. I took it.

Allen Farrell
July 2001

INTRODUCTION

What was it about CHUM that made it so memorable to so many people? I'll state categorically that it was because CHUM was an original.

If other stations across North America ran contests — and they *did* — CHUM launched *more* contests, *bigger* contests, *wilder* contests. While a number of stations encouraged their jocks to make public appearances, CHUM announcers were constantly flingin' their fandango in their listeners' faces, lounging in their laps, and — dare I say it? — creeping into their listeners' hearts. Cliché, thy name is Farrell.

Just as cat fanciers tell us that the Siamese is more "cat" — fiercer, sexier, more family oriented, and more territorial — CHUM was simply more station.

And when our direct competition tried something, anything, of merit, we'd slap them upside the head with a wet flounder and give them the old raspberry on-air. (It was a wet *seal*, actually, that we'll harp on later.) But if a competitor's efforts were tepid, we'd ignore, ignore.

To attempt to keep pace with CHUM (as CKEY tried unsuccessfully to do), you'd need a staff with the fierce competitiveness of a hockey team in the finals, the passion to give 150 percent, the brass to embarrass themselves in public, the hubris to take unheard-of programming risks, and the gall and grit to drop their pants and moon the competition, make love to their listeners, never cheat on them, generally work like husky dogs in a sled race, and persist and persist and persist.

CHUM was not a rock 'n' roll station. Huh? Sure it was Top Forty — or, rather Top *Fifty* — but not in the way rockers were defined across the continent. CHUM broke all the rules and created a few of its own.

The veracity of this was borne out at a clutch of major conferences in the U.S.A., where thousands of radio managers and their staffs roared in laughter or sat back in amazement at, and great appreciation of, CHUM's

audacity and originality. CHUM, perhaps more than anyone, was asked time after time to play samples of the station's rule-breaking, offbeat approaches to entertaining listeners and building audiences.

It's a mug's game to claim that CHUM or any station was the best. Best at *what*? When? In what kind of competitive market? Programming what? For how long? Ad nauseum.

But by any standards, CHUM had it all: leadership, vision, financial management, super-aggressive sales, programming insight, catch-fire competitiveness, unreasonable expectations of performance, and perhaps the finest pool of on-air and behind-the-scenes talent ever housed under one rocker roof.

The result was audience and industry acclaim, plus extraordinary business success. And a whole lot of great memories. Ask anyone who listened.

The CHUM story began with the creation of a 250-watt radio station in Toronto in 1945. Named CHUM, and located at 1050 on the dial, it was labelled a "dawn-till-dusker," a station licensed to broadcast only when the sun was officially "shining."

This struggling little station became the cornerstone of what was to become an astonishing company.

As of the year 2001, the CHUM Group boasts radio and television stations coast-to-coast in Canada. They encompass 28 radio stations, seven television stations, and 30 specialty services.

I had the privilege — and the fun — of serving CHUM as promotion director for nine years, beginning in 1958.

My intent is to tell the CHUM story from both the inside and out, to provide solid substantiation for CHUM's claims to greatness — and to do this with much the same sass, impudence, humour, irreverence, and what-the-hell attitude CHUM brought to the air. I include many quotes from those who helped build CHUM, those who still work at the station, and those who listen to it. From time to time, I simply invent conversations that happened — or *may* have happened — or *should* have happened. What *does* happen is an attempt to put your sweaty fingers on the pounding pulse of radio during those dizzy days.

FIRST DAY AT THE FUNNY FARM

"Rockin' Robin" was boppin' on my Volkswagen Bug radio. The record was back-tagged by an announcer — *I think* he was an announcer — who, in a style that defied description, declared he was the Amazing Al Boliska and launched into a gag so old it had prostate problems.

It was late September 1958, and I had been in Toronto for a whole day and a half. Today was to be my first day working for CHUM.

I summed up what I had learned so far: Etobicoke, where I temporarily roosted, was pronounced "Etobe-coe," not "Etobe-coke"; Spadina Avenue was "Spa-dye-na," not "Spa-dee-na"; and Yonge Street was pronounced "Young," not "Yawnge," boring as it had been on the weekend. I also knew that CHUM Radio was located at 250 Adelaide Street West.

Nervous, I had arrived a bit early, and instead of going right in, I crossed to the south side of the street to get a better look. First impression of the CHUM facilities was of a large, loose packing-case stacked askew over the glories of Steve's Open Kitchen. Steve's was primarily a coffee and short-order joint and its exhausted six-time-loser cooking oil coated the air and clung to anything it touched.

It was time to face the music, so to speak, so I checked out my appearance in the ungreased portion of Steve's windows. A fresh, young face topped with an Ivy League haircut looked back at me. My fashionable New York–cut suit was well-pressed and met muster, and my shoes gleamed in the early morning sunlight. The comedy dates J.J. Richards and I had recently played at the Petroleum Club in Edmonton (as Farrell & Richards) demanded we be ahead of fashion, so I knew I looked sharp. I was reet. Cool. And definitely zoot.

On that positive note, I stepped cautiously into the Stygian gloom of the stairwell leading up to CHUM. The steps were badly warped and covered with deep worn patches. Climbing them in the near dark approximated the stomach-lurching vertigo one got the first time in the Fun House at a fair.

Reaching the summit, I found myself under the inquisitive stare of receptionist Betty MacCallum. She greeted me and invited me to sit down in what was then laughingly called the reception area. Since there were no chairs, I perched myself gingerly on a stack of magazines, first dusting it off to protect my dudey duds. It turned out that the man who had hired me, Al Slaight, was out on a call, and someone else would squire me around and get me settled.

An attractive, well-turned-out young woman soon appeared, introduced herself as Lyn Salloum, and asked warmly if I would follow her, please.

First person I met had an office just off reception. A grinning, rather excited man jumped up, came around his desk, pumped my hand enthusiastically, and said, "I'm Phil Stone." Then, pausing, as if for effect, he added, "Of course, when I'm on the air, I'm Still Phone. Heh, heh. Still Phone." I made a mental note to get used to this eastern humour.

We moved on towards the announce studios. Peering through the glass, I made out a middle-aged, shortish man who sounded as though he was in distress. In a style that could be described as Early-American Choking, he was advising listeners, "If you have a house to sell, you should call Mann and Martell." The announcer identified himself as "Your little pal Harvey." Lyn said his full name was Harvey Dobbs.

Someone had just come out of the studio and was standing there with a sort of bemused, distracted air. Lyn said it was Al Boliska. She made the introductions, and I was interested to match up the person with that rather strange voice I had experienced on the way in.

From the way Boliska stood and the manner in which he was dressed, my first impression was of Little Boy Lost meets the Flea-Market Man.

Al hung his head shyly to the side, much as a timid, nervous dog might. His face was smudged with a two- or three-day growth of beard and there was a spot of jelly on the side of his mouth, a memento from his breakfast doughnut.

Encased in unpolished, scuffed shoes, one of which had a loose sole that flapped, Al's toes turned in, in an "Ah shucks, ma'am" manner. The shoes were partly obscured by grease-stained, baggy pants held up by hard-pressed buttons. Two inches above, a gut protruded, topped with a brushed-wool sweater that might have been woven by drunken sheep.

In his right hand, Al was holding a large coffee cup that he was nervously squeezing. Unobserved by him, coffee was running down inside his shirt and dripping profusely off the elbow of his sweater.

Tearing my eyes away from this spectacle, I put out my hand and said, "Hi, I'm Allen Farrell."

In response, Boliska thrust his coffee-cup hand towards me, slopped liquid over his wrist, hastily transferred the cup to his left hand, wiped off his right on his pants, and placed this sugary, sticky mitt in mine. "Welcome aboard," said Al in a bashful, friendly way. He held a kind of sickly smile for a few seconds, then ran totally out of conversation. Just as I was about to jump in, he said, "Well, you'll probably want to meet the rest of the guys, so I'll . . . just . . . uh . . ." With that, he sort of shuffled around the corner, trailing drops of coffee.

Lyn looked at me and said, "Don't worry, we can always find him. Just follow the coffee spots." Little did I know how prophetic that statement was.

So far my impression of CHUM and CHUM people was that they were amiable, but rather down-at-heel. Lyn brought me to a brief stop to say hello to a smiling Millie Moriak buried in a mousehole-sized record library, and to Fred Snyder, chief operator, who was recording commercials. Lyn then gave me a fast look around the second studio, which was distinguished only by an open beer-case on the turntable.

Next I was whisked off to the Copy department. Here I received a second personality impression, P.B. (post-Boliska).

While I was shaking hands with copywriter Madeline Shoveller, a largish person charged into the room and ran around behind my back, mumbling something. Puzzled, and a bit alarmed, I tried to turn and face this berserker, but he was too fast for me and again ran around behind my back. Only now, I could hear what he was saying: "Where's the knife?" We continued our pas de deux until I faked one way and turned the other to face this mystery man. I was looking at Larry Solway.

Before I could ask him what the hell he was doing, he said, "You're Farrell, right?" I nodded and he rushed on. "You write, right? And create gags? And you're also an actor? Right?" I allowed as that was true and added, "So — ?"

Solway's terse reply: "So, everything! So . . . am I!" Pointing behind me: "So, where's the knife you're going to plunge in my back?"

As he waited for an answer, I had focused on his nostrils, which were dilating and contracting with alarming velocity. I felt he might become airborne at any moment. Lyn Salloum stepped in and diplomatically suggested we had other people to meet.

We continued our odyssey. I was told that

Allan Waters — whoever he might be — was out of town and that I'd meet him later in the week.

Finally we stopped before what I thought was a storage closet. "Here's your office," Lyn said cheerily. It was a space approximately 12 x 9 feet, but "space" was a misnomer, as it was full of things.

One was hundreds of horny pictures. They depicted a purple monster with one eye and a long horn. Lyn smiled, "That was CHUM's Draw the Purple People Eater Contest. We had no place to put the entries, so . . ."

Another was a desk which, Lyn informed me, was only half mine. It seemed a John Spragge used it nights and on weekends, so we would share drawers, if you'll pardon the expression. The space was also full of mail bins for contest entries. And it doubled as a place for announcers to hang out between shifts.

Unhappily, that was only part of the story. This den was also inhabited by another creature. CHUM's lack of recording space had forced someone called Harvey Kirck and some old Ampex equipment into one corner, where he was taping at the moment. Harvey knew I was new, sensed I did not know my way around, and so, when I was talking to Lyn, and as he wanted to record an interview, he simply shouted, "SHUT THE FUCK UP!" And I did.

As Lyn blushed and I recovered my composure in silence, I mentally tagged this office as an upholstered sewer overlooking the mattress factory. In reality, its windows looked out on the large, stinking garbage cans from an adjoining resaurant — where garbage was a *spécialité de la maison*.

Still wearing my suit coat to show off, I was sweating profusely in this un-air-conditioned, hot, sticky atmosphere, and before Lyn could stop me I opened the window, only to be blindsided by the rancid miasma that had arisen. As I stood dumbstruck, words seemed to appear over the fetid fog that read, "Get out while you still can!"

A "SHUT THE GODDAMN WINDOW, TOO!" from Kirck interrupted the reverie. Lyn left me to settle in, and I sat with some rather glum thoughts at a desk that was 50 percent mine.

After Kirck left the office, I called my wife and, in a rather nervous tone, told her I'd made a dreadful mistake. My rough plan was to stick it out for a while and look around for work in an ad agency or a less zoo-like radio station.

Noon finally arrived, along with Al Slaight. He told me he was glad I was there and sounded like he meant it. After about 15 seconds of amenities, he launched into what we were going to accomplish — he on programming, me spearheading the promotions but working closely with him as we built audience.

Perhaps noticing my enthusiasm didn't match his, and seeing my eyes reading either "Tilt" or "Acme Glass Company," he stopped abruptly.

He asked, "You aren't looking around here, are you? Surely you're not being intimidated by these surroundings? Tell me I haven't made a mistake."

As I was about to demur with no little embarrassment, he added with some force, "Listen to me. We're going to turn this town on its ear. We'll drive the ratings up and take this radio station to a new plateau. And you sure as hell are going to be part of it. Right?"

I nodded a numb assent. So, fixing me with a serious eye, he took a breath, opened his briefcase, and went on. Handing me a thick file, he said, "This is the dreariest contest in the history of radio. We have it on the air. Fix it." More files and . . . "Here is a supermarket promotion that's dying even as we speak. Jazz it up." More files, more files. "Now this . . . is something that's supposed to be comic. It isn't. It's sad. Make it funny. As for this . . ."

And so it went for about five minutes: contests, promotions, slogans, and gimmicks that were supposedly dying on the vine, jocks who needed hype, and a fresh look for the CHUM Chart.

And Mr. New York–Suit's job? Fix 'em. Fix 'em all.

I gasped, a bit panicky, "And when do you want all this?"

Slaight replied with a phrase I was to hear often for years to come: "What's wrong with right now?"

Juggling an armful of files, I staggered back to my 50-percent desk in my 10-percent office, where I flopped into my chair of no defined percentage and sat panting. First checking that Harvey Kirck wasn't planning to blast me or some announcer about to take a break in the room's only other seat, I again called home and said rather humbly, "I've changed my mind. I've just met with Allan Slaight and, frankly, although this place gives a dump a bad name and some of the people are serious weirdos, all things considered, I don't feel I'm good enough to work here. I'm real worried. However, I'll give it a shot."

I peeled off my sharp jacket, loosened my silk tie, rolled up the sleeves of my white-on-white shirt and worked until 11 p.m. on my first day on the job.

I'd joined the CHUM gang, and late that night, as I drove home, I thought to myself that if they wanted crazy, I'd show them what a bona fide lunatic was all about. It felt wonderful.

PRIVATE COMMERCIAL BROADCASTING STATION

LICENCE No. **127** 19**45-46**

CALL SIGN... **C.H.U.M.**

installation and equipment at the location specified therein.

[signature]

for Controller of Radio.

DEPARTMENT OF TRANSPORT

DOMINION OF CANADA

LICENCE TO USE RADIO

Issued in accordance with the provisions of The Radio Act, 1938, and the Regulations made thereunder.

York Broadcasters Limited,
Hermant Building,
21 Dundas Square,
Toronto, Ont.

is hereby authorized to establish and operate a Private Commercial Broadcasting Station at

Township Lot 5, Concession 3, East of Yonge Street, Township of North

York, County of York, Ont., Lat: 43° 41' 11" N, Long: 79° 20' 21" W

from the date hereof until the thirty-first day of March, 19**46**., subject to the provisions of The Radio Act, 1938, and of The Canadian Broadcasting Act, 1936, and to the Regulations heretofore or here-after made thereunder.

The frequency and power of the station shall be:

Frequency	1050	kilocycles.
Tolerance	20 cycles	
Authorized power	1000	watts. (Daytime only)

of emission..A3

Chapter Two

A STATION IS BORN

POWERFUL MEDICINE: JACK Q'PART AND THE BIRTH OF CHUM

CHUM Radio came into the world on October 28, 1945, in Toronto.

GEORGE JONES (chief engineer): The original licensee was York Broadcasters Limited. The studios were located in an office suite in the Hermant Building, 21 Dundas Square. The transmitter was on Lawrence Avenue, just east of Don Mills Road on the present site of Don Mills Collegiate. CHUM was licensed to broadcast daytime only. This meant the longest it would be on the air would be in June, broadcasting 4:30 a.m. to 8 p.m. The shortest would be in December, from 7:45 a.m. to 4:45 p.m.

Moreover, CHUM had only 250 watts of power (soon to be increased to a still puny 1,000 watts). CHUM's influence was limited, to say the least. In fact, even in times when you could hear CHUM, you still couldn't hear it.

The licence-holder was Jack Q'Part, a successful entrepreneur whose main business was creating, manufacturing, and marketing patent medicines. The prime reason for the creation of CHUM was to help promote the sales of his concoctions. Part had a small advertising agency which complemented his manufacturing activities and also pumped out ads for competitors' patent medicines, such as Templeton's TRCs.

Like other early-20th-century alchemists, Jack Q'Part travelled gypsy-like around the country flogging his panaceas and nostrums. CHUM was his foray into modern marketing methods to reach a broader audience.

Stop that cough, stop that cold
In the nick of time.
Don't delay, it doesn't pay,
Take Mason's 49.

Wheeze and sneeze and even freeze,
You'll soon be feeling fine.
Call your drugstore, an'
Be sure to ask for Mason's 49.

— *Jingle for a cold remedy heard on early CHUM Radio*

Jack wired the exciting news that he had established a new radio station to Allan Waters. Allan who? Allan *Waters*. Allan had worked for Jack Q'Part before World War II called him into the RCAF. And this same radio station would ultimately inspire Waters to take the greatest flyer of his young life.

PLUCK, NOT LUCK: ALLAN WATERS

Picture a rather low-keyed, conservative man. Envisage someone who took great pains to improve and develop himself. See a salesperson, a family man, a person whose word was his bond, and you have a thumbnail sketch of Allan Waters.

ALLAN WATERS: Business is funny. People say, "Oh, you were lucky." Well, I have a favourite saying: "I don't think there's such a thing as luck." One way to make your own breaks is to do things fairly and properly.

There's no doubt Allan was strongly influenced by his dad, who had come to Toronto from England, taken a sales job in haberdashery, and worked in it successfully all his life. This influence carried into Allan's first serious part-time work, at age 13, when his father helped him get a job at Siberie's Menswear on the Danforth. For three years, Allan helped out with duties ranging from straightening the stock to sweeping the floor. But he relished those busy times when he had a chance to serve the customers. His sincere and friendly manner had him making sales from the very get-go of his career. Pay for an afternoon and evening? Two dollars. Cash. Nice pocket money, but not enough for an itch he couldn't quite locate.

Teaming up with his school pal Jimmy Sharples, Allan plunged into his first business venture. A consumer of magazines even then, he believed he had sussed out an opportunity: miniature radios. The magazine ad copy assured would-be Rockefellers that THIS IS THE OPPORTUNITY OF A LIFETIME. All you had to do was order and pay for a batch of

these miniature radios, mark up the price, advertise them, and GET! RICH! QUICK!

The young fellows formed a company called Shar-Wat and borrowed money from their fathers. Allan must have been pretty persuasive at 17, because he coaxed $300 out of his conservative father.

Allan and Jimmy wrote and placed ads in magazines. Almost instantly, orders came in briskly along with cash, and the boys eagerly shipped out radios by the mittful. Only one problem: the miniature radios didn't work well. Sometimes hardly at all. Soon refunds were flying back to irate customers. Shar-Wat closed quietly, up to its neck in debt and bum miniature radios. Allan headed back to part-time work at Siberie's and pondered how he'd repay his dad out of two dollars a week.

Two lessons emerged from the failed enterprise: believe in the power of advertising, and always research apparent opportunities meticulously.

First item on Allan's agenda after graduating from Eastern Commerce High School was to find a job, any job. He had to make some money. After all, he was in love with Marjorie Shearer, whom he had dated in high school. He answered an ad and was hired on as a clerk by the Atlas Insurance Company on Adelaide Street, where he toiled in boredom for about a year.

WATERS: Nice people, pleasant atmosphere, but the work was deadly dull.

Waters packaged himself with a two-page letter and a photo and fired them out to 10 advertising agencies. Would they hire a young keener with lots of ideas? Most sent polite refusals. One who didn't was Jack Q'Part's agency, located on McCaul Street. Part could use a decent, ambitious young man to help his patent medicine business grow. Waters joined Part and worked mainly in the agency's production end, bringing copy, photos, and layout together to create finished print ads.

This touch of security allowed Waters to marry a young woman as pleasant and down-to-earth as she was striking. Allan and Marjorie were a handsome couple.

Wes Armstrong (centre), Allan Waters (second from right), and RCAF buddies

World War II soon snatched Allan from his connubial bliss. He joined the Royal Canadian Air Force. He was 21.

In the RCAF, Waters wanted to fly, but less-than-perfect eyesight grounded him. There was nothing wrong with his ears, though, and this ex-teenage promoter of miniature radios became a wireless radar mechanic.

When the war ended, Corporal Waters, having spent four years in the service, returned to wife, hearth, and the happy task of rejoining Part, selling and hustling health products with names like "Sarnak."

AUTHOR: What was Sarnak for?
WATERS: For a number of ailments.
AUTHOR: Did it work?
WATERS: People said they liked it. And they felt much better.
AUTHOR: What was in it?
WATERS: Mostly alcohol.

PART DEPARTS: WATERS BUYS CHUM

When Jack Q'Part created CHUM, he decided to bring his agency, manufacturing, and radio businesses under one roof. He assigned Waters the task of supervising the building of new premises at 225 Mutual Street. There, Allan proved he could pound a nail as effectively as he could pound the pavement making sales calls.

The patent medicine business flourished. But CHUM was ailing. And it'd take more than a good slug of Sarnak to make it well. Furthermore, that rascal Murphy and his Law dictated that, just as Part's patent-medicine business was thriving post-war, Jack would run into serious marital difficulties. It was necessary that he divest some of his holdings.

Waters had long been determined to own something, an enterprise he could build. He inquired if he could take the patent medicine business off Part's hands. This was a field he knew and understood. Part refused, saying it was too valuable to him. So Waters asked for the radio station. Part agreed. When they came to terms, with Part helping Waters as much as he could, an important piece of broadcast history quietly took place.

Although elated by the opportunity, Waters was aware he knew squat about the broadcast field. Even that knowledge didn't prepare him for the rough ride ahead.

First things first. Before Waters could take ownership, he had to secure the financial side. And he needed help.

WATERS: As a partner in the accounting firm of Ewen & Forbes, Alex Forbes started doing the

CHUM audit in 1952. When I acquired CHUM in 1954, Alex went with me to the lawyers and the bank. None of them was enthused about the proposed deal, particularly as CHUM owed the bank $70,000, the company was losing money, and I certainly had none. Rather reluctantly, the bank went for the proposal that Alex put forward, which involved lending us additional money. When Alex and I were standing outside the bank at 20 King Street West, I asked him if he thought we could make a go of CHUM. He looked me right in the eye and said, "Sure we can." And we did!

This vital transaction not only illustrates Waters's sales abilities, it points to one of his key qualities: loyalty. In 1962, Forbes became CHUM's CFO, financial adviser, and director until Alex's retirement. Waters stayed with the Royal Bank and has had a career-long relationship.

As of December 11, 1954, Allan Waters owned CHUM Radio. He was also responsible for a heavy debt, a monthly payroll and operating expenses, a mixed bag of talented and talent-free staffers who lived on the pov-

erty line, and the damnedest hodgepodge of on-air programming imaginable.

OLD CHUMS: NEW BLOOD

CHUM, from its origins in 1945 right up to '57, when it rocked around the clock, had all the earmarks of small-town radio in an urban setting. Here was a boonies-type station struggling in a big city. Piping out a weak signal from dawn till dusk, unable to attract advertising, paying poverty wages, living minute-to-minute with creditors' cool breath (chilled by cold hearts) keeping one awake, CHUM was typical of stations in rural towns such as Port Scrofula, Ontario; Dribbling on the Vest, Nova Scotia; and Humping Buffalo, Alberta. It was poor and pressed.

Yet, like their cousins the artists — actors, dancers, painters, and all that gang — people fought to adopt this hardscrabble life. Good people. Talented people. Outstanding people.

MONTY HALL (TV host): When I came down to Toronto from Winnipeg in 1946, I was soon

Bob Hall with race results

contracted by CHUM to do a morning show. Then, at three in the afternoon, I'd also do a show from one of the theatres downtown. Lots of women in attendance, lots of prizes. I guess it was the forerunner of *Let's Make a Deal*.

Bob Hall, brother of Monty, also worked at CHUM.

BOB HALL: One manager had a reputation for being disagreeable. Early CHUM announcer Larry Mann once said to me, "Never take off your hat when you come in in the morning because you might be fired by noon." (This is the same Larry Mann who later headed for Los Angeles and who has been in so many Hollywood films.) CHUM could be a pretty wild place at times, with occasional couplings on the console. Also, if I came in early and the lights were off, I'd know it was the Toronto Police Morality Squad, shall we say, "previewing" some naughty films they'd confiscated the night before.

A great cast of characters passed through CHUM in its pre-rock days. Most did their damnedest for the station and for themselves, exhibiting their talents on-air and energetically attempting to build and entertain an audience.

B. HALL: CHUM was the first to do live horse-racing broadcasts, sponsored by — of all things — Howard's School of Safe Driving. Our intro to the race would be, "Now, we take you to Woodbine (or Dufferin or Thorncliffe Park) and Canada's outstanding racing commentator, Foster Buck Owens!" He called a great race.

Other early CHUM personnel (among many) were Gord Atkinson, a world authority on Bing Crosby; Barry Phillips, who did a show with Monty at the Berkeley Hotel called *Breakfast at the Berkeley*; Leigh Lee, one tough program director (Leigh had married on-air personality and station manager Bob Lee); and creative director Cam Langford (Cam was a paraplegic due to a car accident. When the station moved, Cam, in his wheelchair, had to be hoisted on a chain up the elevator shaft to the offices). Vern Hill announced the country program *CHUM Valley*. Later, Josh King would handle the country show. The will, the energy, and the talent were there — but there was little revenue.

B. HALL: People didn't want to pay CHUM for advertising; they wanted to contra [barter] everything. Only upside was we didn't pay for the Checker Cabs, the Silver Rail, the Brown Derby, or the Palace Pier. Everything was

contra. It was great for impressing girls, but hell for CHUM. I was hired, fired, re-hired, and quit. But the bucks I made at CHUM gave me my law degree. I look back at CHUM as halcyon days.

A notable member of the CHUM gang was Phil Stone. Having had a column in the *Toronto Star*, Phil brought a writing background to this, his first job in radio. Phil wrote commercials and planned station promotions, until he finally became a sportscaster and was soon known as CHUM's voice of horse racing.

PHIL STONE: We carried the results from both American and Canadian tracks. I was on the air every half-hour from about 1 to 6 p.m. We pretty well cornered the horse-player and bookie market.

When interviewed recently about CHUM's race results, Phil spontaneously burst into the following old introduction to the feature: "Good afternoon, sports fans. Once again, it's time for racing news, as the *Daily Sporting News* brings you the late race results, jockey changes, and the prices paid. Just remember, the *Daily Sporting News* is on sale each day at over 400 news stands and news dealers. Get your copy." Not bad for a man of 84!

Phil was an upbeat guy who loved a joke. Jewish, he'd often turn a gag on himself. He'd sidle up beside you and say, "Did you ever see a Jew Jitsu?" Phil remembers Harvey Dobbs joining CHUM.

STONE: Dobbs was not only on-air — he'd also sell commercial time. Dobbs was dedicated to good music and, although he tolerated Tony Martin and Bing Crosby, the music we often were playing, he was shell-shocked when Waters later played us a rock tape from WQAM.

Both Phil and Harvey rode the rock rocket until it was time for CHUM to youth-enize the station.

GO WEST YOUNG MAN: 250 ADELAIDE STREET

It's been said that the love of money is the root of all evil. In my experience, it's *lack* of money that's the rotten root. It certainly continued to be for that lolling-tongued, frisky, lost puppy called CHUM. Despite energetic sales efforts, advertising revenues remained tantalizingly out of reach. CKEY and CFRB were the top dogs in Toronto, and they were burying meaty bones all over the yard. Some mornings on Mutual Street, when Allan

Phil Stone warns athletes of the dangers of playing hockey against CHUM

Waters came in early, he'd find announcers carrying typewriters. He put it down to them seeking space to work, until he discovered it was a regular practice for the staff to hock the typewriters (and other equipment) to the local pawn shop for a day or two so they'd have groceries until payday. Monthly sales were only $9,000 to $10,000, while expenses reached $13,000 to $14,000 a month.

Part told Waters to sell the Mutual Street building. This was a difficult task because it had been partly customized for the radio station, and had oddly shaped rooms. Eventually, Allan sold the building to RCA. That chore completed, Waters moved CHUM to 250 Adelaide Street West. These digs were cramped, crumbly, and crummy. But they served as the launching pad for what would be a broadcast phenomenon. Besides, the cockroaches were right friendly.

Peter Nordheimer joined CHUM, little dreaming that in the near future he'd be a rock jock, with teenagers camping on his lawn to get a peek at him. For the present, Pete had just finished a stint in the boonies.

PETER NORDHEIMER: One of my early stops on the way to fame without fortune at CHUM was at CJCS, Stratford. I think almost everybody had a sort of pit stop there, even Jack Kent Cooke. My young operator had a wonderful voice and I encouraged him to get on-air. He did, at the CBC. His name: Lloyd Robertson.

Pete was very shy, but had a natural, pleasant manner about him. The gals at home liked his mild, sincere delivery, and he would ultimately find himself in an early afternoon slot, participating in some of the zaniest promotions ever conceived. For now, on Adelaide Street, he filled the announcer's chair whenever he was needed.

Announcers continued to play and do pretty well whatever they pleased. If someone was in a Hawaiian music frame of mind, they'd lei it on ya. Other personalities would team up to create a program that would eventually, like old soldiers, just fade away. Almost none of this was sponsored.

There were only four consistent sources of revenue, little though it might be. Johnny Lombardi bought blocks of time and resold them to the Italian business community. The

music was, of course, Italian, with Johnny announcing. Capish? Similar blocks of time were sold to German broadcasters. Auf Deutsch, natürlich. Phil Stone used to drive the German announcer to schnapps when he interrupted him in English twice an hour with the race results (another precious source of revenue). Occasionally, CHUM also broadcast in other languages, including Chinese. Perhaps the most valuable revenue of all came in the form of recorded sermons, often from Southern preachers. (These good ol' boys would begin their pitch for Christian cash offerings by saying, "Just put your hand on the radio as a point of contact.")

BETWEEN ROCK AND A HARD PLACE: WATERS DROPS A BOMB

CHUM's illness was chronic. What ailed it could not be remedied by a shot of Jack

Winners take home discs from an Elvis contest

Q'Part's Snake Oil (no matter how much alcohol was in it). The station needed a full blood transfusion. Word of a breakthrough cure-all that had breathed life into a number of languishing American stations crept into Canada via the trade mags. The name of this potion was Top Forty. Its active ingredient: rock 'n' roll.

On holiday in Miami in the winter of 1956–1957, Waters mixed business with pleasure and gave an early Top Forty station, WQAM, a hard listen. It wasn't exactly his musical cup of tea.

WATERS: "Hard" was the word. It was like rocks smashing together. Very hard to listen to.

CHUM librarian Millie Moriak, Marty Robbins, and production manager Phil Ladd

Nevertheless, the Waters nose sniffed opportunity and sent its owner into action. Back in Canada, his first step was to call together his on-air staff. He announced that CHUM was considering going Top Forty. Before anyone could close a gaping mouth, Waters played a tape from a Storz station. (Todd Storz, along with others like Gordon

Silver, all in a triple-testicled baritone, the effect was overwhelming.

Allan asked them to listen to other tapes, and for their comments and suggestions. He left the room wondering if he should call an ambulance. What *is* the best remedy for group shock? Meanwhile, Waters hired Phil Ladd, an American with Top Forty experience. As

On holiday in Miami in the winter of 1956-1957, Waters mixed business with pleasure and gave an early Top Forty station, WQAM, a hard listen. It wasn't exactly his musical cup of tea.

McLendon, was a founding father of Top Forty Radio. He ran a number of successful radio stations using this format.)

The CHUM staff sat listening, slack-jawed, glassy-eyed, and staring as if they'd been poleaxed. The tape exploded with rapid-fire jock-patter, upbeat station jingles, call letters repeated incessantly, cornball comedy lines, shouted news snippets, screaming oscillator sounds, and crazy contests and talk-over introductions to the dreaded rock 'n' roll. It ended and there was a ringing silence.

To announcers who traditionally tender-tonsilled the mike, breathed syrup into syllables, and purred softly furred introductions to programs with names like *Candlelight and*

well as taking an on-air shift, Ladd would serve as production manager.

A month later, Waters called a meeting of the CHUM on-air staff, plus a few production people. They filed into the room and sat. Still. Some wondered if they'd be offered a blindfold. Others contemplated their requests for a last meal.

Allan Waters had left his usual smile behind. Today, his bearing and his expression were serious. Very.

He gave the following address, which he had titled "Confidence":

"We are not going to have a lot of discussion at this meeting. I don't want anyone here to be trying to think about what is wrong with what I'm saying or how they can do something better than what I'm stating we are going to do. Our last meeting produced quite a lot of discussion from all of us but has produced few ideas from any of you. Our last meeting was held February 11, and at that time I suggested you listen to tapes that were available from successful American radio stations. I think one or two might have done a little listening, but that's all. The facts remain the same: CHUM is a poor third, or fourth, audience-wise in Toronto. CHUM has been that way for 10 years now, and I don't know about anybody else but I'm ashamed of it.

"Now, with a 24-hour operation, if we can't become a strong audience-factor in the Toronto market in 18 months, then I'm going to sell the station — or give it away. Now, I haven't been in the radio-station business as long as anyone in this room, but if I was in the shoe business and operating a poor shoe store, then I think I'd find out who is running a good shoe store and copy his style.

"That is why I've had tapes made of a number of the leading American radio stations. Since our last meeting, I've played these tapes to a few people in the Canadian radio industry. Without exception, they endorsed the idea of patterning the NEW CHUM after these stations. So, as you probably all suspected anyway, CHUM is going to be patterned after a Storz station. As Storz owns five stations and is *first* in each market, it's actually not a bad pattern to follow. In case you don't know, he is: First in Minneapolis, First in Omaha, First in Kansas City, First in New Orleans, and First in Miami.

"Based on a close analysis of his operation by competent advertising people, his success is built around the following:

1. **Exciting news all day and night, with regular newscasts at five minutes to the hour;**
2. **Playing the top 40 hit tunes all the time, plus some standards;**
3. **Concentrating on "personality" shows;**
4. **Using announcers with enthusiasm and zip in their voices;**
5. **A fast and exciting pace all the time;**
6. **Unlimited on-the-air promotion.**

"Now, we are going to listen to a couple of tapes. Don't try and figure out what is wrong with these tapes. Take it that they are *right* and figure out if you can do as good a job.

"Now, let me say here that I want to go with the people we've got here now. If you want to, you can all do a similar-type job to what Storz is doing. If you *don't want to*, then we are all in trouble and, quite frankly, if you do decide you *don't want to*, then say so now so that I know where I'm going.

"Another point. Don't get the idea this is a 'flash in the pan' idea of mine — it is not. I'm going to pattern CHUM after a Storz operation even if I have to go through two or three staffs to do it. Nobody is going to be pampered; you are going to be told bluntly when you 'get off the track.' Now I don't know how people feel about the place you work, but when I worked for others I wanted the place I worked for to be the best. We all have the opportunity now of making CHUM Toronto's top audience station, but I'll tell you one thing: we won't accomplish it without hard work. Now, April is test month for all of us. We've got one month to sound like a Storz station. All the tapes we have are available to you to listen to any time here in the station. I suggest today would be an excellent time to begin."

Having said his piece, Waters left the room to a stunned silence.

STONE: We were numbed by the effect of Allan's speech. We were actually going to do this inconceivable thing. One person left the meeting in tears. One left to puke. One simply left. Left the station, that is. The rest of us headed for the tape machines to listen to the Storz air checks we'd been avoiding.

On May 27 of that year, CHUM officially hit the airwaves as a Top Forty station, broadcasting 24 hours a day at 2,500 watts. To accomplish this, CHUM moved its transmitter to Algonquin Island. Now CHUM could broadcast northward, and with more power. (Some of the Island residents, though, complained that they were picking up CHUM in their teeth fillings and bedsprings. One woman commented that, as she was about to sit down on the toilet, it roared, "And now, CHUM 1050 news!" Apparently, she was quite flushed.)

Chapter Three

ALL SHOOK UP

THE CITY THAT ALWAYS SLEEPS: TORONTO IN THE 1950S

Toronto in the '50s was a study in dull. Perhaps "study" is too dynamic a word.

A book was written whose thesis was that everyone hates Toronto. It was adapted into a radio play and was particularly well-received in the West.

A gag that was a Quebec favourite turned on a contest in which the first prize was a week in Toronto, the second prize, two weeks in Toronto, third prize, three weeks, etc.

The city was nicknamed Toronto the Good, which inspired the response, "Good for what?" Only travellers who had already done to death the Saskatchewan Hoe Handle Counting Festival and the Beautiful B.C. Backslapping Jamboree were desperate enough to vacation in the Everest of Ennui, the Yawn Bonny Banks, the Taj Mahal of Tedium — Toronto!

In all fairness, Toronto's early history had been as turbulent, violent, and topsy-turvy as any pop-historical novelist writing a best-selling bodice-ripper could wish. But the populace appeared to be tight-jaw determined to forget its raw, feisty, frontier roots.

The turn of the 20th century saw Toronto struggling to rid itself of prostitution and the evils of strong drink. Poor people were banned from churches if they smelled bad (the people, not the churches). Besides, the wealthy had rented the best pews.

Toronto had a huge churchgoing population. Hence, another name for Toronto: The City of Churches. (Later, on CHUM, John Spragge would say that Toronto's biggest — and sometimes only — excitement of the week was Dowager Demolition Derby each Sunday. Rosedale matrons who didn't drive all week would do wheelies and generally jockey their block-long limousines recklessly around the Timothy Eaton Church parking lot.)

After World War II, the Grey Lady reasserted herself. Men would have the jobs.

27

Women — no matter what they did during the war — were to become homemakers, have babies, and learn to change diapers, create a home for him, and stretch meals by making creative casseroles with tuna fish.

In the new affluence, Torontonians were encouraged to marry and have families — and buy more goods. Betty Friedan's voice (*The Feminine Mystique*) was being heard by some women, but Friedan was not as commanding a presence as Timothy Eaton and his dour, Scots Presbyterian ways. Some women, however, were damned fed up.

The Lord's Day Act held Toronto, the Queen City, in thrall. It was damped down by Blue Sundays; the rest of the week wasn't so red-hot either.

Sunday in Toronto in the '50s meant cinemas closed, garages closed, sporting events closed, stores closed, restaurants closed. It didn't matter about the restaurants, as there really weren't many to speak of. Want to go out for a decent meal? There was the Royal York, the King Edward, and the Lord Simcoe hotel restaurants. Oh, yes, out on Bloor Street West sat the Old Mill. George's Spaghetti House was open. Sizzling meat was available at The Sign of the Steer, the Chez Paree, and another steak house or three. Jazz devotees hit the Colonial or the Town Tavern. That was about it. But never on Sundays. Sunday was Pray Day.

And how was the food cooked? Like much English cooking at the time (with notable exceptions), it set new standards in well-done beef and overcooked vegetables.

As for downtown Toronto activities, at the foot of University at King Street at 9 a.m. on a Sunday, you could virtually shoot the proverbial cannon either way. Not only would you not hit anyone, you wouldn't see anyone. Toronto (even on some Saturday mornings) was like an early sci-fi film where the city had evacuated everyone to escape the Amazing Growing Sandman.

Somewhere in this sleepy hollow, CHUM perked along, a pre-rock anomaly.

Toronto prided itself on being a business city — a place where the duty of money-making was given the concentration, time, and respect it deserved. "Hog Town," too, was a designation applied to Toronto. Some say this was because Toronto tried to hog everything. Some say it was simply because of the early pig farming. (Ever get the feeling Toronto should have been known as the City of Names?)

Toronto, in 1957, suffered from terminal earnestness. Here was a serious city, a place of parts and prominence, a sedate seat of grave men and firmly principled women who brooked no jackanapes.

However, help was on its way with potent medicine that would, over the next few decades, cure more than the agonies of psoriasis: immigrants.

Redolent of garlic, basil, rich food — and vino — Italians came and started to build the city. French Canadians began to flee the backward, insular blindfold of nationalism, sashaying down Toronto's avenues in Montreal chic, seeking outdoor cafés on Sunday afternoons. Toronto's standing olio of English, Irish, Jewish, Chinese, and Poles was further spiced by more of the same, plus a spectrum of Asians. Affluent or poor, they brought the gifts of their cultures, sometimes a more cosmopolitan way of thinking — and food and meal preparation. Finally!

To this simmering mixture of old-time Toronto, social change, growing affluence, and an inexplicable sense of expectancy, CHUM added Top Forty radio. Muddy York met Allan Waters. The result — Muddy Waters?

THE DAY THE HIT HIT THE FAN: CHUM GOES TOP FORTY

'Twas the night before CHUM went rock. Toronto blinked in the gloom, teetering dangerously close to the brink of change. Many citizens went about their lives, unaware of the gathering storm. (Catchy phrase.)

Couples took advantage of the deepening dark and laughed and kissed and loved. Or at least held hands. After all, this was Toronto.

In the gardens and ravines, raccoons, skunks, and foxes tiptoed silently on padded paws.

Night's inky presence spread. Sidewalks were carefully rolled up. Beds turned down. And as a black veil settled on the Grey Lady, Jimmy went to sleep in his own little room.

Toronto the Good, smug and snug, slept, little suspecting it was to experience a bumpy night. And a rude awakening.

At 6 a.m., May 27, 1957, CHUM went rock, not with a whimper, but with a bang. Top Forty hits only, round the clock. Music rockin', jocks talkin', time clockin', and news sockin' — First! News! First! Veep! Veep! Veep!

On-air were deejays Phil Ladd, Harvey Dobbs, Josh King, Phil Stone, Pete Nordheimer, and Hank Noble, and on news Harvey Kirck and Rennie Heard.

Rock had been thrown through the stained-glass window of Toronto's stately edifice and its foundations began to crack.

And how did tight-assed Toronto react to CHUM and Top Forty radio? Well, it depended upon which Toronto you referred to. WASP Toronto, like another stodgy dowager of old, turned down its mouth and was not amused. It prayed that this pop pestilence would not cross the border from the decadent U.S.A., but its heavenly message went unheeded. The rough beast that was rock 'n' roll had slouched into Toronto. And found a home on CHUM.

Newspapers sneered that the so-called rock explosion was nothing more than a squib that would sputter out like a guttering candle. Politicians viewed it with alarm. Men of the cloth put aside old enmities to unite in the common cause of denouncing rock 'n' roll. Rock, they thundered from the pulpit, lures the witless onto the royal road to perdition. It erodes ethics, they chided in the churches. It minimizes morals, they echoed round the temples. It's blasphemous, they moaned in the mosques.

Educators pronounced rock 'n' roll the gravest threat to a literate public since Dubble Bubble gum. Sociologists, psychologists, consultants, and other unemployables rose to declare that rock was the root cause of everything from bedwetting and penis envy to chronic nose-picking and the growth of hair on the palms of the hands.

Fathers fretted and threatened to lock chastity belts onto rock-crazed, overheated daughters. Mothers laced their sons' soups with saltpetre. Sexy music was raising its snugly head.

Advertisers called CHUM, voicing their disapproval — many cancelling much-needed accounts. Fulminating friends called Allan, sometimes hanging up, friends no longer. Strangers, too, phoned Waters and begged him in the sainted name of Lawrence Welk to eschew this tainted music and return the station to the path of musical righteousness.

Some tried to persuade Waters to drop rock on moral grounds, others appealed to him as a hard-headed businessman. After all, it was common knowledge that rock was just a fad. That year, as we smug ones know, dear reader, was 1957.

And who were the depraved artists who had inspired these foaming mouths and gnashing teeth? The first CHUM Chart, on May 27, 1957, declared Elvis Presley's "All Shook Up" the number-one record, and the King's pelvic pumping had many parents, well . . . shook. The performers who sang the other nine songs in the Top Ten were Pat Boone, Andy Williams, the Everly Brothers, Sal Mineo, Gale Storm, Marty Robbins, Charlie Gracie, Perry Como, and Johnny Ray. Today, perhaps only a monk or

"CHUM's weekly Hit Parade" available every Saturday at your favourite Record Bar.

"CHUM's Hit Parade", compiled according to Record and Sheet Music Sales, Coin Machine Operators and Radio requests as determined by the CHUM weekly survey.

CHUM'S TOP TEN:

week of May 27, 1957

	TITLE	ARTIST	No. OF WEEKS ON CHART
1.	All Shook Up	Elvis Presley	1
2.	Love Letters In The Sand	Pat Boone	1
3.	I Like Your Kind Of Love	Andy Williams	1
4.	Bye Bye Love	Everly Brothers	1
5.	Start Movin' (In My Direction)	Sal Mineo	1
6.	Dark Moon	Gale Storm	1
7.	A White Sport Coat	Marty Robbins	1
8.	Fabulous	Charlie Gracie	1
9.	Girl With The Golden Braids	Perry Como	1
10.	Yes Tonight, Josephine	Johnnie Ray	1

FOLLOWING FORTY:

11. Little Darlin'	24. Wonderful! Wonderful!	38. After School			
12. Come Go With Me	25. Rosie Lee	39. Little White Lies			
13. Why Baby Why?	26. Young Blood	40. One For My Baby			
14. Gone	27. Valley Of Tears	41. Rock Your Little Baby To Sleep			
15. Round and Round	28. Freight Train	42. Mangos			
16. School Day	29. Marianne	43. Mama Guitar			
17. Party Doll	30. I'm Stickin' With You	44. Flip Top			
18. So Rare	31. Love Is A Golden Ring	45. Jim Dandy Got Married			
19. I'm Waitin'	32. I'm Sorry	46. Bernardine			
20. Butterfly	33. Empty Arms	47. Pledge Of Love			
21. Mama Look-A Booboo	34. Teen-Age Crush	48. I Just Don't Know			
22. Four Walls	35. Lucille	49. Harem Dance			
23. Sittin' In The Balcony	36. My Love Song	50. Gonna Sit Right Down (And Write Myself A Letter)			
	37. Jamie Boy				

Dial 1050 — CHUM — for Hit Parade music, 24 hours a day — News Bulletins as they happen — Newscasts hourly at 5 minutes to the hour.

someone who knits nose-warmers for a living would consider these artists wild and wicked, but the opponents of rock in the 1950s railed on.

Ah, but there were those whose brains had not jelled into head cheese, those with attitudes that had not ossified — the kids. What a rush for them! Their own music. Their own station.

Teens ignored the fact that a fair number of really old people, say 18 to 24, also welcomed rock. They'd been listening to American stations and following the hit parade scene for some years. Now they, too, had their own music and their very own radio station. And with the wild enthusiasm and talk of these two groups, the atmosphere slowly turned more positive. Way more.

ELLIOTT-HAYNES DAYTIME SURVEY CHART, TORONTO
7:00 A.M. TO 6:00 P.M. AVERAGE MONDAY TO FRIDAY • JANUARY 1958 THROUGH AUGUST 1960

CHUM

STATION B

STATION C

Their own guide to what was hot and what was not. What made it super cool-o — *Bonus! Bonus! Bonus!* — was that their parents and teachers hated it. How groovy could it get?

PHIL STONE: We were harassed from many quarters for about six months. People's hostility scared me so much that I cancelled the deposit I'd put on a new house. But when the positive change of public attitude came, it rushed like a tidal wave. We showed up strongly in the ratings. We became an unbelievable number two. Then number one! First in the ratings in Toronto? Fabulous!

LET THE GOOD TIMES ROLL: DAVE JOHNSON

He was the best of jocks. He was the worst of jocks. Johnson's life was a Tale of Two Pities. First was his bottle-battle with demon rum. Second was his weight.

FRED SNYDER (chief operator): Dave was pretty well self-taught. He'd been an operator at CKEY, then went on-air at CKOY, Ottawa, before he came to CHUM. We became damn good friends. I was one of the few people he ever told he was an orphan. His eyes used to tear up when he'd relive going to the movies as a kid, tied to other orphans by a rope. He had a lifelong yearning to have family and be part of a family. But even at CHUM he still felt apart . . . and back in that bloody orphanage.

At his best, Dave Johnson may well have been CHUM's purest disc jockey in the clas-sic Top Forty sense. Fellow deejay Mike Darow could have been a close second on days when program director Allan Slaight commanded him to just play the music and keep down the chatter. But most times, Mike's enormous voice and showbiz personality shone through. Bob Laine could have been a contender, but he very correctly toned it down and talked fairly intimately to his night people.

Al Boliska was a clown. Later, Jungle Jay proved to be a comic. John Spragge chatted warmly to a home audience, with charm and wit. Peter Nordheimer had been Mr. Nice Guy. Bob McAdorey was mischief personified. And Brian Skinner was . . . Skinner. Duff Roman, too, could cut it: he knew a hell of a lot about groups and the local recording scene.

Johnson, however, was a smile and the music. His laugh was irresistible, the most infectious in the industry.

Dave Johnson goes overboard with gals from the Boat Show

BOB MCADOREY: Dave could have tutored any of us about how to be a better, straight-rock jock. He had no jokes. He had no anecdotes. His only attempt at humour was when he'd "find clues to a contest in the Clues Closet." Dave drove his show, a huge, ear-to-ear smile on his face — just Johnson and his listeners

Francis tolerably well), she'd ask for Dave to perform the interview.

Meeting Dave, bands, groups, and singles would often say, "Hey, he's a good guy." He was.

Dave could keep it tight. Given a feature like "Johnson's Juke Box," where listeners

Connie Francis, the world's biggest recording star at the time, liked Dave Johnson, and when she'd visit (CHUM knew Francis tolerably well), she'd ask for Dave to perform the interview.

and the music. Dave sounded like he was having a private party (chuckles). And sometimes he was.

Even blasé recording stars liked being interviewed by Dave. Not carrying any egotistic baggage, nor making attempts to show off and upstage the entertainer, Dave won over the most jaded personalities. He focused all his attention on drawing out the person he was interviewing. Connie Francis, the world's biggest recording star at the time, liked Dave Johnson, and when she'd visit (CHUM knew

tried to guess the chart number of the next record Dave would play, he'd wrap the contest up in a snappy manner with no extraneous, draggy commentary. The fact that he had one of the hottest operators in the business, Claude Deschamps, didn't hurt either.

Dave hosted a program segment called "The Hi-Fi Club," sponsored by Coca-Cola. This package came complete with membership cards, special privileges, contests, and prizes.

A happy spinoff was a weekly Hi-Fi Club Dance a few blocks up from CHUM on

Merton Street. It soon developed into one of the finest teen dances the city would ever know. Hi-Fi Club members got in at a reduced price. Coca-Cola was on sale. Only a limited number of kids were allowed. It was absolutely safe, booze- and drug-free, and the hired local constabulary ensured no undesirables were admitted.

The dance was a blast. Johnson hosted. He introduced live bands, featured the favourites — the top, most danceable hits — and record guys popped by with 45s not yet heard. Many a future chart-climber was introduced at this dance.

Later in the evening, other CHUM jocks would drop by, often bringing visiting record-stars or personalities. Musicians would visit Dave and sign autographs. Then came big trouble.

The musicians' union had dictated that union musicians couldn't play anywhere there were records spun. So, non-union bands were hired and paid over-scale, or in excess of what a union group would charge. The union execs went to Waters and told him that, if we didn't hire union bands and not play records, they'd cut off all CHUM's access to visiting stars.

It didn't matter to them that Dave and I ran the dance, not CHUM; that we wanted to hire union musicians; that it couldn't be a Hi-Fi Club dance without records; and that the kids loved this formula of live bands and top hits. The union pressed its threat to CHUM. We folded a super dance that CHUM loved, Coke loved, parents loved, and the kids were nuts over. The owners of the Merton Hall, who had been jealously coveting the perceived potential revenue, jumped in and tried to run the dance. It closed again in a month. Who said, "What goes around, comes around"? And it did. Later, at the Gardens.

Dave was sensitive about his rotundity and we were, by and large, doggone insensitive.

In a contest built around the theme from *The Magnificent Seven*, part of our lyrics ran, "Seven swingin' deejays, now seven singin' deejays. Fat Dave Johnson and Bobbo Laine, their singin' will give you a pain . . . forever."

In our promotional announcements, we might describe an announcer as "Wild Man" Al Boliska, or "Big" Mike Darow. Dave's descriptive phrase nearly always centred on his avoirdupois.

To the boys' credit, they did everything to try to convince Dave to lose weight. They cajoled, they kidded, they went on diets and invited him to join them. Nothing.

MILLIE MORIAK: Dave was a loveable guy. It was a little-known fact that he was crazy about opera. I suspect he was quite sentimental at heart, and those big, sweeping operatic love and tragedy themes and arias really got to him. A group of us from CHUM formed an opera club, and we'd meet regularly to groove on what Dave would call "Tasty Music."

"Taste," as in great-tasting food, was dear to Dave. He was a gourmet cook. To see Johnson at his very best, you had to be invited to one of his summer backyard barbeques. There, Dave was in command; he was Monsieur le Chef, par excellence.

As Mine Host, he wouldn't let you lift a finger (your pinky excepted). Placing an ice-cold beer or cool summer drink in your hand, he'd direct you to a comfy chair where you could soak up the sun, get cheerily snozzled, and watch the Master perform miracles with the meat. Unabashedly outfitted in a huge apron and hat and with Puccini playing in the background, Dave would conduct the preparation of the meal. All the while, newcomers to Dave's Dining al Fresco would exchange knowing looks that meant they'd never seen him so content.

With the same broad grin and high energy he brought to the microphone, he'd ferry fantastic food from the barbeque or kitchen to your plate, always with a "You've got to try this . . ." or "Tell me those aren't the most succulent stuffed mushroom caps you've ever savoured." And when Johnson served Rib-eye steaks à la Loretta (his wife), blessedly conjoined with a generous goblet of an extraordinary Côtes de Beaune, 'twas, as they say, to sigh 'n' die for.

However — wait for it — it was Johnson's preparation of lobster that made palates palpitate and grown men cry in paroxysms of orgiastic ecstasy. His words still resonate in our gourmandizing pleasure passages: "Serve lobster with a simple green salad only: romaine lettuce tops, dash of fresh dill, hit of crushed ginger juice, fresh black pepper, with a dribble of balsamic vinegar. Stop. The focus must be on the lobster. Forget all that butter and garlic. Simply steam the lobster and serve plain on a separate dish — with only a natural dressing." A natural dressing, for those who haven't memorized their James Beard, is the undigested seaweed you find in the cavity of the lobster. Dave would tell guests what it was only after they'd eaten and rhapsodized over it. It was Dave's *chef-d'oeuvre*.

Dave Johnson, wherever you may be, "Cheers!" and *Bon appétit.*

DOWN LAINE'S MEMORY: BOB LAINE

When bleak midnight tolls the witching hour you may spy the night people skulking in the shadows, scurrying to their unnamed rituals.

Lonely as a waterfront security guard, hopeful as a panhandler, wistful as a cruising cabby, they toil in the gloom. For these are the people of the night. They keep the city alive. They move us. They keep factories pumping product. They brew strong coffee in the lambent light of a 24-hour café.

To make their tasks bearable and to escape the cold grasp of night, they seek a lifeline. They reach out to radio, to CHUM. And they find Bob Laine. They turn him on. And vice versa.

The following intro kicked off the Bob Laine all-nite show on CHUM for many a moon:

LAINE: Hello, World, this is Bobbo.
WORLD: Hello, Bobbo, this is World.

For you trivia types, the voice of World belonged to CHUM newsman Art Cuthbert, better known as Ron Knight.

Bob came honestly to this profession. At 16, still in school, he read commercials for local stores over a public-address system that boomed through Lawrence Plaza. Gerry Myers, all-nite man on CKEY, heard Bob reading his announcements, liked his voice and delivery, and encouraged him to go into radio. Casting about for work and after a few futile attempts, he received a call: "Would you like to go to Simcoe and be a copywriter?" Laine's eager answer: "Absolutely! Where's Simcoe? And what's a copywriter?"

Simcoe turned out to be CFRS, Canada's Farmland Radio Station, a 250-watt dawn-to-dusker. Sound familiar?

After Bob had spent a mere three days writing copy, an announcer quit the station. Bob was invited to go on-air. This time, instead of saying "What's an announcer?" he said, "Darn tootin'." His boss, Fred Sherratt, thought Bob's birth name (Shlanger) was too nasal and told him to change it. He did — to Bob Laine. Immediately he was mellow-bellowing with the best of them. Ah, radio.

As will become apparent, nearly all aspiring announcers put in their time in the boonies. Not only was this experience worn like a badge of honour, it also made damn good sense, because a neophyte was forced to do everything. One of Bob's jobs was to set up the equipment for a remote broadcast from the Salvation Army each Sunday. While the service was being held, Bob would sit in the back, reading.

BOB LAINE: One Sunday, a man in a Salvation Army uniform tapped me on the shoulder and said, "You'd better look up, son. The Captain is talking about you. In fact, he's making you an honorary private." I said, "He can't do that. I'm Jewish." And he said, "Too late."

All jocks, starving as they paid their dues boonie-side, assiduously scanned the trade mags for potential jobs. Laine spied one at CHUM, applied to program director Phil Ladd, and got the job in Toronto, man, Toronto! And Bob Laine took over the all-nite show on CHUM in May of '58. Actually,

Bob Laine started at CHUM the same day as Allan Slaight. (That has absolutely nothing to do with anything.)

At the time Laine joined CHUM, Hank Noble was the all-nite man. Earlier, when Bob was still at Bathurst Heights Collegiate, Hank had taught the eager youngster how to operate the board at CHUM. At that time, announcers spun their own discs and generally handled all operational tasks. As fickle fate would have it, Bob took over Hank's midnight to 6 a.m. duties.

LAINE: Noble was also a singer and performed as Billy Guitar. Under that name he'd recorded a tune, "Here Comes the Night," and it got airplay on CHUM.

When Laine joined CHUM it was in the rundown, rickety Adelaide Street location that had wrecking-ball operators slavering in anticipation. Bob worked alone all night. The back door would not lock and barely closed. Probably neither Waters nor the landlord had the money to fix it. However, the building was warm and it invited many a late-night

Bob Laine "keeps his trap shut" collecting money with Dave Johnson

guest. On a regular basis, Bob would open his studio door only to find a derelict or two passed out in the hall, hands still firmly clutching a bottle of Old Sailor.

Perhaps more alarming was the fact that word had got around to the back-alley cats that a radio station's rear door was open in the middle of the night, when the rest of Toronto had long since shut down. Laine had finally had enough when, as he took a break, he discovered about 15 revellers partying on the CHUM premises. Laine was always a trendsetter, and here was Bobbo's Booze Can. But Bob refused the proffered drink and instead wrote a memo to Slaight begging him to hire a newsman or operator to keep him company. Slaight agreed and Bob got an operator — Dave Shaw. (This section was to be titled "Bob Laine — Amahl Alone and the Night Visitors," but it was deemed a tad outré.)

It was not only outsiders who haunted the corridors of CHUM at night; sometimes it was staff. Newsman Jack Kusch was heard ploddingly tap-tap-tapping a message on a typewriter one morning about 3 a.m. Seems he was a bit worse for wear from a party, and some Ryerson buddies had dropped him off at the station. With the unerring instincts of the inebriated, Kusch travelled right round the halls of CHUM, found the only piece of rug in the building — in Waters's office — and

puked mightily on it. The tap-tapping was the resignation he was ponderously pecking out. It was not accepted.

Laine remembers the CHUM years mostly with affection and torrents of laughter, but it was not all fun 'n' games. One night there was a tragic plane crash. An Air Canada flight from Montreal went down north of Toronto. When he asked what he should do, he was told to play soft music and, after the next of kin had been advised, give the names of the dead over the air. Problem was, next of kin did not cover other close relatives and friends. Bob spent the night on the phone with shocked and tearful people asking him if some person or other was dead.

LAINE: I was an emotional wreck. Try telling a person a loved one has died and hear their scream of pain. When I got off the air at 6 a.m. I had no idea what to do with myself. I just wandered the halls, distraught. I don't even remember getting home. But the tears, those I'll never forget.

Bob left CHUM in 1960 to get off the all-nite show and for a hefty raise.

LAINE: Some hefty raise! When CFGM, Richmond Hill, offered me the morning show, they increased my salary. So, how come

I couldn't afford anything? Seems I forgot that Waters paid us profit-sharing four times a year. Turned out I'd taken a pay cut. Now you know why I'm not as rich as Midas.

Gerry Bright was assigned the all-nite show when Laine left, and he worked hard and performed at a journeyman-like level. But he was not Bobbo. And, while many stations could not give a hoot-in-your-hat about the around "The Voice." The audience was told an announcer — called The Voice — was taking over the all-nite show. "Guess his name. Win big bucks." Bob would arrive at CHUM about 11:45 p.m. in a limo, wrapped in mysterioso and wearing a hood. Gerry Bright did all the talking, saying, "The Voice tells me the next record will be . . ." or "The Voice says it's precisely 2 a.m." And so on. Silly? Weird? You bet. But it drew mail. After about two

He was young, nineteen, and single. Why would anyone be surprised when his buddies bought a hooker for him and one night hoisted her up the ladder to the platform?

all-nite show, CHUM viewed it as a section of their programming day. It should be promoted. And make some money.

A sponsorship deal was set up with Craven A cigarettes, who expected us to beat some drums and, I guess, send up smoke signals. Slaight called Laine and asked him to come back.

LAINE: I was very cool. Very aloof. Very stand-offish. I said quickly, "When?"

Laine's return precipitated one of radio's stranger broadcasts. The promotion was built

weeks a winner was announced, Bob Laine was welcomed back into the CHUM fold, and all was right with the world.

WORLD: "Welcome back, Bobbo."

Although Bob might have considered himself tucked away anonymously in the corner of the night, in reality he was more foreground than 99 percent of all-niters in radio. Fact was, he was better known and more prominent than many — if not most — daytime announcers in Toronto. The reasons were simple. Bob was a member of the on-air

CHUM team. He had a gleeful sense of humour and a wacky way of looking at comedy. So he fit right in when we took our circus out-of-station. He could be counted on to participate fully in CHUM Champions activities and add his own touch. And he probably set new standards for bitching about it.

The youngest of all the jocks, Bob was in step with the thinking of the youth segment of our audience. All right, he was a big kid. Weren't we all!

Some nights, CHUM listeners could not find Bob Laine. He was lying down on the job, fast asleep, 35 feet in the air. He was the focus of an early CHUM promotion. It was the fifth anniversary of the Lawrence Plaza at Bathurst, and Bob was living atop a scaffolding for five days. He was young, 19, and single. Why would anyone be surprised when his buddies bought a hooker for him and one night hoisted her up the ladder to the platform?

LAINE: I was in a tent and reading by the light of a lamp when a lovely young woman slipped in. One thing led to another, and we were just getting very comfortable, when the phone rang. It was my buddies. I was furious — until they told me to turn out the lamp because there was a perfect silhouette of us in action showing through the tent.

Even today, Bob can't abide the song "Me and My Shadow."

AL IS IN WONDERLAND: AL BOLISKA

Al Boliska hit Toronto's airwaves with all the impact and outrageousness of a custard pie in the face. And the mess he left in his daily wake stuck like a gooey, splattered meringue. Unique, funny, irreverent, upbeat, and sometimes reckless, for many listeners Al personified the CHUM they loved.

Boliska grew up in Montreal, and one of his better dialects was French Canadian. In Montreal he worked off-air in news for the CBC, who predicted he'd never make it as an announcer because he didn't have the voice. In 1953, developing his offbeat radio style at CKLC in Kingston, Ontario, he often startled his listeners by originating his show from the Kingston pen or the rafters of the local community centre.

Along with friend and operator George Nicholson, Al moved in 1956 to CKSL in London, Ontario, where he took over the morning show.

BOB MCADOREY: I worked with Al in London. That city had never heard nor seen anything like him. Nobody had; he was an original. He was astounding and unpredictable. He turned the town and radio upside down.

In September of '57, Al and George were hired by CHUM for the morning show. From the first moment he opened his mike and his mouth, CHUM listeners experienced a new standard in strange. Strange — but funny as hell. And just the ticket to help build talk and new listeners. Hey! You just have to hear this guy! He's nuts!

Everything was fodder for Boliska's comic cannon.

SHEILA BOLISKA (ex-wife): Al used to refer to me as "Fury" on the air. He'd say, "If driving, stay off the 401. My wife, Fury, is going shopping."

Al was Top Banana in his morning burlesque show, and his operator George Nicholson played straight man. Boliska created a daily on-air feature, "The World's Worst Jokes." (For your dining and dancing pleasure, some he might have told are included in this chapter.)

AL: George, do you know how to break up an Italian wedding?
GEORGE: No, Al, how do you break up an Italian wedding?
AL: You yell, "The cement truck's here!"

(This is a repeat of a gag sprung on Johnny Lombardi on Boliska's first day on the job.)

In addition, Al would use George as part of a break between pieces of music or commercials:

AL: This . . . is the Amazing Al Boliska!
GEORGE: And this is Just Plain George.

Another regular on Boliska's Boffo Bandwagon was CHUM's janitor and handyman Al Devereux. Devereux had never been close to a mike, except when he was cleaning the studio. That meant nothing to Boliska, who dubbed Devereux "Officer Tie Clip of the Toronto Police." Al would invite Officer Clip into the studio each morning. There, in a rather monotone voice augmented with recorded sounds, and in a definitely unprofessional manner, Officer Clip would deliver

42

Lou the Butcher feeds Boliska kishka and straight lines

traffic reports and follow with a short joke. While George ran up recorded laughter, Al would praise and thank the officer and send him off to his beat on Yonge Street, again with appropriate sound effects.

This feature continued without incident until a novelty record, "Who Stole the Kishka?" hit the charts. The trouble had started when a meat-store operator styling himself Lou the Butcher visited Al to sample kishka on the air. This developed into a popular regular fixture, with Al having Lou do meat or deli gags.

Everyone loved this except Al Devereux. To the CHUM staff's enormous amusement, Devereux had become jealous of Lou. Whenever Lou was doing his bit with Boliska, Devereux would stand in the adjoining studio, muttering about Lou's comic delivery — or lack thereof — and tell anyone who'd listen that Lou could use some lessons in comedy timing.

We were rather disappointed when Boliska dropped the Lou the Butcher feature as the kishka record faded in popularity. Lou returned to where his only showcase held lamb chops, and Officer Tie Clip regained his confidence and climbed back onto his high horse.

AL: George, did you know that most disc jockeys are half Irish and half Finnish?

GEORGE: So, what does that mean, Al?
AL: George, it means we're all alcoholics, but we're real quiet about it.

Like all true funnymen, Boliska had a clown's oversensitive nose, sniffing for potential humour. And if it meant embarrassing someone — a group, a sponsor, or CHUM itself — tough! Al always put the corn before the consequences. He was totally focused on entertaining his listeners and always leaped for the laugh before he looked.

Revenue from commercials is the lifeblood of a radio station, and every dollar's worth is hard fought for and hard won. Even in the early Boliska years, CHUM was still rocky financially. Commercial sponsors were a sacred thing. CHUM continued to wait for new sponsors with the anticipation of an old-time bridegroom on his wedding night.

LAINE : News ran through the station — we had a new sponsor, Chrysler! This was major. Boliska, introducing the commercial, said, "Today, we have a beautiful, full-size Chrysler in the studio. I'll turn on the engine, and you just listen to this baby purr!" Following the sound effect of a starting motor, Al threw a garbage can across the studio and continued to kick it, making a horrible racket. Chrysler cancelled its spot — not only on CHUM —

but on radio. Boliska had kicked off the campaign. Literally.

Al held on to his job, and had pretty well forgotten about the incident, when CHUM landed a prize commercial plum: Woolworth's. This retailer had two chronic image problems. The chain's Great Depression background gave it a reputation for selling cheap goods. Also, many young people had grown up stealing from Woolworth's stores. Woolworth's was known in some quarters as Shoplifting Shangri-la.

CHUM had the answer. Larry Solway and Garry Ferrier teamed to write a wonderful, upbeat ad campaign with the slogan, "Like it? I bought it at Woolworth's!" Each spot contained three examples of different people wearing a new piece of clothing. Someone would compliment them, and each person would say, "Like it? I bought it at Woolworth's!" Sample spots were played for Woolworth's, which embraced the theme and signed up with CHUM for a considerable campaign. This was a major score. CHUM had brought Woolworth's into radio. It could use this victory to sell other reluctant clients. Listeners responded positively to the ads and bought from Woolworth's. Here, ostensibly, was a sales story with a happy ending.

Then, one fateful morning, the mirthful mind of Boliska clicked on and twigged to the potential for a laugh. After the spot ran on his show, he turned on the mike and said with great conviction, "George, how do you like my new sweater?" George said, "It looks great, Al." Boliska then said with gusto, "Like it, George? I stole it at Woolworth's!"

Toilet time. Can you say "cancellation"? Ah, me. Who needs a major account anyway?

AL: George, do you know what a dying lawyer said to his doctor?
GEORGE: No, Al, what did the dying lawyer say?
AL: He said, "Give it to me straight, Doc. How many billable hours do I have left?"

Al had this thing about coffee. He spilled it. It was whispered in the station that Boliska dumped more coffee than the rest of the station drank.

Typically, he'd walk into a room with you for a meeting, put his coffee down on a chair or table, and then sit on it. As the hot liquid scalded his skin, he'd leap up saying, "Ah, oh, ooh, what happened here?" Then he'd look around sadly and accusingly as if you or fate or someone had deliberately done this to him.

MCADOREY: Al Slaight was holding forth at an announcers' meeting, but no one was looking

Whipper Billy Watson, teed off at Boliska's jokes

at him. We were staring fixedly at Al Boliska, who, with eyes shut, was picking absently at his Styrofoam coffee cup. Slaight's dissertation was cut short as Al's cup finally burst open and spewed hot coffee right onto his crotch. We watched in silence as Al, jumping about, glared at us, daring us to laugh, while he used his shirt-tail and tie to sop up the spilled coffee. A soggy mess, he sat back down, motioning a bemused Slaight to continue. If anyone had suggested his caffeined crotch was Al's own fault, Boliska might well have sulked the rest of the day.

Childlike when reprimanded, Al would try little-boy-shy tactics. (He referred to himself as "Ol' Loveable.") When he couldn't get around you with this ploy, he'd retreat into himself and go mute. It was, however, difficult to stay angry with him. First of all, he worked very hard.

Radio announcers were notoriously lazy. They'd sit on their nether regions and use their voices for a living. CHUM jocks were exceptions, mainly because they were driven mercilessly to prepare, prepare, prepare — and to involve themselves in difficult and potentially embarrassing promotional situations. But even in the CHUM hotbox, Boliska stood out as one of the best-prepared jocks in radio.

Working 6 to 9 a.m. and noon to 1

Monday to Friday, plus a six-hour Saturday shift in the early days, was demanding enough, what with getting up at 4 a.m., but Al never bitched about fatigue. Instead, he used his open morning hours to prepare the next day's material, searching for the next novel and comic twist and working with George to produce new bits. He treated each day as a fresh opportunity to entertain. No one would ever accuse Al of doggin' it or of taking shortcuts.

Even Slaight tempered his criticism of Al because, although he'd muff a promotional announcement or commit some enormous gaffe on the air, he'd also often recover in a winning manner and use the moment to bring fun to the show. While some of his goofs resulted in major embarrassment for the station and you wanted to beat him with a baseball hat, even hypercritical bastards like Slaight and me couldn't fault him for lack of preparation. Mind you, when Al slipped up, he did it in grand style.

For one popular on-air promotion, in which a listener called in and identified a celebrity, the jackpot had topped $5,000 — a lot of money for a struggling CHUM to cough up. The voice of the celebrity — in this case, Frank Sinatra — was heavily disguised to keep the promotion running and create maximum listener excitement.

One morning about 8:45 a.m., I wandered into the operating studio to talk to Just Plain George. Boliska spotted me, turned on the mike, and said, "Well, our promotion guy has come into the studio, and I know why he's here. He wants to remind me to plug our exciting contest, The Sound, the Song, and the Celebrity. So, be sure to call in during the *John Spragge Show* and you can win $5,000 if you identify our celebrity as Frank Sinatra."

George and I dropped our jaws in unison. Boliska, realizing what he'd done, blanched and signalled for music. The studio phone lit up. It was Allan Waters. Did I really mean for Al Boliska to reveal the celebrity? "No, Mr. Waters." "Why did he do it then?" "It's just Boliska, Mr. Waters." He hung up. The phone lit up again. Slaight. Boiling. "Farrell, why in hell did you have Boliska give away the answer?" "I didn't." "So why did he do it?" "It's just Boliska, Al, just Boliska." His phone slammed down.

And when a thoroughly pissed-off and reluctant John Spragge played the game early in his show, no one was surprised when a listener identified Frank Sinatra as the celebrity and won the $5,000 plus. Switchboard Betty permitted me to take all the irate calls from listeners, especially those who'd played the game before Al had blown the bundle.

AL SLAIGHT: Boliska was a strange chap with a unique style. He was sort of the little guy out there fighting the machinery. He had a lot of appeal. Now I have a question. Is it true he invited friends from CHUM to his house and charged them for parking?

Occasionally we wanted to string Boliska up. So what? The CHUM audience loved him. And for more reasons than his on-air hijinks. Al was a terrific performer in public. This prompted us to build both on-air and out-of-station promotions around him and the listeners' expectations about what he might do next. Getting talk is at the very core of developing an audience. We built CHUM's appeal and Boliska's reputation by exploiting Al's ability to deliver comically when placed in zany situations before a live audience.

When the potholes in Toronto were a civic disgrace and motorists were bitching, CHUM had Al throw out a challenge to the city. Either they fixed the potholes, or *he* would. When nothing happened, we hired a truck, filled it with tarred gravel, and had Boliska shovel this goop into potholes in downtown Toronto. Mike Darow did a running commentary, cutting into the *John Spragge Show*, and our news department picked it up as a light kicker. Civic officials were embarrassed. Fumed. Phoned. Wrote letters of protest to CHUM. Al read them on the air and challenged the officials to get off their assets and fix the potholes. Boliska and CHUM had taken up the cause of the average person. This action sat well with our listeners. It was to become a technique used over and over as the years rolled by. CHUM would fight Goliaths and tilt at windmills while our audience cheered us on.

AL: George, did you know I was once in the origami business?
GEORGE: What happened to it, Al?
AL: It folded!

North America's rock-station world was so rife with lunatic morning jocks that at major programming conferences in New York or Chicago there was an unofficial but highly anticipated "Who has the craziest morning man?" contest. One year the winner was an L.A. station whose morning man was drunk by the time he got off shift at 9 a.m., drove his car, and knocked down the daughter of the city's police chief. Al got an honorary mention for the body of his work.

(As an aside, Canada's true microphone madman and radio rascal worked not in commercial radio, but for the CBC. His name — Allan McFee.)

PETER DICKENS: There was a kind of charming, absent-minded-professor mien to Al. We both lived in Guildwood Village, both worked the early shift, and he would sometimes give me a ride to work. His rattletrap car could better be described as a death trap. It never occurred to Al to have it serviced or repaired. One morning, late, we were firing towards Adelaide Street. Al was having a bit of trouble seeing because he'd just washed his socks and underwear that morning and was drying this laundry by flying it from his radio aerial. We didn't miss our turnoff, though, because Al's steering gave out and the car, by itself, without Al touching the wheel, turned and careered into a parking lot. Shaken, I resolved to drive myself to work in the future.

The filling-the-potholes gag had gone over well, but it didn't really demonstrate

Boliska's abilities as a performer before a live audience. However, wrestling in Maple Leaf Gardens could. And before you could say Gorgeous George, it did. Phil Stone introduced us to fight promoter Frank Tunney, and we arranged a preliminary match between the British Empire Champion Whipper Billy Watson and Al Boliska.

This was the first time CHUM on-air staff

Bob Laine, Peter Nordheimer, and Neil Thomas, followed in costume, carrying Al Boliska on a litter. To suggest huge muscles, Al was muffled in an overstuffed costume, and he was throwing flowers and kisses to the cheering crowd.

The match itself was choreographed, with some action looking amazingly real. Wrestling crowds are something else and they cheered

Phil Stone introduced us to fight promoter Frank Tunney and we arranged a preliminary match between the British Empire Champion Whipper Billy Watson and Al Boliska.

would perform as a group. When they were told, in a briefing session, to pick up their costumes at Malabar and meet at the Gardens for a rehearsal, their shocked and ashen faces were a sight to behold. Tunney reminded us to wear high boots because wrestling fans — particularly grannies — liked to burn your legs with cigarettes as you walked in.

Night of the match, our procession was headed up by lovelies: gals we named CHUM Chicks. Announcers and newsmen, including

on Boliska, who bounced off ropes, exercised in the corner, mugged to the crowd, and Chaplin-like, caught his foot in the water pail. He drew laugh after laugh.

That night we were convinced that Al could cut it in public, and that our team could work for humorous effect. Tunney and the Gardens learned about the early power of CHUM. With our participation, the match drew four times the usual attendance. This fact was not wasted on the people who

Al Boliska muscles in on the wrestling scene

promoted Gardens events, and the match kicked off what was to be a long and mutually rewarding relationship.

So, there was Al the professional, who worked hard and prepared his shows well. And there was the on-air madcap so popular with CHUM's listeners. But there was also another person — Al the loner.

PETER NORDHEIMER: Al was a friend of mine. But I was always aware that he had that sad-clown quality. On the air, he was great. But off-air, he became another person altogether — seemingly aloof, but actually painfully shy. I'm not saying he couldn't be friendly, but as soon as he shut off the mike he seemed to shut himself off, too, and become someone else.

Al Boliska exhibited the same characteristics as some of our most famous funny people. Consummate professionals when doing their prime job of making people laugh, away from the microphone, stage, or camera, they were almost invariably dour, silent, morose, and, often, rude. The late great Danny Kaye was described as "a depressive, with a public capacity for joy." It's well established that the wellspring of comedy is not happiness but anxiety and those terrible twins, fear and anger. Accompanying this angst is a longing to be loved and accepted and a compulsion to

please. They find these in laughter, applause, and acclaim. Away from the heat of their medium and their audience, in the cool of everyday life, they often revert to introverted and cold behaviour. Al Boliska was no exception.

His years with CHUM passed. But it seemed that, as his popularity grew, his capacity for any kind of criticism waned. Off-air, he limped along with the walking wounded. He seemed to anticipate criticism and took offence at each imagined slight.

Happily, this did not affect his on-air performance. His show could stand up in any market that featured rock radio with jocular jocks topped by a maniac morning man. Despite some strain, CHUM and Al continued to grow ever more popular together.

It was taken as gospel that the way to build ratings was to pump up the audience for the morning show. Etched into our brains was the adage "As goes the morning show, so goes the day," suggesting that once listeners tune in, you have a chance to hold them.

Perhaps that explains why Slaight took such a tough tone with us about Boliska. Al had stormed out of an announcers' meeting, lost his voice, and stomped upstairs to Slaight's office to quit. Slaight had had enough. We'd put too much into Boliska to lose him. After coaxing Al back into the fold,

Slaight read us the riot act. We were to bury the hatchet, quit sniping at Ol' Loveable, and act in a purely professional manner towards a pivotal member of our team — no matter what he might do.

Al's old friend McAdorey and I took up the challenge. We invited Al to lunch up the street at the Swiss Chalet. There, in a reasonable tone, both sides aired their gripes. Al was particularly adamant that everyone stop kidding him about being clumsy. "I'm not clumsy," he said, daring us to argue, "I'm just trying to do my job." He added hotly, "I may be a bit casual, but . . ." Mac and I hurried to agree with Al and assured him there would be no more of that uncalled-for and unwarranted chatter. Smiling, mollified, Al shook hands with both of us. He then excused himself to go to the men's john, which sat at the bottom of a long flight of stairs.

Mac and I were about to congratulate ourselves on handling that situation well when there was a shriek and the damnedest noise: *Tumble, rump, dump, rata-tata-rata, ka-clomp, splat, groan!* We rushed over to the top of the stairs. Al had tripped and fallen down the entire flight and was now lying on his back trying to focus his eyes. We charged down. "Are you *okay*, Al? Does anything hurt?" Boliska struggled to sit up. "Not one word," he croaked. "Not one word!" Mac and I swore on scout's honour we'd never tell about this incident. And being the trustworthy sweethearts we are, we never have.

Chapter Five
FIRST WE TAKE TORONTO

STATION IDENTIFICATION: TAKING STOCK

Allan Waters's bold scheme was working as far as building a viable audience. Despite the startlingly strong listener-rating numbers, however, new advertisers were slow to sign on. Building sales to pay the bills and grow was to prove a long, laborious process. Advertisers and their agencies simply did not grasp the changes that were happening in music, the media, and the world in general.

Nonetheless, by the spring of 1958 Allan had accomplished nothing short of a miracle. He'd Pied Pipered a grey, mousy Toronto into the rock era and CHUM's ratings had skyrocketed. This had shaken up a complacent CKEY, which was soon rocking, too.

Waters had jump-started the on-air sound with an electric, madcap Al Boliska, a hard-driving Dave Johnson, and a solid all-nite Bob Laine.

His gang had unleashed the CHUM Chart — an instant hit that transformed record stores into promotional vehicles for CHUM's lineup of music. This was definitely quid pro quo as CHUM — and rock — breathed a blast of super-heated air into a heretofore sad, sagging record industry.

Now a 24-hour station, CHUM's power had increased to 5,000 watts. George Jones had further engineered it so the transmitters were much better situated to send a more effective signal.

CHUM's retail sales manager Wes Armstrong was, person by person, building a stronger sales

Left: A new Toronto landmark; Above: Allan Waters accepts award from Dr. Stewart of the BBG

team and relieving Allan of some of the pressure of landing local advertising.

National sales were on the cusp of growth, driven by the almost maniacal energy and drive of sales reps Bill Stephens and Ernie Towndrow. But even their awesome capabilities were deeply challenged. CHUM — and its boisterous orphan rock 'n' roll — desperately needed respect in the community. Even more important, respect from advertisers and ad agencies. CHUM, somehow, had to demonstrate its influence and power in spite of a teen-rock reputation that stuck like snail slime. Simply put, many advertisers and agencies did not believe CHUM could deliver an adult audience with buying power. CHUM's competitors, naturally, endorsed that misconception.

Financial control was in the steady hands of Alex Forbes, a Scotsman (who better?). This was vital because debt load and operating costs always romped ahead of revenue from advertising. CHUM literally operated on a week-by-week, if not day-by-day, financial basis. Forbes's judgement and business acumen would prove particularly effective when there were actually some substantial finances (read revenues) to control.

While practically checking behind the couch cushions for nickels, Waters still had to find the wherewithal to add several more balls to his juggling act.

The most important task on his to-do list was to uncover a hot program director who could finish the job of finding on-air personalities that fit a Top Forty format, then sharpen the sound and build the station into something unique, special, and attractive to both listeners and those who wished to push their products and services.

Stephens and Towndrow whispered in Waters's ear that they might have the answer to his quest. Stay tuned . . .

SOCK IN THE HITS: ALLAN SLAIGHT

If Allan Waters manufactured the CHUM automobile and kept it serviced and well-fuelled, Allan Slaight was its V8 engine with explosive horsepower and overdrive. Slaight made CHUM accelerate. He came to the job from being national sales manager of CHED, a very successful Top Forty station in Edmonton.

AL SLAIGHT: I got out of high school at 16. I tried university. I didn't like it and it didn't like me. The first time I entered the halls of CHAB, Moose Jaw, I fell in love with radio. After working at CHAB, I wound up in Edmonton about 1950 at CFRN, in '52 at CJCA, and '54 at CHED on-air as news director. CHED went Top Forty. I became national sales manager.

I met Bill Stephens and Ernie Towndrow and they recommended me to Waters.

Waters had pretty well decided to hire me. I came down in May of '58 for an interview. I had had a capped tooth since about grade four in the front of my mouth. I was giving Waters an impassioned presentation as to why I should be the man for the job when the tooth decided to split in two. It fell into my mouth and subsequently into my hand. Underneath it was this little, brown, runty stub that had not been exposed to the air for years but still had nerves in there causing me considerable pain. I mumbled my way through the rest of my interview with my lips curved in and only breathing about every two minutes. It was probably because of that that Waters had pity and hired me. I glued the broken tooth back on and flew back to Edmonton to prepare my move.

Al was hired as program director. Imagine his surprise when he was introduced to Phil Ladd, who was the production manager. He was told that Ladd was his boss. It seems these titles meant different things in other parts of the country.

Al had little, or nothing, to worry about. Ladd just didn't fit the vision of the station Slaight (and Waters) wanted. Phil went on an extended holiday in the summer of '58 — it seems it just kept on extending.

SLAIGHT: One of my first concerns was to get the music formula right — well, as right as any of us could conceive. CHUM started as a reasonably pure Top Forty station. It seems along the way Phil Ladd had altered it. My assumption is he was thrown by CKEY's adjustments to their music philosophy.

Instead of concentrating on playing our top 50 hits, Ladd started to dilute the impact by introducing the formula of "1, 2, 3" — playing a hit, then a new record, then an old record . . . or something like that. When I took over the job, I deferred to Jerry Forbes of CHED, Edmonton, who reminded me that the Storz and McLendon stations, leaders in the U.S.A., just played the hits. So, we went back to focusing on them. Dave Johnson

Allan Slaight with comedy writer and performer Bill Dana

was told to play only the top 50 every night — plus we initiated some truly wild promotions, and CHUM took off again like an arrow.

After the music mix, Slaight's second priority was to pick up where Waters and Ladd left off — creating a more youthful, Top Forty–comfortable, on-air staff.

He removed Harvey Dobbs, who went into full-time sales and did a sensational job. His morning shift was given to John Spragge, who would follow Al Boliska.

Phil Stone came off the air next and focused on PR and Public Service. Mike Darow slid into his 4 to 7 p.m. slot. Al was reasonably comfortable with that lineup and we began to promote it in earnest.

Allan Slaight could be one tough mother. He wasn't interested in your track record or what your potential might be. He demanded excellent performance as of the current moment. Too bad if a jock introduced a record beautifully 10 times in a row. If he flubbed it when Al was listening, Slaight would phone and dress down the deejay, accusing him of being the world's sloppiest flub artist.

And if Al was tough with his call-ins, they paled beside his memos. To say that Slaight was

intemperate in his memos would be like saying Vlad the Impaler was kinda cranky.

Why did Al write such searing memos? Because he could. Raised in a newspaper family in Moose Jaw, one of the first skills he learned was writing precise copy. Inventive, articulate, aggressive, and with a well-stuffed vocabulary, when Slaight laid his hand to a critical memo, it often held a lash. Al sometimes forgot that the prime reason for the memo was to motivate the recipient to take his advice.

If this was Slaight's only business fault, and it probably was, it looks small, indeed, measured against his contribution.

LARRY SOLWAY: Slaight had a mailed fist . . . but still a fundamental sweetness about him. He was congenial, loved a laugh. He was as responsible as anyone for the high morale we had at the station.

Like most successful people, Slaight had enormous energy. It was bandied about the street corners that if Al didn't outthink you, he'd outwork you. Most times, to the competition's chagrin, he'd do both.

He could energize the station with just one pass-through. Say a new jingle package was being considered. Al, armed with sample tapes and a portable machine, would charge through the halls. He'd pull a couple of gals from the traffic department into a meeting room, play the jingles, and ask their opinion. He'd repeat this action all through the station. No matter that these people had nothing to do with programming, nor purchasing jingle packages. This was not showboating — he was seeking any idea that would improve the package.

His attention to detail could drive you bats, but it kept us all honed and at the ready. Bring him a fresh idea or some new way to tweak CKEY, and his face would light up. "I like it, I like it," he'd exclaim. "What are you going to call it?" You'd tell him. He'd laugh and reach for his dictaphone. "Great, great." Shooing you from his office, you'd hear him scheduling promotional announcements for this new idea, leaving you almost enough time to write and record them.

Al invited me out for a drink one day after work. He said it was time we got to know each other a little better. And so it was — I'd been there nearly a year.

Once settled with a Scotch at the Northgate Hotel, I took the initiative and asked Al about his life out west. I inquired what he did besides radio.

Al hesitated, then told me he had a lifelong passion for magic and that one year he'd toured Saskatchewan with a magic and mental-telepathy show.

That stopped me cold. Angrily, I asked him what the hell he meant by making fun of me. We were supposed to be getting to know each other. As my boss, he shouldn't insult me.

Al, his eyes wide, asked me what the blazes I was talking about.

I replied that he knew full well that I had toured Saskatchewan with a magic and mental-telepathy show. So, yes, he was taunting me. That couldn't be a coincidence.

It was. Allan Slaight and Allen Farrell — one year apart — had both travelled with a magic and mental-telepathy show across Saskatchewan. Al operated out of Alberta, and I, with magician "The Great Eli" (Bill Eliason), from Vancouver. Now, what are the odds of that? Perhaps it explains how for years to come we could practically read each other's minds regarding promotions.

SOLWAY: Allan Slaight is the best radio man I ever met . . . in . . . my . . . life! I have enormous respect for him. He had an unerring sense of what would work. And on his feet, discussing radio or CHUM's qualities, I've never seen his equal.

(Though let's not forget he temporarily banned the play of Rolling Stones records on CHUM.) Now, for my next trick . . .

DANGEROUS DAN MCJINGLE: PIERRE BERTON

"There are strange things done in the midnight sun . . ." and even stranger things on CHUM. We contracted Pierre Berton to provide commentary. (No self-respecting radio station would hire a newspaper man.)

Berton hated rock. He was annoyed by CHUM. But we loved *his* work. Pierre's daily column in the *Toronto Daily Star* was consistently entertaining and is remembered to this day as brilliant. Especially close to our hearts was a ridiculous radio station he'd invented for his column called CHOO, obviously a send-up of CHUM. One of Berton's classic lines was "We'll return with music on CHOO after the singing of the news."

After some negotiation, Pierre became a familiar and integral part of the CHUM sound, which provided another outlet for his opinions and talents.

On CHUM's 40th-anniversary video, Pierre summarized his CHUM experience: "I can't believe that I actually did 11 commentaries on the news, every . . . single . . . day, five . . . days . . . a week! I must have been out of my head. They didn't pay that great. They ran my comments twice, so I was on CHUM 22 times a day."

The Berton presence was something special, so we decided to package his comments with a singing jingle. Musical station idents were pumped out by jingle mills stateside. They'd conceive a theme, write lyrics, and lay down a musical bedtrack. To peddle their jingle package, they'd create a demo, often using the call letters and personalities' names from a high-rated, leading station in a major U.S. city. The jingle company would flog this demo to sell the new package in many American cities.

They approached Canada in a similar manner, using CHUM as the hot-rocker demo. Slaight carved many a tough financial deal on the premise that if CHUM bought a particular jingle package, it would sell easily in other cities up here in the pink section of the map. This proved to be true for a number of jingle series.

The Berton feature was too good to miss, so Al had the jingle adapted from the package to provide an opening and closing for Pierre's commentary:

He's back again, here's Pierre!

OPENING (sung): "He's back again, here's Pierre . . . CHUM's Mr. Berton is on the air!"
CLOSING: "So, down comes the curtain on Pierre Berton . . . on C-H-U-M, Ten-Fifty, Toronto."

"You turkeys! I've just driven through the States and what did I hear? [Singing, sorta.] 'He's back again, the weather man,' 'He's back again, Irv Schwartz with sports,' and 'Down comes the curtain on Joe Obscure.'

Berton hated rock. He was annoyed by CHUM. But we loved his work.

Pierre almost swallowed his dog-eared copy of Robert Service's poems when he heard his jingle. "Down comes the curtain on Pierre Berton," he thundered down the phone to Slaight. "Sounds like I'm dead."

Al, highly amused, was ostensibly sympathetic. He stressed to Pierre how CHUM had gone to enormous trouble and expense to have those specially customized musical pieces produced. How about a bargain? You allow us to at least recoup our expenses by playing them for a while and we'll look at dropping them later.

Pierre understood money. He wanted to be fair. He reluctantly agreed. Soon after, he again hailed Slaight. He didn't need to use the phone — you could hear his howling from Kleinburg:

Customized for me, my foot! Great expense, my Aunt Fanny."

VOX POP: THE CHUM CHART

They're paper. They're prized. They exist in several sizes and many colours. They're collected. A set in mint condition is reputed to be worth beaucoup de gelt. No, they're not stamps, you crazy person who failed to read the title of this section — they're CHUM Charts.

The idea behind these petits pamphlets was to tally and report the sale of hit-parade records in the Toronto area. While CHUM was preparing to spring rock 'n' roll on an unsuspecting populace, it also assembled the first CHUM Chart. The first step was to contact as many record stores as possible, ask for their co-operation, and provide them with a sheet on which they would indicate their pop music sales for one week. This information was tabulated by CHUM, printed up imme-

diately, and returned to the record outlets in the form of the CHUM Chart.

PETER NORDHEIMER: When the CHUM Chart first came out, we were very short-staffed. So, the job of delivering them to the record outlets fell to the announcers. I covered the Queensway and all of Etobicoke. As an incentive to owners who had never heard of CHUM, we promoted the names of their stores on-air. The response made believers of them all!

The chart's acceptance with listeners, record store owners, and customers was immediate and a bit overwhelming. There was an instant demand that sucked time away from deejays and other personnel already struggling with the very real challenges of becoming a Top Forty station.

The producers of the first chart intuitively built into it the basic elements that pretty well remained from its first issue on May 27, 1957, to its last on April 26, 1975. (It was then printed in the newspaper until 1986.)

In addition to a listing of the standings of record sales for the past week, it was also a dandy mini-package of promotional items: jocks, contests, recording artists, games, and hoo-hah. People couldn't wait to paw through it each week.

If you think the Top Ten list originated with David Letterman, think again! Let's see if we can recapture the spirit and content of the CHUM Chart by offering up its top ten qualities.

A couple o' cool cats: Millie Moriak and Clementine

10. **REFLECTED EACH WEEK'S LOCAL RECORD SALES**
9. **ITS CREATORS WERE QUITE BONKERS**
8. **OFFERED CONTESTS AND KEEN PRIZES**
7. **EDUCATIONAL. ALSO PUBLISHED IN LATIN AND SWAHILI (NAAAH . . .)**
6. **PROVIDED PHOTOS OF TOP RECORDING STARS**
5. **FUN 'N' GAMES (IT CONTAINED FUN. AND GAMES.)**
4. **FEATURED HOT NEW HITS AND ALBUMS**
3. **SPOTLIGHTED CHUM DEEJAYS — OFTEN CLOTHED**
2. **PROMOTED CHUM-SPONSORED ARTISTS IN CONCERT**
1. **FREE! YOU MOOCHING, TEENAGE SNARF, YOU!**

A jazzy cat was featured on the cover of early issues. Her name was Clementine. Much of the artwork was provided by Fred Snyder, CHUM's chief operator, who had studied at the Ontario College of Art. Like so many CHUM people, Fred was multi-talented and contributed to the chart for many years. His humorous cartoon games always tickled the teens. To draw attention to the chart, a staffer recorded sayings in a cat-like voice. Listeners were asked to guess who it was, the answer being "Clementine." The cat's voice was that of Madeline Shoveller, a CHUM copywriter. Soon, she and Fred Snyder would marry.

In the fall of '58, when CHUM began to push hard with the idea that the station always got it first and did it first, we adopted the phrase "Always a Jump Ahead" and traded in Clementine for an unnamed kangaroo, designed by artist Ben Wilson. Ben joined CHUM later as an in-station artist, and not only designed the next cover, which featured full-body caricatures of our jocks swinging on a musical note, but was responsible for the chart's overall look for years to come. When CHUM abandoned the caricatures, the cover went into general use, sometimes featuring photos of the jocks, or promotions.

DAVID STILES (CHUM listener): At night we'd sneak the latest chart under the covers along with our transistor radio. It drove my parents nuts. They hated what we listened to. It was great!

The charts often supported on-air promotions, and these messages went directly into literally thousands of schools, homes, and businesses. We kept it light, kept it funny, 'cause CHUM listeners loved to laugh. Feedback has it that the April Fool's charts are particularly prized by collectors.

BOB MCADOREY: We strained our butts to make the CHUM Chart as accurate as possible — knowing full well we couldn't have a perfect reflection of record sales. I got the feeling that a few stores were a bit casual in recording and reporting their sales. So, I made up a record:

"God Save the Queen" by Mack Truck and the Gas Fumes . . . and put it on the chart. Damn if it didn't move up. Now, A&A, Sam's, Eaton's, and many big players didn't bite, nor did many of the outlets, who assumed we were fooling around, as usual. But there were enough peripheral stores who reported sales of that unlikely record that it charged up the chart. I think I took it off when it was around #32. We had a quiet chat with the offenders.

SAM (THE RECORD MAN) SNIDERMAN: We worked directly with the chart to market our 45s. I had a huge blow-up of the CHUM Chart in our pop music section, one you just couldn't miss. Records were slotted by current numbers for easy reach. I think this became common practice in many, many stores.

At one time, CHUM was producing 50,000 charts each week, and getting them into stores all over Ontario (100,000 charts per week during the CNE). In addition, we had an impressive mailing list of stations, music-oriented publishers, and other organizations.

SLAIGHT: The CHUM Chart evolved into a tremendous responsibility we didn't seek out. We had done the research, including contacting all the record stores as to their sales, and computed the findings. Many stations in other markets would simply take our chart — perhaps with a few local changes — and make it their own. Again, without aspiring to, we had a huge influence on pop music in Canada at that period.

What had begun as a promotional vehicle to help sell rock music on CHUM — and build audience — turned out to be an expensive long-term commitment and a memorable piece of growing up for thousands of people.

STAN FAIRCHILD (CHUM listener): I was a junior rep for our cottage association. My job was to buy the music for our clubhouse dance hall. So I'd head out to a record store with $50 and two or three CHUM Charts from different weeks. I'd just hand over the charts to the clerk with the numbers circled of the 45s we wanted. Worked like a charm.

Harvey Kirck — a one-person interview team

FIRST! NEWS! FIRST!
THE NEWS DEPARTMENT

If CHUM were to produce a retrospective about its news department, it might take a deep breath, examine the body of its history, jog its memory cells, stimulate its funny bone, and shake its skeletons out of the closet. Thusly:

ANNOUNCER: Good evening. My name is Lamonte Blanc. Tonight, C-H-U-M brings you a special program. Written by some guy who needs the money, and edited by Bertrand Russell, "All the Noose That Fits" is the story of the greening of the CHUM news department. The regularly scheduled *Dave Johnson Show* and *Speak Up, You Dreary Bastard* with Larry Myway will be heard tomorrow night at their unusual times. Here, with his panel, is host Harvey Kirck.

KIRCK: Good evening. Before I introduce my distinguished colleagues, allow me to wander a bit afield regarding myself, radio, and CHUM's early days in news. From the time I was a kid, I wanted to be in broadcasting. In '48 I started at Sault Ste. Marie, then in stations in Barrie, Calgary, and CKEY in Toronto. Then, to CHUM. Since CHUM was daytime only, I didn't have a hell of a lot to do. I wanted to get rich doing commercials,

and this gave me time to perform live, memorized commercials on CBC TV for Westinghouse. I worked with Laddie Dennis, the Betty Furness of Canada. (Remember her opening the fridge door?) I underwent this ulcerous ordeal for about two years.

As for CHUM news, we weren't a serious player.

Then Allan Waters bought the station and everything changed. First thing to make it all

go was a 24-hour licence that George Jones and Waters worked so hard to obtain. Waters didn't know bugger-all about the broadcasting business, or very little. But among his strengths was the smarts to hire and surround himself with good people. Pat Bennett joined

soon as news director, as did Jack Kusch. And I brought in Spragge, right out of Ryerson. He was a keener. Then came Earl Bradford and Peter Dickens at about the same time.

This is a good spot to introduce my friends here on the panel, ex-CHUM newsmen, Denis Woollings . . .

WOOLLINGS: Hello . . .

KIRCK: . . . and J.J. Richards.

RICHARDS: Hi.

KIRCK: Denis, any remembrances about Peter Dickens?

WOOLLINGS: First of all, he was our morning man, and a damn good one.

RICHARDS: Dickens was one of the best. I always wondered why he didn't go into television. He spent his entire career in radio.

WOOLLINGS: Remember his temper? When he got angry, he'd start by throwing sandwiches, then move up to staplers. He developed a great throwing arm and the sports guys used to track and post his sandwich-throwing as an ESA — Earned Salami Average.

RICHARDS: Dickens's temper? What about Kirck, here? I remember you accusing Slaight of turning the newsroom into a fish bowl because he wanted the window blinds open on Yonge Street so fans could see the jocks in their booth.

KIRCK: Well . . .

WOOLLINGS: And the time you called our pro-

Peter Dickens throws his voice

motions guy a prick and damn near started a punch-up because of the outfits he put some of you in.

RICHARDS: How well I remember it: black silk Bermuda shorts, knee-high socks, cummerbunds, white short-sleeved shirts topped with hip, crossover bow ties, and capped off with a black bowler . . .

KIRCK: My point at the time was that when you're trying to build a respected and authoritative news voice, you don't go out dressed like a clown. In retrospect, I know both guys were promoting us, but . . .

RICHARDS: Harvey, you also mentioned Bradford. I can still see him nibbling on vegetables all day because he claimed he was deprived of them as a kid. Good voice, though.

KIRCK: Who else was with us?

WOOLLINGS: There was Neil Thomas and Derek Lind.

RICHARDS: Right. Neil had a wicked sense of humour and would write headlines that Derek would read cold and destroy himself. One time the Queen was in Toronto and her vessel, *Britannia*, was moored in the harbour. What Neil wrote and Derek read cold was . . . "Ottawa — the PM promised tax cuts in the next budget . . . Halifax — fishermen protest dwindling stocks . . . Toronto — I don't care what your name is. You can't park your blue boat in my harbour!"

KIRCK: It seems to me I remember Slaight appearing instantly to brace Lind, but instead he just burst out laughing and walked away. Denis, anything memorable in your background before you joined CHUM?

WOOLLINGS: No, just the usual round of moves. Everybody did it, the jocks and the newsmen. Radio stations were generally run by cheapos whose first nickel was still warm in their pocket.

I came right out of school at 17 to a station that specialized in hiring young kids, CFCO, Chatham. It was 1955 and I earned the grand total of $28 a week. The Teamsters came in and the station used it as an excuse to introduce two new wrinkles. One, a good-behaviour bonus of an extra two dollars a week if you didn't smoke and didn't say your name on the air. The non-smoking was self-explanatory, but the real reason for not mentioning your name was you couldn't develop a following. If no one knew who you were, the station could replace you easily with another kid off the street. I moved myself out and hopped a broadcast train that took me to Toronto, with stops in Kirkland Lake, Timmins, North Bay, and Regina. As I said, lateral moves were the only way to get a raise.

The second wrinkle was a two-dollar sick bonus. They paid you two dollars because you hadn't been sick that week. However, if you did get sick, they didn't pay you any-thing. The theory being that you had saved up all those two-dollar bonuses and were well-heeled enough to live without salary.

KIRCK: J.J., you want to share a little of your pre-CHUM history with our listeners?

RICHARDS: Sure. Compared to you both and most of the CHUM news people, with per-haps the exception of Spragge, I had little radio experience. I'd spent a little over a year doing a morning show at a government radio station, CKUA, in Edmonton.

When I got here, I got a job as morning announcer at CHWO in Oakville. Darow was

CHUM newsmen Derek Lind, Bill Drylie, and Earl Bradford

now a part-timer at CHUM as he looked for singing work. As for moving to CHUM, there was a huge warehouse fire in Oakville one night and my style caught CHUM's attention.

KIRCK: J.J., how would you rate the CHUM news organization?

RICHARDS: I don't know if that's a fair question. As you know, I left the CHUM nest when I headed out to the West Coast. Later, I joined CHUM's CFUN station in Vancouver as news director and commentator. This, I think, makes my view prejudiced and suspect. But if we look at the work history of individuals, we see many of the early news guys go on to excellent careers. Look at yourself, Harv, and the work you did as news anchor at CTV. Dennis is still in the game, still writes and delivers an authoritative 'cast. Dickens and Taylor "Hap" Parnaby went to 'RB, Art Cuthbert and Sheldon Turcotte to the CBC, and Tony Parsons is anchor at CKVU in Vancouver. And that's only a few of them. Stan Ranton, for example, a first-class reporter, became speech writer for prime minister Pearson. As for CHUM and its associates, I believe they deliver some of the highest-quality news services on the radio. And then there was crusty Bill.

KIRCK: Who?

RICHARDS: Bill Drylie.

KIRCK: Right. You know Waters hired him out of the Toronto *Star*. A newspaper man in radio! Drove the radio community crazy. Especially the Americans. Practically unheard of.

WOOLLINGS: Didn't Drylie complain to Slaight about those news slogans they foisted on us? "News Comes Alive at Fifty-Five," and "CHUM — Terr-if-ic in Ter-affic in Toronto"?

KIRCK: I hated them, too. Mind you, I didn't like Drylie, either, and he didn't care for me. Got to hand it to him, though. He sharpened up the news operation. I was gone within a year.

RICHARDS: Say what you want about his temper, Bill Drylie was a consummate professional. Bill could really write. He had the ability to put into words everything he saw and make it work. He brought that authority you always said we needed.

KIRCK: Yeah, but they didn't put him in a monkey suit and tell him to hand out badges from the back of the trailer at the CNE.

WOOLLINGS: Bill loved to tell the story of when CHUM sent him to cover southern U.S.A. race riots. He described a scene right out of B movies. The setting was deep in Cracker County, near the towns of Bigotry, Ignorance, Loutsville, and Inbreeding. There, the definition of a virgin was any girl who could outrun her brother. The local constabulary did everything they could to hassle the reporters. After informing press scribes that the phones were temporarily out of order and that the hotels were all full, they dragged the news-hounds down to the local jail, where they "examined their press credentials." I think Bill described the cops as something dragged in from Central Casting: overweight, under-brained, beer-bellied, red-necked, black-hating slobs. They took down the usual details from Drylie about his name, nationality, and the station he represented. Then the interrogator said, "Hat?" And Drylie said, "No." The cop repeated, "Hat?" Drylie snapped, "I don't wear a hat." Frustrated and red-faced, the cracker cop explained, "When ah sayee 'hat,' ah don' mean what chew weah on your head. Ah mean, how towel are yew?" "How towel?" said Drylie. Then he laughed, sharing it with the other reporters, "You mean 'height.' How tall am I?" This pretty well ended the interrogation and Drylie was one of the first news people that was directed out to the airport, located close to Gritsville on the Lynchmob.

KIRCK: Great story, but past my time at CHUM.

WOOLLINGS: Going back to what J.J. said, Drylie was one piss-cutter of a writer from a journalistic point of view. CHUM had pioneered the short, sharp, crisp news style in Toronto, but he moved us up several more notches. Bill had the best attributes of a city editor, keeping abreast of the news and knowing where to go to get the story. We actually became efficient and had our people working at a whole new level.

RICHARDS: I don't know who was responsible, but we found ourselves with a full-complement newsroom: parliamentary reporters in Ottawa, international stringers, and local, on-staff reporters.

KIRCK: Yes, but that was later. Hearkening back to the earlier days, although both 'EY and 'RB had better staffs of news people, it took CHUM to personalize the news. The other stations were not only more stiff, they focused on high-falutin' issues, government policies, and other earnest topics. CHUM hit some of those highlights, but homed in mainly on Toronto and, to some extent, Ontario. We looked to bring ordinary individuals' stories to our listeners. CHUM news was more local, more human, and much warmer. It fit right in with what the rest of the station was doing with personalities, music, and out-of-station promotions. Eventually, we strongly influenced the content and tenor of other Toronto radio stations, which

the newsroom and said, "What the hell are you doing here?" Slaight had never told him. So Drylie and I had this little bit of history right from the beginning.

One day I was having a kind of argument with Drylie. Just a normal journalist-type spat over some kind of story treatment. During the course of the argument, I used the word

> Say what you want about his temper, Bill Drylie was a consummate professional. Bill could really write. He had the ability to put into words everything he saw and make it work.

reluctantly began to provide some local news and colour. Denis, how did you get aboard?
WOOLLINGS: I set my sights on working at CHUM. I called Bill Drylie and auditioned. Drylie said, "Good, I'll call you, but there's nothing right now." Later, I got a call from Slaight, who said, "I want to hire you." I said, "Great — but is that okay with Drylie?" Slaight said, "Drylie's out of town on vacation. I don't give a shit. Come on over." Drylie got back and quite literally walked into

"fuck." Not "fuck you," just "that's not the fucking truth." Drylie said, "What? You can't use that kind of language to me." I said, "What the hell do you mean? You use that kind of language yourself all the time. You're nothing but that kind of language."

Drylie said, "If you're going to use that kind of language to me, you just put on your coat and hat and get out of here."

So, I walked over and grabbed my coat off the rack and said "I haven't got a fucking hat."

And exited with as much dignity as I could muster.

I was just married to Joan Binder, who worked at CHUM. I called her and said, "I don't work there any more." She was a bit upset. I said, "Don't worry about it, I'll get a job by the end of the day."

I started calling around — 'RB, etc. — and everyone had the same story: Yeah, could be interested, but don't need anyone this minute.

Meanwhile, in between calls, the phone rings. It's the telegraph company. The message read, "The kids are crying. And I'm lonely. Come on home. Love, Mother." I called up Drylie and I said "Mother?" And he snarled, "Yes, goddammit, get back in here." Back I went. That's kind of sloppy stuff, but we got to be pretty aggressive at times. Remember J.J.'s exclusive?

RICHARDS: I blush to say there were so many of them. I will say I wasn't the only aggressive reporter, not by a long shot.

ANNOUNCER: We remind you that you're listening to "All The Noose That Fits," a retrospective of the development of CHUM Radio News. This portion of the program is brought to you by Schmedlap's Suppositories. Remember our slogan: "Kiss Bleeding Piles — Goodbye!" Here again is your host, Harvey Kirck.

KIRCK: The Toronto police were in a position to alert us to potential news items and provide useful information. No station had a better relationship with them than CHUM in the late '50s, early '60s. Each day I'd go down to the police department and read the blotter. Got to schmooze with a bunch of the guys. I pushed Waters to fund a pre-Christmas party for the cops in the basement of Nanking Restaurant. In attendance would be anyone from our station who wanted to come and over 50 of Toronto's Finest. We did that for about five years. Also, when we had stags, we always invited a couple of cops. You fellas remember that stags in timid Toronto were strictly taboo, especially if there were films that didn't show Bambi or women in less clothing than the temperature might indicate.

Sometimes a couple of other cops would "raid" us, only to find their buddies there and a glass of mother's ruin placed quickly in the raiders' hands. Any films we might have rented or tapes we prepared they "confiscated" (temporarily) to show to the guys at the shop. And were they ever great to us. Then Auntie Lloyd screwed us up.

WOOLLINGS: Auntie Lloyd? Do you mean Lloyd Lockhart?

KIRCK: Yeah. I don't know if it was his idea or not — I don't want to blame the wrong person — but Lloyd was running a kind of special affairs for Drylie. And those Leaf Gardens cops who . . . Denis, you tell the story.

WOOLLINGS: Okay. In a nutshell, there were a lot of complaints that the hired cops outside the Gardens were giving preferential treatment to the wealthy and influential regarding stopping and parking. CHUM, always for the underdog, planned a sting. One evening when the crowds were pouring into the Gardens for a game, we had Jack Kusch drive west along Carlton and park near the front doors. He was

driving an older, rather battered car. He was also wired for sound. Immediately a policeman hurried up to him and, in a voice that brooked no objection, sternly ordered Kusch to move it — and fast! Kusch, very politely, told the cops he was waiting for a sick aunt. The cop told him he didn't care if he was waiting for the Second Coming, just move that heap out of here. Very politely, Jack did as he was commanded, and drove away. We had all this on tape, of course.

Lloyd Lockhart took up the taped commentary, saying that he was driving in close to where Kusch had been — only now actually blocking the crosswalk. Lloyd, dressed in a chauffeur's outfit, complete with cap, was driving a shiny black limo. The same policeman approached him. With caution and a smile, he asked if he was waiting for someone. Lloyd, affecting a phony accent, almost snarled that he was, indeed, waiting for Lord Boomingbum of Bath. The cop touched his cap and walked away. Soon, he returned, and almost cringingly asked if Lloyd would mind

moving a few feet ahead to park, as he was blocking the crosswalk. With ill humour, Lloyd complied. And just parked there.

All this was taped, edited with comment, and run twice each hour around the clock, discussing the unfairness of this discriminatory practice by the police. It was whispered that the cop in question had been torn a new one and was pounding a beat among the oil tanks and sewage disposal near Cherry Street. We were also tipped that he was just waiting to find a CHUM person in any misdemeanour.

KIRCK: Cops are very loyal to each other and friends. And word went out that we'd broken the rules.

RICHARDS: With the jokers we had at CHUM, everyone broke the rules.

WOOLLINGS: Then there was the Art Cuthbert name debacle that left us all confused. Let's see if I can get these newsmen straight: Jack Kent Cooke hired Art Cuthbert at CKOY, Ottawa. Jack didn't like Art's name. He did, however, like the name Ron Knight, which was the name of a newsman at CKEY. So Art Cuthbert changed his name to Ron Knight. CHUM hired Art Cuthbert, with his new on-air name of Ron Knight. Then CHUM hired the real Ron Knight, who had to change his name to Steve Hunter. At this point, CHUM also hired Norm Hunter and renamed him Norm Hooper. To further confound CHUM's personnel department, we also had Bob Laine, Bob Payne, and Bob McBain.

ANNOUNCER: You have been ignoring a special broadcast by Radio Station C-H-U-M. Your host has been Harvey Kirck, and still is. The regularly scheduled program, *The Dave Johnson Show*, will return tomorrow night, followed by Larry Myway and his special phone-in topic, "The Marquis de Sade Sure Knows How to Hurt a Guy."

I'm Lamonte Blanc. Goodnight.

Mayor Nathan Phillips (left) joins Peter Dickens (right) to welcome "The Walking Doctor"

Chapter Six

ON-AIR TALENT II

HAWK IN A HOMBURG: JOHN SPRAGGE

A banshee howl of anguish screamed through the halls of CHUM. The mournful cry pierced the door of the room where our 9 a.m. meeting was about to begin.

"Hmmm," commented Slaight casually, "sounds like Hawk's here." We nodded our agreement.

"Now," said Slaight, as if we hadn't just heard that woeful wail, "what's first on our agenda? Oh yes, keeping the announcers' studio neat and tidy."

BOB MCADOREY: John Spragge was neat. I mean, he was fastidious. We all wore suits, shirts, and ties to work. But John dressed like a banker. He wore a homburg at a time when most men were considering not wearing hats at all. He used to tell his wife, Beverly, that he was going to the office. In reality, he was heading down to the CHUM circus. When faced with the bloody mess Boliska left in the announcer studio each morning, it was like Felix Unger staring at the garbage dump.

When Boliska turned over the studio to Spragge at 8:55 a.m., John had only five minutes to seat himself, clear his head, pump up his energy, and greet his listeners right on the hour. This was a daily chore for all announcers and not a particularly easy one — especially if you had to swamp out the studio after the last jock.

When Boliska vacated the studio, John would open the door, only to find it filled with cigar smoke and the smell of something you couldn't quite put your finger on. (Nor would you want to.)

MCADOREY: When Al finished his shift, the studio was a wreck. There'd be an overturned garbage can with its contents and other papers all over the floor. The air stunk. And the announce desk — it was awash in spilled coffee. Worst of all, our log — the long white

R.J. Kearsey wears a touch of mink

pages that contained everything we were to play except the music — this important document would be soaked in coffee and often had to be peeled, dripping, from the desk. Poor Spragge faced this mire, this Boliska bog, every day.

Sometimes there'd also be something creepy, crawly, and indescribable on the announcer's chair — a miniature, muffiny monstrosity that had mutated over the last three hours. Boliska could instantly transform any area he worked in into a giant petri dish. Spragge's daily, never-ending trial was akin to Sisyphus's, doomed forever to roll a boulder to the top of a high hill, only to have to do it all over again. If we are to wax mythological, perhaps a better metaphor would be the sixth labour of Hercules, where he diverts rivers to clean the Augean stables. What makes that story more apt is the loads of horse-pucky that clung to the studio after the Boliska show.

One morning, long before John's battles with bacillus Boliskii, Spragge was writing an exam at Ryerson Polytechnic Institute, when a professor interrupted him for an urgent phone call. It was Harvey Kirck at CHUM, where John had been working part-time in news. There was an emergency. Could Spragge come in to work at noon?

John answered that he was in the middle of an exam — but — if they'd agree to hire him full-time, he'd hie his young ass over to CHUM and do the noon gig. If not — nope! — and he'd take his last exam, scheduled for the next day.

JOHN SPRAGGE: What makes a 20-year-old act that way? They said, "Fine, you're on full-time staff." I didn't write another exam, and I didn't pass. And my wife has never forgiven me.

In the spring of '58, Spragge began to work five afternoons a week as a newscaster. Later, he hosted a weekend feature sponsored by Weston entitled "Holiday with CHUM." This was a summer show, featuring things to do, places to go, and traffic reports (much like the CKEY *Rolling Home* show).

SPRAGGE: Before I had my own show, Kirck had me doing morning drive-in traffic reports. I was living at home, still young, and would often sleep in. I could see the 401 from our home on Sandringham Drive. So I'd head out in my pyjamas to a CHUM cruiser and fake the first traffic report, shave, fake a second, and by the third I was on the road. One morning Kirck called while I was shaving and dreaming up my second report. The gist of the call was to ask me what the hell I was talking about. There'd been a serious accident and I'm merrily telling motorists all is well. I fessed up. He reamed me. Then he asked how long I'd been faking. I told him from the beginning. Harvey cracked up. He loved it. But from now on I was to actually get out on the road. Picky, picky, I say.

That Thanksgiving, Slaight approached Spragge to ask if he'd like to take over Harvey Dobbs's shift, 9 a.m. till noon. John would and did. And CHUM's fourth young newer-generation jock was in place, along with Laine, Johnson, and Boliska.

Spragge turned out to be an excellent choice, playing mainly to the gals at home with features like CHUM's "Housewives' Hit Parade," with women sending in votes for their favourite tunes each week. Slaight tagged him "Hawk," for a reason that eludes everyone.

A regular attraction for Spragge's women listeners was movie previews. These were generally light comedies with Rock Hudson as the hunk and Doris Day as the eternal virgin. Popular, these previews often filled two theatres above Yonge and St. Clair, with John

hosting the events, awarding prizes, and keeping it fun.

In the summer of '62, one preview, *A Touch of Mink* with Cary Grant, really pulled in the response. Al Boliska emceed, while John broadcast from the theatre lobby. Grand prize? A gorgeous mink stole.

John was committed to bettering himself through hard work. He asked for and received permission from Waters to be processed through a full commercial-radio training. In addition to his shift, he worked in every department of CHUM on his own time and for no extra money. This proved to be

Elephant and John Spragge (that's John on the right)

excellent for John's long association with radio.

John's sense of humour could cause him to self-destruct. One day he noticed a dusty pile of old 45s — duplicates and dogs — in the music library. (Wide-awake, observant John.) He picked them up, all 150 or so, and headed towards the garbage disposal. (Responsible John.) Walking down the hall, he tripped. (Same old John.) Seeing the records in a mess on the floor, his humorous side spontaneously combusted and he jumped on them and, whooping, kicked them joyfully in all directions. (The John we love.) He then noticed he was directly in front of Lyn Salloum's open door, where she and Allan Waters were staring at him. (You've-just-joined-the-club John.) "They're all broken," he said lamely to Waters. (Fast-thinking, professional quipster, John.) Soon we were lunching at Senior's, sharing mustard, swapping stories, and hoping that Waters really did have a sense of humour.

TWO MIKES AND TWO TURNTABLES: MIKE DAROW

With excitement mixed with the sinking, butterflies-in-the-stomach feeling one endures at the sound of the words "Five minutes to curtain," Mike Darow, J.J. Richards, and Trevor Evans climbed into Darow's big old Chrysler and floorboarded it from Edmonton down to Toronto in record time.

It was 1958. Trevor found work at CFTO and soon was Kiddo the Clown. J.J. landed at CHWO, and Mike just sort of hung around CHUM until they gave him some part-time chores to do, knocking on doors as part of sales promotions.

Mike Darow was born Darow Myhowich. Growing up in Edmonton, Mike displayed four outstanding characteristics or talents. First, he was very tall. (Later on, J.J. Richards would tag Mike as "Six-foot-five — plus hair.") He had a big, resonant speaking voice that nudged him early on towards a career in radio. Among a surfeit of goodies, he was also blessed with a truly fine singing voice that led him to professional offers before he was out of his teens. He could croon like Vic Damone in the style of the period. But his power, many-octave range, near-perfect pitch, and a sense of humour pulled him towards a career in musicals. That being said, his outgoing personality and true love and appreciation of people were traits that distinguished him, even when he reached prominence in the Big Apple.

In Canada, Edmonton was perhaps the best city for musicals, but everyone worked for very little. Great groups like the Orion Musical Theatre helped prepare both Mike Darow and Bob Goulet, who had left for Toronto earlier.

Darow had paid the usual radio dues with a stint of starving at CHAT in Medicine Hat, styled "CHAT in the Hat." CHAT was famous — or infamous — as a training school, where you learned to be an announcer and how to live on hope and fried air.

But as a slick — and slender — pro, Mike caught a job back at CFRN as an announcer, styling himself Mike Darow, M.D., the Doctor of Music. His show was called *Two Mikes and Two Turntables*. (Ooh, we loved those cutesy-pie labels!)

While Darow built his Edmonton radio audience and was in great demand singing around town, he was heard by a CBC-TV producer. Mike was flown to Toronto to sing on television, coast to coast, with Juliette and the swinging Jack Kane Band. His TV appearances drew excellent mail. He was asked back several times and was being groomed for bigger things. Meanwhile, he put his show business career on hold and performed front-and-centre on the radio stage.

When Phil Stone came off the air, Mike was the obvious (and excellent) choice for his replacement, 4 to 7 p.m., where he meshed well with the new generation of jocks and the CHUM sound.

Mike's height, good looks, and easygoing nature made him a perfect host when we had to squire some stars around town. As part of a promotion, he escorted Jane Morgan (*The Day the Rains Came Down*) to an opening of the new musical *Camelot*. Jane in her stunning gown and Mike in his tux made a terrific entrance as they swept down the aisle of the O'Keefe Centre. Later, Jane told a record rep that it was refreshing to be escorted by a radio announcer who was charming and not overweight, acned, and in love with his own voice. Why, Jane!

Another tall gal was Mary, of Peter, Paul and. Performing at the Colonial, Mary noticed Mike sitting at a ringside table, softly humming along with them in harmony. At the end of the number she pointed at Mike and said, "You. The hummer. Stand up." Mike stood and mumbled out that he did not think they could hear him and that he was sorry. Mary came down and stood beside Mike, measuring

Mike Darow with Jane Morgan at the opening of *Camelot*

herself against him. "I suppose you're married," Mary said. Mike allowed that he was. Mary climbed back onto the stage and said to the audience, "All the tall, good-looking ones

are married." Then to Peter and Paul, *sotto voce*, "And he can carry a tune, too."

One incident endeared Darow especially to his fellow deejays.

Elvis was great. Elvis drew listeners. Elvis

was the Prince of the Pelvis, soon to be crowned King. That meant the turntables of CHUM were gyrating with his songs morning, noon, and nighty-night-night. It also meant that the jocks were damn sick of hearing him.

Mike spun yet another Presley platter. Elvis moaned, "It's now or never . . ." With that, Darow dragged the needle across the record, *riiiiip*, shouted into the mike with his biggest showbiz voice, "NEVER!" tossed the disc into the corner, and segued into another artist.

Elvis fans screamed. Phone lines caught fire. Al Slaight was tearing into Mike just seconds after the palace revolt. Although the other jocks loved Darow's dastardly deed, there were mortgages to pay and children to feed.

Mike never repeated the stunt. Makes you wonder, though, what he might have done with "Wooden Heart" or "Return to Sender."

Mike Darow and Marge Waters, Allan's wife, found they had a mutual passion: Stan Kenton, famed progressive swing bandleader. Darow promised Marge he would track down some Kenton records for her. Every time she came to the station and saw Mike, she would kid him about not finding the records and hint she would be complaining to her husband Allan.

It was all in fun, but something had to be done. Darow dropped everything and found the Kenton records. But how to present them?

CHUM No-Stars Boliska and Darow show their style against Toronto All-Star soccer team at Varsity Stadium

This called for a statement. After his shift one night, Darow simply commandeered a group of us who were just about to head home. Nope. It seemed that we were destined to form a parade. Crammed into silly hats and

Allan opened the door and stared at our motley crew. Before he could recover, we said, "Can Marge come out and play?" Allan called Marge to the door. We drew our swords and held them up (did I mention that we were

outfits left over in the prop room, and carrying instruments, we marched down the street to the Waters home. Neil Thomas played his bugle. CHUM Chicks in costumes who had just come in from a Candy Cane Cuties promotion swayed and sang. And with me dancin' and drummin' and Darow hummin', we high-stepped up to the Waters's door. We knocked.

wearing swords?), Darow ducked under them, knelt, and handed Marge the LPs, saying, "For you, my lady." With that, we snapped off a ragged salute, turned, and double-timed it back down the street. A "Come back!" from Allan Waters stopped us and we returned to share libations with the Waterses to assuage the strain of our performance.

Guy in the Sky Mike Darow relaxes 60 feet in the air

A slick CHUM retail salesman, the type we termed "a well-scrubbed vulture," assured us we could bank a bundle of commercials if we would have one of our deejays live in a car 60 feet in the air until Golden Mile sold 300 cars. The year was 1963.

Who would do this uncomfortable and potentially dangerous stunt? Answer: Mike Darow. He had the guts and the temperament. Also, Darow adored making money. Mike exemplified the old showbiz adage "A gig is a gig." What's more, there was a bonus in it for him, which the Darows would find particularly welcome because Cathy was pregnant. The baby was due any time.

She was what? What would our listeners think if we kept a man away from his fruitful wife at baby

time? Especially if it was to raise filthy lucre for a Scrooge-driven employer? Not much. Not much nice, anyhow. So we decided to keep it a secret.

Humming a few bars of "Green Sleaze," a

day before the promotion was to start, we inspected the site. It was scarier than a tax review. The 60-foot metal scaffold was held by cables anchored to the ground. After scoffing at our querulous questions, the riggers attached huge banners reading "Mike Darow — CHUM's Guy in the Sky." A wind picked up and the whole shebang threatened to fly to Peoria. Holes were frantically cut in the canvas and the Good Ship Darow seemed becalmed. They then bolted a station wagon on top of the scaffold. The car was the exact length and width of its precarious platform and fit so snugly there was no ledge — just a straight plunge to the car lot.

Experienced riggers and other steeplejacks who wouldn't be living in the car gave it the thumbs-up — and up Darow went to settle in for the ordeal.

Climbing up to visit Mike was a daunting adventure. Most of the CHUM staff couldn't do it. Spragge climbed up several times and Mike silently gave him full marks. The best

Riggers prepare a sky-high home for Mike Darow

of us was photographer Neil Newton, who swung in fearlessly like a tintype Tarzan. Since I had to go up daily, I'll tell you that what was terrifying about it was that the rear door of the station wagon stuck out and you had to let go of the scaffolding and reach out before you could climb in.

This was a pants-changing manoeuvre.

It was baby-birthing time for Cathy Darow and I drove her to the hospital. I approached

Mike Darow is 60 feet in the air . . . living in a car . . . at Golden Mile Motors.

BIDDY (glancing at the security guard): And Mr. . . . ah . . . Darow changed his name while he was up there, eh?

MOI: Definitely not. Sure, he was taking trombone lessons, but . . .

BIDDY (as if talking to a small child): This woman is not Mrs. Farrell. And she's not Mrs. Darow. So who, precisely, is she?

A slick CHUM retail salesman, the type we termed "a well-scrubbed vulture," assured us we could bank a bundle of commercials if we would have one of our deejays live in a car 60 feet in the air until Golden Mile sold 300 cars. The year was 1963.

admissions and was drawn into a comedy routine with a hawk-nosed biddy who, I believe, was suffering from unhappy hemorrhoids.

BIDDY: What is your name?

MOI: My name? Why do you . . . ?

BIDDY: Sir, give me your name.

MOI: Allen Farrell . . . but . . .

BIDDY (writing in the form): Mrs. Farrell.

MOI (starting to panic): It's not Mrs. Farrell. She's not my wife. (Biddy gives me a tough look.) She's Mike Darow's wife.

BIDDY: Ah, so it's Mrs. Darow.

MOI (my voice becoming squeaky): Definitely not Mrs. Darow. (over-explaining) You see,

MOI (with a sickly smile): She's Mrs. Myhowich.

With a world-weary shake of the head, she filled in Cathy's form and Mrs. Myhowich was taken away to perform nature's miracle. Mike stayed up there for several more days before Golden Mile sold their quota of cars. I filled in for him, on the home front, taking flowers to Cathy, making kootchy-kootchy-koo with baby Alissa, and becoming familiar to the other women in the room. I took Polaroids and ran them up the scaffolding to Mike.

Soon as the promotion was over, Mike hurried down. He was briefly interviewed by

J.J. and then hightailed it over to see Cathy at the hospital. As he gave her a hug and a kiss and fussed over the baby, I noticed the other women in the room giving Mike the hairy eyeball. Because of our secrecy, Cathy had never spoken of Mike. And so, when one of the women got up the courage to quietly ask me who he was, I said, in a very loud voice, "Him? Why, he's the father of the child." And then I scurried from the room.

In the end, CHUM picked up a thick wad of advertising dollars, Golden Mile Chevrolet sold lotfuls of cars, and CHUM — and Mike Darow — was the talk o' the town. Whether Cathy Darow will ever forgive us is still open to question, however. Mike said a number of times that leaving CHUM was the toughest thing he ever did. But in 1965, the New York stage and TV beckoned, and he answered. CHUM's problem was how to fill his size 12 shoes and enormous heart.

MISTER MISCHIEVOUS: BOB MCADOREY

Bob McAdorey had an Irish leprechaun-like bent toward mischief. "Lord love ya," he'd say,

before taking you or his audience down some trail to trouble. Take "The Case of the Probed Proboscis."

CHUM guys and gals were always out on some public promotion or other. Photos of the event were taken for publicity or to show a client. We were forced to scrutinize them carefully if Bob was in the shot because, just before the camera clicked, he'd jam his finger in his nostril and simulate picking his nose. (This would really impress a food advertiser.) Some days the heat from photographer Neil Newton's frustration could fog his film. We pled. We cajoled. We threatened. Still the next photo session would be ruined, finger-up-the-nose-wise.

Finally, we assigned staff to watch his tricky finger critically during photo shoots that included Bob. You'd hear our anti-finger fellows saying, "Who's on nose pick?"

MCADOREY: I was in Stamford Collegiate in Niagara Falls when my guidance counsellor called me in. It was obvious I wouldn't graduate because of my maths and sciences. My teacher said that I was good at English, public speaking, and a pretty good writer. There was an opening at radio station CHVC for a copy-

Above: Dick Hayes took over the 1-to-4 Mike Darow slot; Right: Bob McAdorey prepares for more bull on his show

writer. I applied, got the job, and my meticulous handling of sweeping the floor led me to an on-air shift. Then to London, where I met Boliska. Then CJOY, Guelph.

Bob's entree into radio pretty well paralleled most other announcers'. Their voices — or talents — dictated their life's work.

Very few announcers have university degrees, although some take training in college radio and arts courses. Most enter radio young and are poorly informed. This changes almost immediately.

In short time, announcers build up a kind of knowledge about music. Almost simultaneously, they pick up on current sports they (or their station) report several times a day. Then come current events, politics, financial jargon, and a local, provincial, national, and international picture. This happens mostly by osmosis. Not as informed as newsmen, but you can't be exposed to a half dozen newscasts — or more — per shift, five or six days a week for years, without soaking up a skinful of information.

Like Mac, pop deejays particularly have a highly developed sense of fun and comedy. And, "Lord love ya," with luck, it gets them into trouble.

MCADOREY: I was elected alderman in Guelph while I was at CJOY. I'd built a house, we'd

had a second child, and I was there forever. Boliska called me and said CHUM needed a person for 4 to 7 p.m. Would I send an audition tape? I did, along with a note that said I wanted the outrageous sum of $600 a month. We'd heard that Gordie Tapp was getting $100 a week at CHML. What could anybody possibly do with a $100 a week? Then CHUM called and offered to hire me for $600 a month. Alderman, shmalderman — I agreed. Heavy on the "greed."

CHUM tried never to miss a chance for self-promotion. When it was settled that Bob would join us in the 4 to 7 p.m. drive-home slot, we began an oblique build-up. Each of the CHUM announcers mentioned to his listeners that with Pete Nordheimer leaving, Mike Darow was moving from the 4 to 7 p.m. shift to the 1 to 4 p.m. They added casually that the 4 to 7 p.m. shift was a desirable one — and one each jock wouldn't mind taking on. Over a period

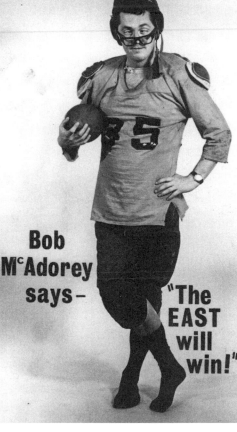

Bob McAdorey says— "The EAST will win!"

of two weeks, this turned into an internecine war, with each announcer jockeying (yeah, yeah) for the drive-home spot. This was good as far as it went — promoting the time slot and building interest — but how could we get out of it? The CHUM announcers sincerely sounded as if they'd be pissed off at anyone who took the shift — particularly an outsider.

So, when McAdorey was announced to our listeners as the winning candidate, we had to get Bob off the hook. The announcers each told his audience they had heard good things about Bob, but they had to be convinced he had the stuff to be part of the CHUM team. They decided to initiate Mac, using Trial by Hot Air.

Mac was ordered to join Bob Laine on the all-nite show. Bobbo peppered Mac with questions about his eagerness to make an ass of himself in public. Would he be willing to log-roll? Scuba dive? Wear red underwear and walk down Yonge Street? Yes, he would.

McAdorey displays his "Body Beautiful" in championship form

Bobbo passed McAdorey off to Boliska at 6 a.m. Al had him reading jokes, improvising comedy with him, and substituting for Just Plain George in the World's Worst Jokes. Boliska also mentioned that he and Mac were old friends. When Spragge came on at 9 a.m., Boliska said McAdorey was doing pretty well, but he wasn't totally convinced yet.

going wild. "Give the guy a break. He's terrific. Cut him some slack."

Mike did. He assured listeners that Bob had passed all their tests with flying colours. He was now part of the CHUM team. An exhausted and grateful Mac said thanks to the jocks and thanks to the audience for their calls and good wishes. Phew! (That evening he only rested

Bobbo peppered Mac with questions about his eagerness to make an ass of himself in public. Would he be willing to log-roll? Scuba dive? Wear red underwear and walk down Yonge Street? Yes, he would.

In truth, Mac sounded terrific. But Johnny really hammered him, demanding he ad lib commercials, talk live to his listeners, and set up a Housewives movie promotion. By this time, listeners had been calling in. They liked Bob McAdorey and said, "Don't you think you're going a little too far? The poor guy has been up since midnight." We paid no attention. Bob then moved into the tender mercies of Mike Darow, who interrogated him about his knowledge of music and made him do intro after intro to records. Now the phones were

and guested on Johnson's show. Then Dave took him out for emergency drinks.)

MCADOREY: I still didn't get on the air for at least another week. Meanwhile, CHUM asked me to emcee a music function at Massey Hall. I walked out cold and said, "Good evening, I'm Bob McAdorey," and the place went nuts. Whistlin' and clappin', and stompin' — a standing ovation. As I said, I hadn't been on the air yet — except for my initiation. What kind of place was this CHUM anyhow?

Mac discovered that CHUM was the kind of place where he'd fit in perfectly. Waters and Slaight now had their complete, contemporary on-air lineup. Another building block was in place. CHUM had funny, appealing men in both Boliska (then Jungle), in the morning, and Mac in drivetime. Bob also had an excellent ear for music. (As for his nose, no comment.) Mac's musical sense landed him the responsibility of being music director of CHUM (while retaining his on-air shift). His combination of music savvy, approachability, and wild humour was noted by Channel 9, and Bob hosted *Hi-Time*, CFTO's TV dance party, each Saturday afternoon. (Worth noting, too, is that along with Mac on CFTO TV, Darow once hosted *Club Six*, CBC TV's teen dance, and Boliska picked up the emcee duties on CBC TV's *On the Scene*. A hearty round of "Hear, hears" and "Huzzahs," please.)

Mac was articulate, comically inventive, and, yes, full of mischief. Listeners enjoyed the absolute glee he exuded as he flirted with dangerous topics or commentary. He was on the skinny side and styled himself on-air as "The Body Beautiful — with the knees that please." We had fun with that, formally "uncovering" his knees in public, with attendant shrieking from the gals.

You might also call Bob unpredictable. One time CHUM received a telephone call from him the day before he was to return from his holidays. Could CHUM send him $500? He had deplaned from an aircraft as it landed on some obscure southern island, and he just didn't bother getting back on. He waved to his wife and friends as they took off. "And oh, by the way, okay if I take another week of my holiday?"

SCHTICK MEN: LARRY & GARRY

Larry was Larry Solway. Garry was Garry Ferrier. They still are. Garry was modest, rather shy, and unassuming. Larry . . . well . . .

Both were bright and uncommonly talented. Each made significant contributions to CHUM, both individually and as part of a team. While still at CHUM, they also played in the big American leagues of commercials and comedy on network radio. Many CHUM employees made a buck or two with outside enterprises, but Larry and Garry set a whole new gold standard.

LARRY SOLWAY: When CHUM went rock, the conservatives in the business — which was everybody — said, "Aw, it can't last. Rock 'n' roll is just a fad." In August of '57 I was interviewed by Phil Ladd, who said to me, "Can you write?" Never having written anything of note,

Garry turns the tables on Larry

I replied, "Oh, ho, can I write!" It seems their creative director, Cam Langford, was having serious health problems related to his paraplegia. Ladd asked me if I could start that day, so I literally walked into the copy department, sat down behind an electric typewriter, and began to write. As early as the next day, I was in the studio with an announcer voicing those 250-words-a-minute, two-voice screamers.

From the beginning, Larry could write an inventive commercial as fast as he could type it. Solway was acting in radio and TV at the same time that he taught at Holy Blossom Temple Religious School, ran a television tube business, and part-timed at CHUM.

SOLWAY: I was one of the world's great part-timers. Slaight put the kibosh on that. He said I was either going to be here . . . or not be here. Cam's health had really declined and CHUM needed a creative director. I came on full-time and I believe I made less money working five full days a week than when I was part-time. Oh, that sly Slaight. The copy department got in step with the rock format and became another asset. With the sales people bugging us for fresh approaches and gimmicks to sell, we piped in some fresh blood — the wickedly comic mind of Garry Ferrier.

Garry Ferrier's prime interest was music. Specifically, jazz. Mainly a self-taught musician, he went from blowing the bugle in the De La Salle marching band to taking master classes in jazz piano with Oscar Peterson. He did take some lessons at the insistence of his mother, but he preferred boogie-woogie to Chopin, and played in a Dixieland jazz band on weekends.

As for radio, he, too, did the boonie bit, and as we join one of the heroes of this chapter we find him as program director in deepest Oakville at CHWO.

GERRY FERRIER: I hired a news director, an itinerant camel driver named J.J. Richards, who had just travelled down from Edmonton with Mike Darow. J.J. ran the 6 a.m. morning news, then drove back from Scarborough for the 6 p.m. news hour and the evening run. Plus the ethnic programming on the weekend. His was the best voice on the station. We paid him a cool $53.10 a week. No wonder Richards grabbed it when Slaight offered him a job after hearing him do some freelance voice reports. J.J. liked the comedy bits I was doing on the CHWO morning show and played a tape for the CHUM people. This led to an interview with Slaight, and I jumped at an offer to work for the summer, giving traffic reports from a cruiser and writing for

Solway in the copy department.

Like everyone else, I did an Ed Sullivan impression: "And now, ladies and gentlemen, let's hear it for Nick McKoski and his trained bears. Somebody clean up that mess."

Larry taught me to write copy his way, the CHUM way: hard-sell, fast, dynamic. And to let my imagination go. CHUM kept me after

them to be as good as anything being produced in North America. This turned out to be true. Advertising agencies, those pools of paranoia that are terrified to let anyone near their clients, began to commission our Terrific Two to create comedy commercials. This began slowly, but then acceptance grew as they called on the agencies playing their samples.

the summer. I began to do voices on spots and write comedy commercials. Larry kept encouraging me. I'd never done this before. It changed my life. I got centred. Maybe writing comedy was something I could do for a living.

Solway and Ferrier teamed up first of all to create comedy commercials for CHUM. With our bias fluttering from the mast, we judged

Almost simultaneously, they began winging comedy bits as they worked in the studio. It began with a takeoff on a news series Harvey Kirck was assembling on prostitutes and Toronto's tenderloin. With Garry as the call girl and Larry as the hard-hitting reporter, the results were hilarious. Slaight directed them to do a new piece every day, which would be repeated. This was to be the first time they

91

Larry & Garry meet Bob & Ray (Ferrier with Bob Elliot; Ray Goulding with Solway)

were identified as CHUM's Larry & Garry.

They picked up the tempo of their careers when Solway was holidaying in San Francisco. He took a few of their tapes and played them for agency giant Young & Rubicam. The timing was perfect. America's number-one commercial funnyman, Stan Freeburg, had refused to do Kaiser Aluminum Foil spots. Larry & Garry were awarded the job, the first of what was to become a number of prestigious American campaigns, including General Motors and a huge one for Coca-Cola.

They thought they'd been flying high — and they had — until Garry took their comedy tapes to ABC Radio in New York. Comedy team Bob & Ray were legends on radio. ABC decided to add comedy to their U.S. network show, *Flair*. Larry & Garry was their comedy answer. And to fine acclaim.

Meanwhile, back at the ranch, they continued to write copy and expand their contribution to CHUM. Garry's comic talents were matched by musical ones. Johnny Horton had a hit in "The Battle of New Orleans." This jingoistic American song prompted listeners to call in. Couldn't we play something where Canada beat the Yanks? Enter Garry Ferrier. He wrote a song entitled "The Battle of Queenston Heights." We recorded it professionally with Mike Darow on lead vocal. Terrific reaction from listeners, with credits going to Garry and Mike every time we played it.

Larry was to become inextricably intertwined and associated with a phone-in program entitled *Speak Your Mind*.

Speak Your Mind was originally a 25-minute show that ran from 10:30 to 10:55 p.m. Its first host was Marcus Long — Irish, and a professor at the University of Toronto. His approach was rather benign, and he took calls from anyone (usually with a beef) and sort of calmed them down with logic and a soft brogue.

Next to bat on the show were June Callwood and Trent Frayne. Sometimes they'd do the show together and other times alternate the hosting duties. The show was newsier under their aegis, with June very strong on issues of inequality.

92

Darow and Ferrier go a little "over the top" to promote Garry's record

SOLWAY: It was at the time they could no longer do the show that Slaight came to me and said, "You know a little bit about just about everything!" And I do. Slaight tried me out on the show, alternating with J.J. Richards, who was primarily in news and special events. Slaight chose me for permanent host.

Larry brought an argumentative quality to *Speak Your Mind* that people came to expect from him. He also added the concept of a single topic.

SOLWAY: Slaight wanted me to be tough. No problem, because I'm an intolerant kind of guy. Everyone is entitled to his or her opinion, especially me. Slaight liked to hear me hanging up on people. That was showbiz. I didn't like hanging up as much as I loved winning an argument. I'm not sure whether I was a creature of Slaight . . . or of my own honesty.

Speak Your Mind continued on, challenging our only talk competition, beating out 'EY's very capable Brad Crandell in the numbers. Its popularity saw CHUM expand *Speak Your Mind* to two hours, 10 p.m. to midnight.

SOLWAY: I was known to some people as "The man you love to hate." I didn't particularly like that. Not at all.

With everything else he was doing, Larry took on a two-person dialogue feature. Pierre Berton and Charles Templeton were making a success of it on CFRB. A topic would be chosen or a question posed and Berton would take one side of it and Templeton the other. CHUM blatantly copied it.

Across the microphone from Solway was ex-mayor Phil Givens. What did I name their pieces we ran each day? "Give 'n' Take." The feature was well received and had a decent run. Of course, we took every opportunity to promote Givens, including him (or a ringer) in our out-of-station events like the broomball game with the policewomen.

FERRIER: Solway was really into *Speak Your Mind* and, as an actor, was developing this on-air persona that was close to a cobra with a fang-ache. Me, I figured I was one of the luckiest guys in the world. Waters had just given me a profit-sharing cheque. I never felt I deserved it. I thought, "God bless the man. He's spreading it around. He has my respect and love." (Laughs.) That's what money does for Ferrier. I'll follow you home.

Garry, knowledgeable about jazz, knew little about classical music. Solway used to tutor him in the copy department. A picture worth framing was the two of them listening

to Richard Strauss while writing commercials for Cayuga Raceway.

CHUM was approached by the police department to assist them in an awareness campaign regarding traffic deaths in Toronto during October 1961. We entitled it "The Black Flags Are Flying." Every time a traffic death occurred, both CHUM and the police flew black flags (like those on funeral cars). CHUM would also air dramatic announcements regarding the fatality and our need to be careful.

We searched for some music that would set these serious messages apart from our usual froth. Larry Solway instantly suggested "Fanfare for the Common Man" by Aaron Copland. It was perfect.

Not only did our listeners comment favourably on this campaign but it went on to win U.S. awards and inspired a number of stations to adopt it. They all wanted to know the name of that extraordinary music.

Ferrier was modest almost to a San Andreas fault. Comic Vaughn Meader had a huge album hit with an impersonation of President Jack Kennedy. Kennedy was riding the myth of Camelot and material about him was gold. The comic megillah of the album was Kennedy (Meader) answering questions at a press conference with gag answers. Funny. Lots of airplay, tons of sales.

Larry Solway speaks his mind, and speaks his mind, and speaks his mind

I wrote a Canadian version as a promotional vehicle for CHUM. Garry did the Kennedy voice. Big hit. Astral Records wanted to release it. Did. Excellent sales (a 10,000 advance sale). But the biggest surprise was the newspaper reviews. After some years of CHUM taking a pasting from local scribes, reviews from Toronto were in step with those from Montreal and other cities — unanimously favourable, some, glowing.

A few columnists quoted gag lines they particularly liked, but all lauded Ferrier's impression. One reviewer went so far as to take the CBC to task for not hiring and featuring such an obviously talented young man as Garry.

Larry and Garry did do work for the CBC, but with their hands tied behind their backs. Later, Garry would write successful TV shows for the government mother ship while holding down his job at CHUM. Larry and *Speak Your Mind* moved to prime time and remained an intrinsic part of the CHUM persona.

Individually, both made their mark. Collectively, theirs was a rich commingling of talents and personalities.

Chapter Seven
COMING OF AGE

MOTHER, WE'RE HOME: MOVIN' AND GROOVIN'

Hallelujah! It's moving day!

In 1959, CHUM abandoned its digs on Adelaide Street and set up house in the Ginn Building at 1331 Yonge Street. It is situated a few blocks south of St. Clair Avenue, on what Toronto expert and author Mike Filey says is called Gallows Hill. Was Allan Waters, who always gave us lots of rope, trying to tell us something?

The potential trauma of leaving the downtown Murky Mystery Mansion and being housed all day in a real building prompted management to have counsellors on hand to introduce us gently to our new environment. We held hands as we were taken through the building in groups of five.

"My God, what's that?" one of the CHUM staff shrieked. "That's Mr. Office, dear," said the counsellor patiently. "Ooh," we chorused. "And that?" squeaked another staffer, pointing and cringing against the wall.

"Sweetheart, that is Mrs. Chair, and you needn't be afraid." "Ah," we sighed in relief. "Look at that big thingamabob," exclaimed another of our gang. "Now, now, that's only Miss Desk," the counsellor said kindly.

"Eee," we breathed. In the next few minutes we were introduced to Mr. and Mrs. Washroom, Tippy the Typewriter, and Gabby Gestetner. This was all very comforting, but one question lurked in our collective minds: where were Mr. Mouse, Roger the Rat, and Friend Cockroach? And there was no sign of a bottle in a brown paper bag anywhere. We assumed they were all hidden and that they came out at night. "Yuck," we whispered to ourselves.

In truth, it was wonderful going to work in a building where you didn't need to take tetanus shots. Most of us now had offices to ourselves and there was plenty of space to expand or to throw your old pizza boxes. Parking was limited, but free. The record library was bigger, sales worked out of the second floor, and the

Our new home was most "appealing"

news people actually had a space to themselves. Desks, pencils, teletypes, and everything.

Nearby were a number of places for pleasant walks or to eat and shop, and the Northgate Hotel was just down the hill.

Our fresh and upgraded environment definitely had a salubrious effect on morale (we could actually find and see each other) and was the genesis of a team concept. People came together as a team in departments, each with a clearer, emerging role. Staff socialized in groups. The on-air CHUM Champions concept was maturing from an embryonic stage to something more tangible. Perhaps most important of all, with much of the Top Forty generation staff falling into place, our entity became more cohesive.

Still, we continued to look askance at the "T" word. The phrase "CHUM Team" was not spoken. If it were, it would probably be met with a smirk. Yet, let someone outside criticize or make fun of CHUM, and the staff would close ranks like a herd of bull yaks.

CHUM — and rock — were still far from being acceptable in some quarters, notably the Board of Broadcast Governors (BBG) and advertising agencies. And then — about a year later — there was that snob we encountered at an industry cocktail party. (By "we," I mean John Spragge, Mike Darow, Jack Kusch, and Fred Snyder.)

The boys were doing their best to keep distillers' stocks rising when a stranger inched into their grouping. He had read their lapel tags and murmured, "CHUM, huh?" He identified himself. It was a name like Haddock. He went on, "Since you're with CHUM, I suppose you dig the rock 'n' roll." Exchanging glances that hinted there might be sport here, our fellas agreed that they did, indeed, "dig the rock 'n' roll." Misreading their mood and encouraged by their smiles, with a curled lip, Haddock sneered, "I wonder if I were to give a $100 bill to the evening announcer, would he play a classical record just once?" His superior smile suggested he had just delivered an epigram worthy of Oscar Wilde.

Putting down their drinks (by God, they were serious!), Spragge stepped forward to reel in this bottom-feeder. Their fishing derby went something like this:

SPRAGGE (pasting on a smile a shark might envy): First of all, Mr. H., a $100 bill wouldn't even tempt our evening announcer, Dave Johnson. Dave makes so much money, he might use your $100 bill to light his fine cigars. But if it's money you're interested in throwing around, I'll bet you not $100, but $500 that our evening announcer, as you call him, knows five times more about opera than you'll ever know (making reaching movements towards his wallet). You pick the jury, and I'll lay down the bet.

KUSCH (fed by John's fire): And I'll bet you $1000 that Mike Darow here knows 10 times more about show music than you do.

DAROW (waving his wallet in Haddock's face): And I'll bet $10,000 that CHUM's Garry Ferrier knows 50 times more about jazz music than you . . . and that our promotions guy knows 100 times more about Shakespeare.

KUSCH: And I'll bet you another $10,000 that Larry Solway knows more about everything than you.

HADDOCK (gagged, netted, and wiggling in the bottom of the boat): Well, be that as it may, it bloody galls me to have to teach CHUM's kind of radio in our school.

SNYDER (who stood by and watched the fishing derby and didn't put his drink down): Then why don't you try a more suitable career? Like lard box–folding?

With Haddock skinned, filleted, and definitely on ice, the CHUM boys put their wallets back in their pockets. Sum total of their contents: $12.47. They then picked up their drinks, ceremoniously saluted themselves, and sauntered into the crowd to further demonstrate what a bunch of fun fellows they were.

PAPER TIGER: ARTHUR

Allan Waters owned the station. He was the head man. But, as in many corporations, there was a special person behind the scenes who held the whip hand.

I am speaking of Arthur.

Arthur bossed us all. He bossed Slaight. He bossed Drylie. He bossed Solway. On occasion he even bossed Waters — when he wasn't hitting up Allan for five or ten dollars — money Waters could little afford. Croesus, Allan was not.

Arthur, our janitor, was a petty despot who ensured there was no paper or any other refuse on the floor. Jamaican, 80-ish, he was about five foot four and carried a box about two-thirds his size, suspended by a rubber thong worn over his shoulder.

When we heard him approaching, we would all scramble madly to pick up paper or anything that had hit the floor. Arthur would enter an office and always, it seemed, find some detritus we had missed. This called for a dressing-down from our lord of the litter. We liked Arthur and wore his admonishments like a badge of honour. We'd tell each other, "D'you know what Arthur just said to me?"

Late one hot-sunned, summer Friday afternoon, the streets glutted with impatient, sweaty, cottage-going traffic, Wes Armstrong rushed into my office. He looked grim. "Call an ambulance," he said tightly. "Call the fire department. It's Arthur. He's sick." I did. Then I hurried into Waters's office, where Arthur was sitting limply on a chair, with Allan and Wes standing attentively over him. He began to say, "Mr. Farrell, I don't feel well . . ." when he fell onto his back on the rug, his eyes fluttering. Wes, always a take-charge guy, had the good sense to remove Arthur's now-loose false teeth. A patch of sunlight that had slipped unnoticed through the office blinds covered Arthur like a shroud. A spasm of pain racked his small body. When it subsided, he said quite softly, "I've had it." Then, holding us firmly in his eyes as if to etch us in his memory, he said, "Goodbye" to each of us one by one. And, with a sigh, he was gone.

Arthur had no relatives in Canada. Waters arranged for the funeral in the St. James cemetery. It was quite a turnout. Everyone at CHUM who could get there attended. Even crusty, cynical Drylie. Black flags flying, the CHUM cruisers and private cars crawled solemnly to the grave site. For the first time in CHUM's history, there were no quips, no gags, and no asides. Humour seemed to have dropped out of sight, much like crumpled paper into Arthur's box.

The sunlight was filtered by the dappling leaves on the trees, refracted into many hues of soft green, as Arthur was slowly lowered to rest.

Arthur was family. A friend. And not one of us would ever retrieve a piece of paper from the floor again without thinking of him. We would lose other members of our family to death's grip in years to come. Bill Drylie would be next.

Old Sol slid behind a lowering cloud as our sad procession turned northwards on Yonge, towards 1331 and home.

TURNING THE TABLES: OPERATORS

CHUM operators were the men behind the men behind the mike. They spun the disks, recorded traffic reports and race results, and slotted in the cartridges for jingles, station breaks, comedy bits, and commercials. Operators had to be card-shark quick, smooth, and part mind-reader. They anticipated a jock's mood, matched his style, and waltzed to his rhythm. These were fully clothed turntable dancers. CHUM's air was full of flying balls and our operators juggled them like adroit carnival performers. They included Dave Shaw, Walt Ryan, Peter Crampton, Bob McQuiggan, Ray Kinoshameg, Glenn Russell, and Doug Thompson, who went on to be a hot CHUM producer.

DOUG THOMPSON: Where you really learned to fill in as an operator, seguing to commercial, seguing to station ident, seguing to music and generally faking it with sound . . . was when McAdorey would leave the studio and lead a leering pack of newsmen onto Yonge Street in the summer afternoons. Each day at five, the girls leaving Pilot Insurance would parade by, providing a late afternoon pick-me-up for the guys.

Then there were those operators who did double duty. George Nicholson (Just Plain George) was Ed McMahon to Boliska's Johnny Carson, as well as producing his show. George was also a stand-up goalie for our hockey team and a play-maker on our squirrelly basketball squad. And he found the films for our stags. Oh, George!

Chief Operator Fred Snyder put zing 'n' sting into our commercials and promotional announcements and made us all look good as he recorded our comedy segments. Besides contributing regularly to the CHUM Charts, he put his rural Saskatchewan accent to good use creating on-air characters. As Wilbur Beyer, he announced supermarket specials on CHUM's *Shopping Show*. Then, in summer, he gave tips to anglers on *Fine Fishin' with Len Weed*. Fred/Wilbur/Len would later become Moose Latreck.

Each Friday afternoon at about 5 p.m., Fred would announce that "Eddy's Bar and Grill" was open. This meant Snyder had a twenty-sixer of rye whisky available for sippin' behind the Ampex recording equipment. Production staff were especially welcome to partake, but Fred never sent any parched pilgrim away without a small taste. This ritual was in response to the fact that Friday afternoons were insane in production. Members of the copy department, Solway, Ferrier, Dan Hyatt, and Mary-Helen McPhillips would queue up with all the commercials that needed to be voiced and mixed for Saturday, Sunday, and Monday.

Promotion elbowed its way in, too, with announcements introducing new contests, out-of-station appearances, or other bags of mixed nutsy notions and cutesy comedy come-ons.

Slaight had long before decreed that we were to make commercials and public service and station promotional announcements as entertaining as possible. That meant producing each one with two or more voices, plus sound and music. And with as much shtick as a dedicated listener could stomach.

So Ferdy or Ferd, as Fred was tagged by Millie Moriak and Scoob McInnes, made life tolerable as we toiled late each Friday evening.

Soon, an operator with extraordinary potential skills would lighten the load:

Claude Deschamps. Claude, born in St. Jean d'Iberville, Quebec, came to CHUM as an operator from CJMS Radio, Montreal, speaking almost no English.

CLAUDE DESCHAMPS: Farrell helped me learn English with the help of Perry Mason novels. I was improving, when I discovered Charles Dickens and looked up unfamiliar words. I didn't know it had affected my speech until Allen came into the studio one day, and I said, "Your countenance is extraordinarily robust and commendable." "What have you been reading?" asked Farrell. "Charles Dickens," I said. "Forsooth," he said, "you'd better stick to Perry Mason."

Claude's production skills would be challenged later when we took on the *Dick Clark Show*. For now, he and Dave Johnson became a terrific turntable team.

TOO MANY COOKES: COMPETITION

At CHUM, we looked at the competition in one of two ways: we were either competing for volume of listeners or for advertising revenues.

CFRB fell into the second category, along with print media and TV. Cee-Eff-Are-Bee, spoken with a sense of self-congratulatory staidness, had its own well-established audience. Theirs was a solid staff, led by long-time morning man Wally Crouter, and enjoying depth in news and commentary with Jack Dennett, Gordon Sinclair, and Betty Kennedy. John Spragge once said that folks were milking cows to the sound of CFRB all over Ontario. 'RB definitely saw itself as the cream — even if it was CHUM that was rising to the top.

Originally, 'RB ignored CHUM from a great height, not even doing what high-flying birds do. It wasn't until CHUM began to syphon off some of the national advertising dollars that they deigned to notice us.

Despite CHUM's extraordinary showing in the ratings between 9 a.m. and 3:30 p.m. when (mostly) moms (read, consumers) were at home, the station continued to suffer from the teenage-audience reputation albatross.

CFRB's sales staff — in front of ad agency types — congratulated CHUM on owning the teeny-bopper market. CHUM sales people repaid this compliment in kind, praising CFRB's management for providing ramps for their announcers' wheelchairs, including rubber underwear as part of their pay packet, and installing faucets that ran prune juice and Geritol.

When their sales people characterized our jocks as having teenage stars in their eyes, we reciprocated by tagging 'RB as having an announcer staff with pennies on their eyes.

This battle for the buck soon stopped. Let's call it a draw (as in drawing blood). Besides, it was CKEY territory that was our true battlefield.

CKEY was the dominant force in Toronto radio in the mid fifties. Until CHUM's old Sonic Tonic rocked the Toronto boat, 'EY's audience share roosted eagle-like in the rarefied air of about 45 percent of Toronto. (No station would threaten that record again until CHUM did, in the early sixties, with 42.5 percent.)

In the meantime, CHUM, with 17 percent of the market in mid '58, truly had its work cut out.

CHUM's secret weapon in the early rock warfare was the owner of CKEY itself, Jack Kent Cooke. Jack was an entrepreneur extraordinaire. A self-made millionaire, he owned, among other knick-knacks, *Liberty* magazine and the Maple Leafs baseball team. He was flamboyant, successful, unpredictable, and arrogant.

AL SLAIGHT: Cooke couldn't believe how we were swallowing 'EY's audience. Once, he demanded to sit with the phonists at Elliott-Haynes's survey office. When person after person was asked in mid-morning who they were listening to, and he heard the answers, "CHUM," "CHUM," "CHUM," "CHUM," he nearly took gas.

When it was obvious that CHUM was for real, and the rock of the town, Kent reluctantly went Top Forty with a sound almost identical to CHUM's. He had two advantages: a more mature lineup of on-air staff and the financial clout to promote the station. CKEY picked up some of the listeners they had lost, but not for long. CHUM gained back the audience, and began its long upward climb.

DUFF ROMAN: Everything revolved around Jack's whims. One time he showed up at 3:00 a.m. He had pop singer Kay Starr with him. I'm doing the all-nite show. He said, "What time's the next sports, Duff?" I said, "3:15 a.m." He said, "I'll take care of it." So, armed with sports scores, I introduced him with the name he'd given me: "With the 3:15 sports, here's Biff Burns." Jack started, "This is B-i-i-f B-u-u-rns with all-nite sports." He finished up, collected Kay, and trundled off into the night.

Jack was notorious for coaching even his top announcers during their shifts. 'EY announcer Keith Sandy was a pro's pro. Jack joined him in the studio during a commercial. Just seconds before Sandy opened his mike, Jack drawled, "All right, Keith, say something really funny!" It was said he enjoyed seeing people fall apart before him.

ROMAN: There was no one he was tougher on than his own brother Hal, who supposedly managed the station. Jack we knew only as this eccentric millionaire who'd swoop down on us from time to time, upsetting the programming and individuals. He'd change the format, then turn it back to brother Hal, whom he referred to as "Nooksie." At one announcers' meeting, an order was put in for coffee all around. The young guys pushed back their chairs and headed out to get the coffee. Jack said, "No, no, no, goddammit, you guys are important to this meeting. Nooksie will fetch the coffee." And out would go Nooksie, with a red face, to fetch what the master wanted.

When CKEY went rock, it suffered the same pains that CHUM had when it came to replacing its established announcers. Keith Sandy, Stu Kenny, Mickey Lester, Martin Silbert, and Brad Crandell were extremely popular. Newsmen Franklin Armstrong and Howard Cooney were seasoned veterans, as were Joe Chrysdale, who created simulated sports with Hal Kelly, and Ron Dunn who hosted the all-nite show. (He tagged himself "Rundown Ron Dunn" and could imitate Jack Kent Cooke perfectly.)

Many of these men had to go to make room for Top Forty jocks. Duff Roman, Brian Skinner (the Chinner Spinner), and Larry Teeson were among the early replacements. Later, the great voice of Bill Brady would be heard and the comedy duo of Steve Goodman and Keith Rich would brighten mornings. But in the early days of rock on CKEY, there was mostly the old group doing the best they could under Jack's bent baton. CHUM used Jack's ego to goose 'EY's Cooke.

CKEY ran a contest. They'd call out the name of someone living in the Toronto area. If that person phoned in within a prescribed time and correctly identified himself, he would win a prize. 'EY wasn't getting a lot of results. Then CHUM listened in to 'EY, called out the same name on-air, and said if the listener phoned CHUM immediately he would win a prize. When the listener called in, we told him to phone CKEY to claim his prize. We added, "Be sure to tell them you heard your name on CHUM first. They'll love to know that."

ALLAN WATERS: Jack phoned me, infuriated. Asked if we were going to stop. I said no. Then he threatened to sue me. I said, "That's okay." We continued to rag on him, and, oddly enough, he and I became friends.

Jack gave up the fight in Toronto radio. He had foolishly attempted single-handed combat against a committed army.

ROMAN: When Jack announced to us he was heading for the U.S.A., he strongly suggested we all do the same thing. When we hesitated, he heaped abuse upon us, calling us chicken-shit, idiots, and losers.

LARRY SOLWAY: To save face, Jack always said that he left Toronto and Canada because of greater business opportunities stateside. But we know we ran him out of town.

Hit the road, Jack.

ALL-AMERICAN BOY: DICK CLARK

In 1963, the Dick Clark people had an idea. Why not spread Dick — his name, fame, and talent — around? For Yankee dollars.

His producers set out to create the illusion that Dick Clark was performing live shows with local deejays across North America. In reality, the shows would get taped clips of Dick introducing, and often back-tagging, records. A 12-inch reel was sent to every station that subscribed to this syndicated service.

Fleshing out the Dick Clark participation and helping to build the impression that Clark was right there in the studio were customized voice clips. On these, Dick would give station idents, use the jock's name and "talk" to him

and, perhaps, ask him a typical question, such as, "What's the temperature, Dave?" (Johnson).

CHUM was very interested in throwing something new, strong, and promotable at CKEY. We gave the *Dick Clark Show* sample tape a hard listen.

CLAUDE DESCHAMPS: Dick sounded just fine, but we thought the total production effect was rather amateurish. Slaight, Farrell, and I said "Bush league" almost in unison. However, give it the CHUM touch, and it could be terrific. (Seems we'd missed Humility 101.)

We bought the package, then Deschamps took over and wove his production magic. He was onto the Clark people constantly, wheedling, begging, demanding more customized cuts from Clark: personal asides, his experience with recording artists, by-play with Dave Johnson. Claude asked for — and received — hundreds of customized and personalized comments.

DESCHAMPS: They had Dick asking Dave the time. I switched it, and had Dave ask Dick. This meant Dick had to record every possible minute for two hours. "Dave, it's 8:17 here on CHUM," etc. Then we did the same with temperature. Also, I had Dick do special things like sing "Happy Birthday" to Dave, make

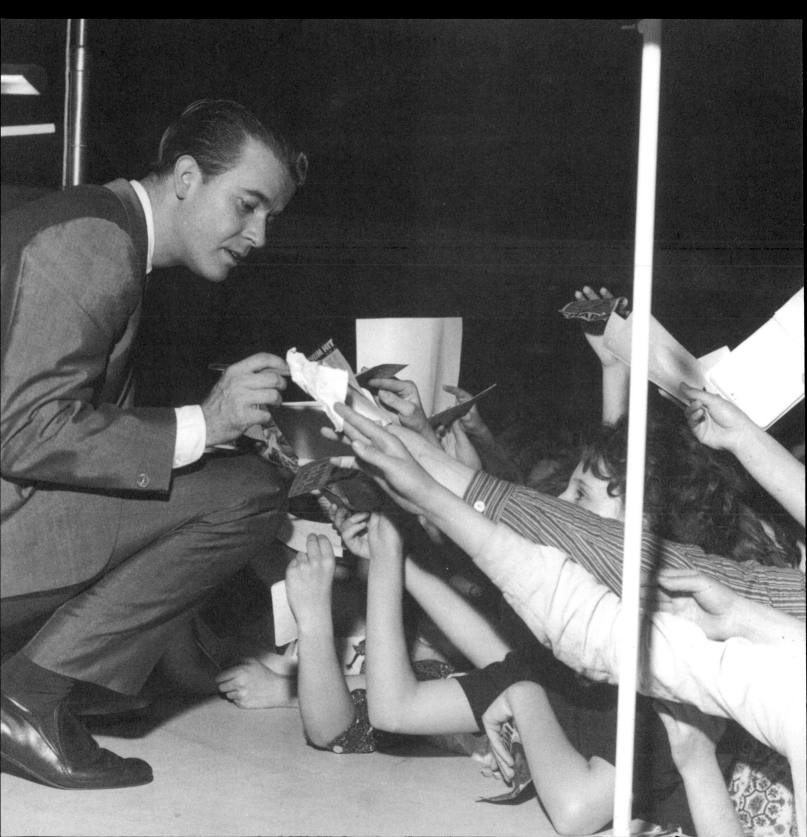

references to other CHUM jocks or features or to Toronto events, and anything else that gave credence to the live quality of the program. Dick was fantastic. Never turned us down.

Claude was often buried in stacks of cartridges in the control room, some with only one line from Clark on them. While the Dick Clark/Dave Johnson show was cooking, Claude resembled a demented octopus taking a Twist lesson.

When Dick heard the CHUM version of the show, he called with congratulations and offered Claude a job with his production company. Problems with bureaucracy and immigration prevented this from happening.

We blasted off the first Dick Clark show with a live broadcast of a ring-a-ding rock hop from the Terrace. Da joint was jammed and jumpin'! There we created a bang-up, blown-up version of Dick's legendary *American Bandstand* TV show for a huge audience. The roller rink rocked as a jam-packed crowd, excited just to be near this most famous of all pop-music radio personalities, got down and shook their booties.

Dick Clark and Johnson co-hosted. In the tradition of *Bandstand*, guest performers were invited to "Sign in, please." And so they did. Freddie Cannon and Bobby Curtola, among others, outdid themselves belting out their charted hits. The Chummingbirds made a guest appearance, CHUM Chicks escorted the artists, and the CHUM jocks turned up the charm and mixed with the crowds. Boliska was in rare form that night, and his antics on the dance floor created a classic comic boogie. The evening was an unqualified smash, establishing Clark as part of CHUM's musical juggernaut.

Later, celebrating and relaxing at Al Slaight's home with a few CHUM types, Dick asked for the show's introduction (which we'd taped) to be played over and over: "Here he is . . ." Johnson's enthusiastic voice proclaimed, ". . . Dick Clark!" The ensuing roar from a jammed Terrace audience tore the air. The walls of the arena had seemed to bulge with the power of the response. Now Dick, with a huge grin, kept repeating, "Just like the old days, only bigger. Let's hear it again!" Nice to know a superstar is human.

MICKEY MOUTH: DAVE MICKEY

No cock o' the walk likes to be interrupted in mid strut. CKEY not only choked off our crowing, they also almost served us up browned and well basted in our own boasting pan.

The name of the new, dominant radio rooster: Dave Mickey. Dave patterned himself after Dick Biondi at station WLS, Chicago.

Dick Clark meets CHUM fans' hands

Dave was young. Dave was fearless. Dave talked faster than a man caught in bed with his neighbour's wife. His real name was Dave Marsden, but he used Dave Mickey on the air.

DAVE MARSDEN: I was 18 years old. I'd been in boonie radio for only one year. Now I was

going on-air 7 to 10 p.m., in Toronto, on a top radio station, against CHUM — *CHUM!* — and the Dick Clark/Dave Johnson show for gee-awd's sake. Thirty seconds to airtime and I was scared shitless! I took my cue, and my tongue tore into my first record intro. I was speaking at a speed even *I* couldn't follow.

Generally, I zipped along at about 350 words per minute. Management told me later they'd clocked me that night around 700 words per minute. They loved it, and told me to keep it up there. Ha! But how?

The kids loved it. Rockin' adults said they hated it, but damned sure tuned Dave in to see how much. Dave Mickey was the talk of Toronto. CHUM was the station with all the commercials, the ratings, that great old gang of familiar guys. But Mickey was fresh. Outrageous. In. Hip.

Buzz: "Mickey crashed CHUM's Dick Clark Cavalcade of Stars reception at the Gardens' Hot Stove Lounge. Were the CHUM guys ever pissed off!"

Buzz: "Did you know CKEY gave Mickey a monkey that lives with him? It's called Mickey's Monkey, after a Motown hit, and it peed down his back while Dave was broadcasting. Too much! He's really putting it to CHUM."

Buzz: "Hey! did you see that — whatta-yacallit — stretch limo he arrives in each night with an armed guard at the CNE? The fans

Brian Skinner and a CHUM Chick oversee an "easy as pie" contest at the Ex

want to touch him. Dave Mickey! Dave Mickey! Dave Mickey!"

CHUM owned the CNE. The phrase "CHUM Checks from the Ex" was as familiar as what Jack and Jill did on the hill or "Thirty days hath September."

That summer 'EY built a colourful exhibit around a circus theme. Each night Mickey would command the centre ring. His performance was augmented by hot bands brought in by Duff Roman, who was still at 'EY. And,

was with Mickey and CKEY in the evenings. We'd been predominant and arrogant for so long that it hurt to eat it. Crow, dirt, whatever. Ironically, CKEY announcers were trying to digest the same spread.

ROMAN: When I joined CKEY, mature announcers with top ratings and great pipes knew they could not do what newcomers like Skinner, Larry Teeson, and I were used to laying against the mike. Now I and my fellow

CHUM owned the CNE. The phrase "CHUM Checks from the Ex" was as familiar as what Jack and Jill did on the hill or "Thirty days hath September."

boy, were they tooting this attraction on the air, as well they should.

Instead of puking in distress, we set to work. Our strategy: focus on adults, families, and the daytime up to 7 p.m., when Mickey came on air. Everyone was pressed into service, challenged to devise special events that would draw our listeners to the trailer and keep them there.

Attraction-jammed days drew record crowds and plugged the Princes' Gates area with people. Every single day at the Ex was filled with a list of crowd-pleasers. Evenings we'd slip into our traditional mode of regular contests, Chummingbirds performing, prizes, and jocular jocks. It worked, but the action

jocks at 'EY (and CHUM) heard Mickey and despaired that if that was the voice of the future, we'd soon be out on the streets or back in the boonies.

MARSDEN: That sojourn at CKEY was one of the most confusing and toughest of my young life. I spent most of my time living with that damn monkey, who tore up my apartment. When I finally slipped out for food or human contact, super-fans would be waiting and mob me. I had a very tiny, but nasty, taste of what real celebrity is all about. God, I was lonely.

Today Dave remembers his brush with stardom as being about as glamorous as hiding under the porch steps to avoid the school bullies. But then, he was the thorn in CHUM's tender bits and a constant source of irritation. What were we to do?

As it turned out, nothing. Mickey left CKEY after about six months. Dave chose TV over radio. He signed a contract with CBC TV, co-hosting *Music Hop* with Alex Trebek.

Ultimately, Mickey did us little harm. In fact, he might have sharpened us up. Having exposed our soft underbelly, however, we wondered why 'EY didn't attack with, perhaps, another motor-mouth. Well, if they didn't have a plan, we sure weren't going to provide one on the back of a CHUM Chart!

TAKE NO PRISONERS: CHUM'S DIRTY TRICKS DEPARTMENT

If you've played basketball, a dictum hammered into your benumbed brain by coaches is "beat the bugger to the spot." The bugger in question is a hot shooter for the other team. The spot is where he or she loves to set up on the court. Beating him means hustling to this favourite shooting position before he does. Thus, in theory, you've neutralized a key competitive advantage.

The CHUM on-air strategy incorporated the spirit of that ploy. Not only did we focus on offence, we also used defensive tactics, attempting to dilute the competition's prime strengths. This strategy included teasing.

But as any schoolchild will tell you, it's no fun teasing someone who ignores you. You must target a victim who will squeal the loudest when you pull his or her tail.

Both Hal and Jack Cooke were excellent subjects — but especially Jack. As a successful businessman, he was unfamiliar with being ridiculed in public. And he was downright enraged when the kidder was CHUM. Who had ever heard of Allan Waters? Or those other losers he surrounded himself with? And what's all this shit about a CHUM seal?

The seal was CHUM's pet device for splashing cold water on CKEY's promotions. Whenever we kidded them on the air we'd end our piece with the seal's recorded "Ork, ork, ork, ork." Our staffers sometimes referred to it as CHUM's "Seal of Disapproval." The true origin of our marine mocker is more fun. "Seal" in French is "le phoque" (rhymes with "Jock"). So each time our whiskered wonder barked on air, we were saying, "'Phoque' 'em if they can't take a joke."

One day in 1959 CHUM Operative 1050 tipped us that 'EY had ordered a trailer to equip as a remote broadcast booth. This was an expense CHUM didn't need. But, to compete — or *lead* . . . damn!

Our operative's report contained the name of 'EY's trailer manufacturer in Peterborough. Dropping everything, we scurried up there and saw the 'EY design and early renovation. Hey! We could improve on that. After Allan Waters and George Jones looked it over and approved a sale, CHUM went into full promotional gear.

We called it CHUM's Satellite Station, asked listeners to watch for it, and told them to look for its space-age design and bright red-and-white colours.

'EY, who wouldn't be taking delivery of their trailer for at least two months, didn't say a thing. We assumed they thought, like everyone else, that CHUM had beaten them to the punch again and that our Satellite Station was whizzing about town, making money on commercial remotes and generally promoting our station. In reality, work on it hadn't begun.

Upside: when 'EY unwrapped their trailer, it was "Ho-hum, CKEY's imitating CHUM again." Downside: when we finally received our trailer and begun towing it around Toronto, we couldn't say much. After all, our more streamlined Satellite Station had been out for six months, hadn't it?

One Saturday morning our phone rang. It was Allan Waters. Had I been listening to CKEY? No. Do so, please, and note their new promotion. Call me back. I did.

CKEY was running a cute, nicely produced little promo to push their theme: "The Fabulous Forty."

LITTLE GIRL'S VOICE: My Mommy listens to the Fabulous Forty.
MATURE (RATHER SEXY) WOMAN'S VOICE: My *baby* listens to the Fabulous Forty.
MUSIC: Stinger

"I heard it, Mr. Waters." Three words from Waters to me: "Go. Get. Them!" And I did. And we did. I wrote 26 versions of the following:

LITTLE BOY'S VOICE: My creaky, crappy crocodile listens to the Sloppy Seventeen.
MATURE WOMAN'S VOICE: My creaky, crappy crocodile's *baby* listens to the Sloppy Seventeen.
DEEP, SNEERING MALE VOICE: Whyyy?

Silly stuff, but you get the picture. Fred Snyder came in to produce, and using people who were in the station we recorded the cuts — sales secretary Shirley Hart as the Mommy, me as the little kid, and J.J. Richards adding the wonderfully sneering "Whyyy?" CKEY cancelled their promotion. We never knew "Whyyy?"

On another occasion in the early fall of 1963, Operator 1050 came through again. CKEY was about to put together a basketball team, made up mainly of their personalities, to go out and play high schools.

Sometime back, we'd heard of American stations doing this on a casual basis, playing a game now and then. Reports were that the events went over very well. We'd kept it on the back burner because we knew what a bugger it would be to execute. Also, we'd do it with a frequency and intensity that the Yanks had never heard of. And now, 'EY was going ahead with a team. Before us, yet.

So, it was Action Stations once again. On the air immediately went promos talking up our non-existent team and inviting schools to play us — if they dared. Implied was that we had been doing this for some time and were just getting around to promoting it because we'd been so jammed with requests.

So, dirty trick #1 was that we scooped 'EY, who didn't come on air promoting their team for at least a month afterward. (Why? I ask you, why?) Again, listeners assumed 'EY was imitating CHUM. "Couldn't CKEY think up anything of their own?"

But dirty trick #2 was much more insidious. 'EY played a few games, but most, if not all, were out of town. Playing games in Metro Toronto was tough enough, and we'd taken on a heavy schedule. We didn't need the added pressure of driving to Brampton. Or farther. Our goal was to stay in Toronto. So, with a black snake in our hearts, we wrote and phoned the presidents of student councils in all the high schools in Metro Toronto. Oozing sincerity and universal largesse, we explained that our competition with 'EY was simply a game we played on the air. We went on to say that both our stations agreed that the important factor was providing each school with fun and a fundraising event. (At this juncture, you may reach for your vomit bag.) We had, therefore, agreed that only one of our stations could come to each school. For example, we said, breathing generosity and fair play, if their school wanted CKEY, we encouraged them to call them. On the other hand, if they should prefer CHUM . . . well, they should put in a request within a few days because our bookings in Toronto were close to closing. Dripping concern, we asked if we could give them a name and a slam-dunk number at CHUM they could contact in case they had an immediate ad hoc meeting and wanted to discuss a firm date.

Result? We tied up nearly all of Metro's high schools. 'EY could hardly get a game without driving way out of town. This, of course, cut down their appearances, while we worked our way through the Metro schools. Personally, I was proud as punch. Although some days I think about "Limbo Rock" and "How low can you go?"

ROMAN: Another time when I was at 'EY, we were proud of our stolen car reports. We fit the missing vehicles into a format that ran as follows: Music, sirens 'n stuff . . . and . . . "Hot Car! Hot Car! Hot Car! Police report stolen a black-and-white 1962 Chevrolet. If you spot this vehicle, call the police. Remember, if you leave your car, lock it and remove the keys." CHUM countered with "stolen dogs" announcements, using similar music and sound effects: "Hot Dog! Hot Dog! Hot Dog! Police dogs report a stolen black-and-white pooch named Spot. If you see this animal, wash the dog and remove the fleas." Some of us laughed. Hal didn't. He pulled the Hot Car announcements off the air.

But what CHUM really yearned for was a major coup that would send listeners flocking to us, having told 'EY to flock off. Ideally, we'd trick our arch enemy into making a serious music change (away from rock), leaving CHUM as the only major rock station, with the attendant option of programming precisely as we cared to. "Dream, dream, dream," as the twinned tonsils of the Everly Brothers might have sung.

To the best of our knowledge, no station had ever accomplished that feat. So what in the sacred name of Chuck Berry gave us the hubris to believe that we mere mortals could? Answer: CKEY's mistaken conviction that we were omnipotent in Toronto pop radio. The two Cookes, nicknamed Frank and Jesse by J.J. Richards, firmly believed that CHUM had a secret programming formula that bordered on the mystic, plus inside information based on divine revelation.

The earthly truth was that we were flying by the seat of our shiny pants. Rock worked — sure! — Waters had proven that dramatically. But, owning an exclusive programming stratagem? You've got to be kidding! Ask the secret of CHUM's increasing success, and our answer would probably have been a firm and resounding "Huh?"

Buoyed by the fact that it is usually appearances, not truth, that count, and after several Old Viennas for courage, we lifted our kilts, showed our hairy backsides to our enemy, turned, and charged. We decided to try to convince 'EY that we were about to change our music from rock 'n' roll to swing. Why swing, rather than, say, calliope music? One: major trade mags in the U.S. had reported that several stations had switched to swing music and were doing all right. (In very small print they added that these were in markets crammed with rock stations.) Two: swing was an easier sell for advertising dollars, particularly to agencies who stuck with whatever

was safe or trendy. And, three (you sly dog): Jack Kent Cooke hated rock and adored the big bands.

We knew that if we were to pull off this one-time-only deception, we'd have to go all the way. This meant demanding of ourselves exactly what CHUM would do if it truly was switching to swing. CHUM would go all-out, balls-to-the-wall. So, with visions of eggs all over our scarlet faces, we not only bit the bullet, but fired at will.

Our bogus campaign began with a theme to give it credibility: "The Sweet Swingin' Sound of CHUM." We aired a teaser: "What is S.S.S.?" Promos followed hard on the teaser's heels: "S.S.S. — coming soon to CHUM." Next came the inevitable and expected contest: "What is S.S.S.? Win keen-o prizes, etc. Coming soon to CHUM." And, to further build believability, S.S.S. was featured on the CHUM Chart.

In the middle of our waltz with Machiavelli, we moved down to the Sportsmen's Show, angling for hunters and others to become new listeners. And smack-dab over our glass box booth we hung a huge red sign: "Listen for the

It's printed. It must be true.

Sweet Swingin' Sound — Soon on CHUM."
Next to us we displayed an array of big-band
LP covers, including Miller, Dorsey, Kenton,
and Shaw. It was a bit of a laugh watching 'EY
staff spies sidle up to our booth to say hello,
all the while getting a big eyeful of our sign
and display. This was the last bit of evidence
the Cookie Monsters needed. CHUM had
promoted it heavily on the air, pushed it on the
chart, and now printed it in public. It must be
true!

Meanwhile, the CHUM staff was giving us
funny looks — particularly the jocks. Because
of the esteem in which they held Slaight and
me, and the deep respect they had for our
strategies, they asked us quietly, "Are you out
of your cotton-pickin' minds?" Or commented softly, "Swing? Swing?! You assholes!!"
As for Allan Waters, who was in on the ploy,
he watched the ratings and waited.

ROMAN: I was still at 'EY at the time. We had
no idea that what CHUM was doing was a
sham. All we knew was that Jack Kent Cooke
swept into town in an uproar. He called us all
together, told us he had done some research or
something and that CKEY was going swing.
It was a black day. No one could believe it. It
was so crushing for us young disc jockeys that
now we were going to play Jack's invention,
"The Sweet Sound of the Sixties." And immediately we were playing swing, creating sugary
programs with harp-interlude intros and even
giving poetry readings. Jack stopped anything
that had to do with rock and demanded we
program around that theme. I remember him
crowing, "We've beat the bastards to the punch!"

CKEY swung like mad with those great
bands, and we allowed them to blow their
brains out. The rumour mill whispered that the
Cookes were boasting to anyone who'd listen
that they'd tweaked CHUM's nose but good.
We played Puss in the Corner and allowed them
to establish that they'd abandoned rock 'n' roll.
By then, Slaight had the station rockin' like hell,
replete with his coveted hardened sound. This
was energized by music contests, chances to
meet rock artists, and anything that emphasized
our dominance as the station with the hits.

CKEY, although puzzled, continued to
swing in the wind for a few weeks, then
switched back to their former rock format. But
CHUM had picked up some new listeners and
had demoralized the enemy. Rating surveys
reflected an increase in our audience.

Chapter Eight

PROMOTE THIS!

AND THE WINNER IS . . .: CHUM CONTESTS

Wiggle those waists. Oil those hips.
Bob those bottoms and enter CHUM's
Hooplarious Hula Hoop Contest!

CHUM wants to see you go round in
circles . . . and win prizes so neat
your head'll spin!

Meet CHUM's Dave Johnson, Mr. Hula Hoop
himself, 10 a.m. this Saturday,
Dixie Plaza . . . and give it a whirl.

Hula Hoopers — see you around!

Yowsah, yowsah, yowsah. Shades of Allan Waters's early patent-medicine activities, contests were viewed as the elixir that would put pep in the step of a radio station. Whether they would deliver cash or just be cute, contests were a cornerstone of CHUM, along with music, personalities, and information.

CHUM followed the shaky logic that, if one contest could act as an iron pill to infuse red blood into anemic ratings or sagging listener interest, then a cartful of contests would make the station positively robust. So, we piled them on. (Yes, yes, I know, we piled *it* on, too.)

Our contest activities were driven by a philosophy that dictated that nothing, *nothing*, was too controversial, cornball, or wacky to air.

A little contest popular in 1958 was entitled "Bucks for Breaks." Listeners would send in a station break, we'd use it on the air, identify the sender, and fire out a dollar. Many of the breaks were really quite clever and they seeped into our CHUM lexicon: "C-H-U-M. We're fit to be tried," or "Got a minute? Put CHUM in it."

One slogan that sticks in memory was "Wanna have fun? Listen to CHUM!" We particularly wanted to use it because "fun" was an Allan Waters byword. When I explained to the listener/writer that we liked it, except that it didn't rhyme, he said,

117

"Whatta you mean it doesn't rhyme? Are you deaf?" Who can argue with such logic? What the hell. We were spenders. We sent him the buck.

Hard on its heels came Bocks for Knocks, an obvious knock-off of knock-knock jokes. Peruse a few ripe samples from listeners:

Knock knock.
Who's there?
Venice.
Venice who?
Venice Boliska going to get new gags?

Knock knock.
Who's there?
Thelma.
Thelma who?
Thelma radio? Are you Cwaythy? I'm lithening to CHUM.

Knock knock.
Who's there?
Dishes.
Dishes who?
Dishes me. Dat is you. And in between is CHUM.

Knocked out? Well, some CHUM critic once wrote a letter to the editor complaining that we were "pandering to the younger sex."

This "Bucks for . . ." concept evolved into Bucks for Yucks (a dollar for each short gag we used on the air), and finally, years later, into the zaniest, most popular listener-response contest we held: Bucks for Clucks. We invited listeners to call in and

"What say my apartment at 6:30 for a little drinkie-winkie?"

cluck like a chicken. The phones went wild. Our switchboard became overloaded. Each time we picked up the phone, on every line, we'd hear "*Cluuuuuck, cluuuck, cluuck, cluck.*" And the occasional "*Cock-a-doodle-doo*" from the over-inspired.

Bell Telephone phoned and pretty well demanded we stop whatever-in-hell we were doing. Seemed the response had "blown out" an exchange, and listeners' clucking was clogging phones for blocks around. We taped the clucks, played them over the air, and finally announced a winner as "The Biggest CHUM Clucker in Ontario."

Contests could be divided into a number of categories. (We never thought that way about them at the time; we were too busy thrashing about and muddling on.) For example, there were station-personalities contests.

A favourite of these was Design a Sign. This multi-faceted promotion encouraged plenty of talk. Al Boliska offered to arrange for 50-foot billboards for each of the jocks. Listeners were invited to design a sign for their favourite deejay. Twenty-five bucks was awarded for each winning entry. The catch was, Al demanded that the jocks paint the winning designs. We arranged for professional sign painters to help them. When finished, addresses were given for the sign locations, and listeners were invited to visit the signs and choose their favourite. There were gag prizes. Locations were rotated. What for most stations (products, etc.) would have been just another "outdoor campaign"

was developed into a listener-involving, fun project that really drew attention to our advertising. The favourite board was one for Mike Darow. It featured a hooded man with an axe against a bloody background and read, "Listen to Mike Darow on CHUM-1050 or you die!" (Boy, some of our listeners were sickies.)

Then there were the jocks' own contests, ones exclusive to a single deejay. Dave Johnson loved a contest called "Title Tales." Listeners were invited to make up a story using 10 titles from the CHUM Chart. With prizes of $5 and $25, who could resist? Let's see: "*The Great Imposter* ran into a *Hitchhiker* playing a *Yo-Yo*. He said, *I Just Don't Understand. Why . . . ?*" You finish it.

There were also some silly "we're pulling your leg" contests:

"CHUM's Five Thousand Dollar Contest! You send us $5,000 dollars. We'll send you 25 words or less. Enter now!"

"CHUM's Clever Cat Contest. If your cat can say 'I always listen to CHUM,' we'll award it $1,000. Let your cat bring you in today!" (Do you believe listeners brought cats in? You bet your tuna fish.)

Subtle, subliminal CHUM advertising

Of course we had retail sales contests, a staple of the era. In Super Shopping Spree, listeners could win three, five, or ten minutes of shopping at a supermarket. The event would be recorded and highlights played back. Dragsters, move over. For real thrills, watch a determined gal and her shopping cart race the clock.

HONEST ED MIRVISH: I've always believed in promotions. I recall clearly two successful ones we did with CHUM. They ran a dance marathon, then a rollerskating contest in our store. There was Phil Stone broadcasting in the windows. Drew excellent crowds and good business.

The CHUM Chart contests were also a hit. Holy Buddy Holly! There were contests on the back of the chart about every other week. Based upon response, the crazier, the better. Especially the April Fools' charts. (See this dot? Hold the dot up to your nose, rotate the book, and stand back for a big surprise.)

There were national sales contests, such as Cars and Cash, sponsored by Instant Maxwell House Coffee and the Jell-O Family of Fine Foods. Advertisers bought a substantial chunk of radio time on CHUM. An instructional/promotional booklet was sent to a great number of Toronto homes. CHUM gave it the full on-air treatment. Listeners could win a '62 Dodge or a '62 Valiant. Plus prizes of $200 per hour and $400 bonus hours! — 14 times each day, six days a week. CHUM maintained it was pure coincidence that this blockbuster contest was positioned smack-dab in an important ratings period.

Mike Darow and Bob Laine with contestants at the CHUM/Honest Ed's Dance Marathon

And, of course, seasonal contests. Crusade for a White Christmas was held one particularly balmy December. CHUM had listeners call in and sing a verse of "White Christmas" on the air. If anything could have prodded the weather gods to co-operate and send snow, it was the amazing extra sharps and flats our listeners glissaded into the Irving Berlin classic.

Oh, stop already. Hard to believe, but there were close to 1,000 contests run on CHUM from 1957 to '67. For years and years, witnessed giant-sized sliced-cheese packages (along with three other jumbo packaged foods) actually being snapped up and sold in supermarket after supermarket, all part of a product promotion with a gangbuster prize, when we received only eight entries. That's the tip for the contest crazies: you have a much better chance than you think with many promotions. As for radio stations, if we don't set up our clients ahead of time, the following could happen.

They ran a dance marathon, then a rollerskating contest in our store. There was Phil Stone broadcasting in the windows. Drew excellent crowds and good business.

CHUM kept up the clarion call to WIN! KEEN! PRIZES!

Strange but true, many product-driven contests move merchandise off the shelves without necessarily attracting a truckful of entries. Apparently the excitement and ballyhoo that surround the ads and the promotion inspire many consumers to buy the merchandise without actually entering the contest. This is a tricky concept to sell to ad agencies and advertisers because it sounds as though you're wimping out and providing an excuse for potential failure. But, it's true all right. We

When I first joined CHUM, a three-week contest had just closed. Product had moved beautifully off the shelves. Now the account exec from the Framis Agency wanted to see the entry-forms. It seems that CHUM's sales rep had kept him happy by saying, "Entries are pouring in!" Now he wanted to see the mail. He was coming over now to get it. Our mail bin held precisely 17 entries. When Slaight said to me, "Handle it," I was wondering how fast I could get out of Dodge. I definitely had to adjust my moral compass.

Mr. Excitable from the agency landed in

my office. "Well, where are they?" Feigning surprise, I asked him how he could have missed those huge cartons blocking our entryway. We headed out to the lobby entrance. Mysteriously, there were no cartons. I questioned Switchboard Betty. With a straight face, she said she'd had them moved to the shipping dock, because they were in the way. Mr. Excitable smelled a scam. And me, my nose was growing. We hastened out to the dock, only to find the doors open. Questioned, our handyman said he thought those cartons were garbage, and had put them on the dump truck. Mr. Excitable knew we were lying. And I knew I'd never grow up to be a real boy.

"How the hell will we find a winner now?" choked Mr. Excitable. After a suitable pause for method-acting puzzlement, I gave an "I have it!" I led him back to the mail bin. "Here's a few we removed early to examine." He took the pathetic pile of entries in his hand, much as he might hold fresh bird lime. "There's something very wrong here," he muttered. Then he left, leaving only a pungent odour of distrust. Later, we heard he resigned from the agency and went on to teach James Joyce. Perhaps it was to help decipher our fink-think. Or to study "A Portrait of the Artist as a Young Con Man."

PETER NORDHEIMER: One of our contests revolved around listeners having their houses cleaned by a pair of CHUM deejays. Al Boliska and I were teamed up. No one was encouraged to take this offer 100 percent seriously. Our winners did. They met us at the door with mops, brooms, brushes, pails, and cleaning agents. We washed windows, walls, and ceilings, vacuumed, polished, and swept. For hours. I remember photographer Neil Newton shooting us cleaning the bathroom and saying to Al, "Can't you get your arm further down into the toilet?" We found out later the other jocks did some perfunctory sweeping or dusting, were served coffee and cake, and went out to lunch with the winners. We simply looked for a shotgun and tried to find Mr. Promotion.

Al Boliska (on ladder) and Pete Nordheimer really clean house for CHUM contest winners

NO GOOD DEED GOES UNPUNISHED:
PUBLIC SERVICE

CHUM was hounded for free airtime by not-for-profit organizations ranging from the Society for the Preservation of Hockey Players' Jock Straps to the Venerable Brotherhood of Single Malt Scotch Sippers.

One well-known Jarvis Street tabernacle for the downtrodden once asked us for a cash donation for the needy. Allan Waters gave his approval on the condition that we check them out. Upon investigation, we discovered they had, in their secretary's words, "taken our ministry south for the winter. It's a mission we take on each year." Further questioning uncovered that they were spreading the Word to the unenlightened in Jamaica, Nassau, and Trinidad and Tobago, all the while spreading the tanning oil, too. It was a dirty job, but . . . We said we'd pass on filling their collection plate until they took their winter ministry to the balmy beaches of Baffin Island.

Radio, by and large, did a reasonable job of promoting public-service organizations. This often meant donating airtime for a func-

tion or fundraising activity being held by some charitable group. Encouraged by the BBG, many big-city stations exaggerated their public spirit by running spots in that prime, high-listener time slot — the middle of the night.

When CHUM took on a P.S. campaign, instead of simply reading the pallid press releases we received, we threw our best creative people at it. And we would often tie a package together with station and on-air personality participation. Our relationship with the Heart Fund ran for many years. It was during a Heart Fund campaign that we met Mike, Mark, and Jack — the Rhythm Pals — three great, talented guys we were to team up with several times. One collaboration involved a song-writing contest on CHUM. The winning original song was titled, "The Ballad of the Dying Cowboy." We recorded this hurtin' tune with Boliska, backed by the Rhythm Pals, with proceeds going to a good cause.

Another CHUM Heart Fund promotion began with each jock soliciting valentines that contained donations. Friendly rivals Dave Johnson and Bob Laine heated up the

Boliska is coached by Darow for his singing debut: "The Ballad of the Dying Cowboy"

promotion with a bet that whichever of the two received the least money would walk north up Yonge Street from Queen to CHUM in long red underwear (in February) collecting money. We, of course, promoted the bejabbers out of this on the air. Thus it was that loser Bob Laine, clad only in his trap-door special and carrying a large sign admitting he had lost the bet, trekked up Yonge to CHUM, asking for donations. A wonderful crowd lined the streets, waving valentines. Bob, with a grinning Johnson beside him, collected more money that day than in our entire campaign.

For Foster Parents Plan, each jock and his listeners adopted a child in a Third World country. Listeners donated the money. When the letters and photos from the kids arrived, the jocks shared them with their listening audiences and partner parents. This was a quiet promotion but one that was very satisfying and that listeners indicated they enjoyed. It went on for years.

One day, flying by the seat of our pants as usual, we aired a regular contest that asked: "What would you do if you won Al Boliska for a day?" Many of the answers were hilarious. Some were unprintable. And a good, nutsy time was being had by all. Then came an entry from a man who said that, if he won Boliska for a day, he would make Al more aware of the work being done with mentally challenged children.

Instead of continuing the easy, comic road, we made this the winning entry and built a whole public-information campaign around it. Al and a CHUM news team spent the best part of a week at the organization's headquarters. Clips of Boliska interviewing or kidding around with these young people were played back on his show each day.

What had started as another loopy, larky CHUM promotion evolved into a rich and very worthwhile radio service. As for Boliska, his unique comic sense prevented anything we might say from dissolving into bathos or false sentimentality.

During the Cold War, CHUM personalities spent time in a bomb shelter. We passed on a message about how to make yourself safer against an atomic attack. It had been proven conclusively that Toronto was on the Soviet list of cities to strike. This was one Hit List we wanted to avoid.

We promoted water safety — specifically, a new method for saving your life, called Drown Proofing. Did we have Bob McAdorey and Mike Darow demonstrating this technique at many neighbourhood pools? You bet your tan line. And what better place to show off your itsy bitsy teeny weeny yellow polka-dot bikini? Eh, guys?

CHUM struck a sweet note with the volunteers of the Toronto Symphony Orchestra by creating a Secret Symphony Shopper. The volunteers held a rummage sale each year to raise money for their really big band. The quality of the merchandise was generally excellent. Attendees were urged to discover who this shopper was, and the first person to discover her would win . . . blah, blah, blah. Worked well.

First day of the sale, Bob McAdorey and I had given instructions to our shopper and she was on her way. It was only about 10 a.m. and we decided to walk around. Two attractive, upper-middle-aged but well-preserved women members of the volunteers spotted our CHUM badges and invited us to have a little refreshment with them. One also casually mentioned that we were good-looking young men. Gallantly we replied that they were fine-looking women. We thought we could use a coffee, so we accepted with alacrity, only to discover that what was being poured into our coffee cups was straight Scotch. We were sitting in a private anteroom with the door locked. One of the women took a healthy belt and told McAdorey he was cute. After two "coffees," the other woman patted the sofa beside her and invited me to "not be such a stranger." As Mac and I bolted from the room, our virtue intact, we could hear the

women's amused laughter. Heading back to CHUM, we cringed over what our Irish ancestors would have thought about our craven behaviour. We vowed never to let it happen again.

Dick Shatto Day was one of a number of promotions we did to publicize and entertain sick kids with visits to the hospital by personalities. (Dick Shatto was a popular Argos star.) Boliska was good with kids — true — but his innate shyness kept him apart in the role of a neutral clown. Funny, yes, but still the aloof performer. It was Mike Darow who really got to the kids. After they got over his size, they soon recognized that he was a kid, too. He was one of them. Mike would actually romp with these young people. "Where's Darow?" "He's under the kid's bed, singing." He treated them all alike, ignored their problems and illnesses, and had them squealing with joy. When playing games with the kids, he'd cheat. And when caught, lie. The kids loved him. And when we left, we'd look at Mike's eyes and softly hum "Misty."

For another promotion for a children's cause, CHUM stated that John Spragge would walk down Yonge Street from Richmond Hill to the CHUM building. And he did. He carried a sign that read "I'm walking for crippled children who cannot." This turned out to be one of the first — if not the first —

CHUM'S
JOHN
SPRAGGE
I'M WALKING FOR
CRIPPLED CHILDREN
WHO CANNOT

walkathons in Toronto, and we were told later that it was the inspiration for some of the major walkathons and their ilk to follow. The only person unhappy was John's brother, a doctor, who was worried that John could have crocked himself. He threatened harm to my precious body if I did anything like that to John again. (Good thing he didn't attend the Sportsmen's Show.)

The CHUM guys also collected toys and gifts for St. Vincent de Paul, visited mental patients with Red Kelly and other Leafs as part of a CHUM/CMHA awareness program, and were trounced soundly by kids in a wheelchair basketball game. The CHUM boys worked the booths in the Hadassah Bazaar and involved themselves deeply in a string of other not-for-profit activities.

Our efforts were acknowledged with several awards, topped off with the coveted award for the station in Canada that had contributed most to public service organizations. What price glory? As Mac might say, "What glory?"

Pressure inspired us to create and sponsor a Public Service Seminar in 1961. From time to time over the next two years, CHUM picked up the tab to fire us around the country with our seminar — a modern medicine show of which Waters and Part would have been proud. It attracted some pretty august audiences, primarily of volunteer corporate heads.

OK, SO WE GOOFED: SOME CLINKER CONTESTS

After all our braggadocio and other Italian dishes about how listeners loved our contests and promotions, perhaps we should fess up that there were a few that were, well, less than superb and drove us to drink. That's our excuse, and we're sticking to it.

Let's revisit a few less-than-finest hours.

One of the first was CHUM's Safe-Cracking Contest.

AL SLAIGHT: I had just joined CHUM. I had talked Waters into a Five Thousand Dollar Safe-Cracking Contest. The plan was to earn advertising dollars from Tip Top Tailors, where the safe would be kept. Waters had no money and had to borrow it from the bank. I assured him no one would be able to open the safe. The money was safe as houses.

We gave obscure and vague clues to the safe's combination. A huge lineup of listeners turned up to try. This stuff was new to Toronto. Several days before the Tip Top promotion was to end, I was busy congratulating myself when the phone rang. It was Bob Laine. He said, "Hi, Al, guess what?" Some guy had popped the safe. Remember also that CHUM was fighting an image problem. Was it a pillar of society that got the

John Spragge performs one of Toronto's first walkathons for a good cause

combination? No, it was a rough biker who announced, when interviewed, that he would buy a new Harley, "and pick up somethin' nice for my chick."

Waters was a class act. He didn't fire me. But he had to scramble to meet his next payroll, that's how tight financially he was.

While Slaight was still cringing about that promotion and Waters was out squeezing stones and advertisers looking for blood, I

our heads that were in another darker area, and not for the last time. You must realize that these were early days, and Slaight and I were only seven years old.

Then there was CHUM's Father of the Year contest. Listeners were invited to write in and tell us why a certain outstanding man should be chosen as our Father of the Year. There were prizes for both the writer and the recipient of the award. This contest had gone over well for two years. This was our third.

Our boys had nicknamed this "pulling a fast one" and "Bossie's hand job."

joined forces with Al. Teamed up, we created a lulu: CHUM's Loot and Literature Promotion.

It was Library Week in Toronto, so why not hide $50 bills in library books and give our listeners clues as to where to find them? thunk we. Our surefire way to promote literacy turned into lunacy. As libraries were rummaged and ravaged, complaints from panicky librarians buried under books had us pull this baby off the air, but fast. The Toronto Libraries never sued us. We convinced them that our hearts were in the right place. It was

We made our choice and announced our winner. Then we received the following telephone call:

SWITCHBOARD BETTY: Good morning, CHUM Radio.
CALLER: Morning. I called to congratulate you on your choice of Father of the Year.
BETTY: Thank you . . .
CALLER: And to ask you how you knew.
BETTY: Knew . . . uh . . . what?
CALLER: You know, your guys never fail to impress me. I realize you have a terrific news

organization with reporters covering the city, but how you could know this is beyond me.

BETTY: Know this what?

CALLER: Oh, come on. You know full well that your winner has been fathering illegitimate children all over the town for 10 years. We thought it was a local secret, but how CHUM found out and had the *cojones* to put it on the air — you've got my unqualified admiration.

BETTY: Thanks for the call, sir. Goodbye.

Did I mention we pulled those congratulatory announcements off the air pretty damn quick? And that we didn't share that gem with Allan Waters?

Not that he needed reminding that even our commercial promotions were not always perfect. Case in point: CHUM's Cow Milking Contest.

This commercial promotion was sponsored by the Dairy Farmers of Ontario. Listeners were invited to guess which CHUM disc jockey could get the most milk from a

cow in a prescribed time. Our boys had nicknamed this "pulling a fast one" and "Bossie's hand job." To give it more flavour, the pull-off would be held live on CFTO TV and Annis Stukus, ex-coach of the Argos, would be the referee. Why? No one can remember.

What we did remember was our live broadcast of an earlier Sports Celebrity Dinner. As the new coach of the Argos, Stukus was asked how he felt. His answer: "I feel like a new bride. Between the dishes and the douches, I'm in hot water all the time." For weeks afterwards we wondered if it was lose-your-licence time.

The contest was held one Saturday morning. All had gone well until McAdorey started to milk the cow. Perhaps displaying a bovine criticism of his technique, the cow in an unladylike way lifted her tail and shot an admirable stream of steaming urine into the air and onto CHUM would-be farmers, especially Mac.

Did the cameraman use his experience and

Bob (cold hands) McAdorey, left holding the bag

know-how and, with compassion for home viewers, turn his camera away? Did the director signal to cut to a commercial or footage of agricultural landscape? Nope. This ninny focused in on the peeing process, treating viewers to a tight close-up of the cow's hindquarters. Only when every drop had been dripped did he pan to the CHUM announcers, who were displaying their lack of maturity and immunity to childish humour: Stukus and Darow had actually fallen across the cow in helpless mirth. Only then did the producer cut to shots of products and a voice-over that talked of the purity and quality of milk. But McAdorey added not one word about how to get cow urine out of your hair and clothes. Back at the station, Mac was accused of milking a gag.

If you get all gooey and warm about Christmas, then how about this well-done turkey: CHUM's Win a Collie for Christmas Contest. It sounded seasonal. A little kid won the collie pup from CHUM just before Christmas. Problem was, everything terrified it (the dog, not the kid). This beautiful dog was just a few months old, but when tied to the leg of my desk, it was strong enough to wedge the desk against the door, effectively locking itself in and us out.

Did I mention its nerves brought on waves of diarrhea which spread all over the floor of my office? To get in to rescue the dog and reclaim my office, I had to go outside, get a tall ladder, climb up onto the roof, and break my window. As I stretched gingerly in to avoid jagged glass, my foot slipped in the mess and I landed flat on my back in doggy doo. My thrashing and splashing caused the Cute Christmas Crapper to launch into new spasms of used dog food. Thousands of years of bonding between *Homo sapiens* and *Canis familiaris* were going down the tube. As I slithered around, attempting to get to my feet, I could hear comments through the glass of my office door. My erstwhile friend, McAdorey, had gathered CHUM personnel to watch this demonstration in dog handling.

MCADOREY: It's the gift that keeps on giving.
SPRAGGE: It's the answer to those who don't give a shit about Christmas.
JOHNSON: How did that dog know how I feel about Farrell's effing [for "festive"] promotions?

Visits to the laundry and the vet later, we delivered this truly sweet animal to the contest winner. But it was simply too nervous. The family returned it to CHUM. Pete Nordheimer and his wife took the doggy and did their level best. To no avail. The dog was just too nervous to be in a home. It did, however, finally end up with a farm family. The story had a happy ending. We only wished the promotion had.

I believe we copied the idea for CHUM's Walking Man Contest from an American radio station. At least I hope so, after living with its results. The concept was simple. CHUM hired a person who would travel around Toronto. We tagged him the "Walking Man." We invited listeners to ask everyone they met if he was the CHUM Walking Man. When someone nabbed him, they'd win $1,000. In truth, the idea was kinda feeble. Dumb, even. And much too limp.

So, we narrowed the focus, saying, "Ask everyone you meet in elevators today" or "Ask everyone on subways" or "at the front doors of stores," etc.

As we made it easier and easier to win, we dropped the prize money accordingly. No takers. We knew we had a lemon on our hands and decided to blow it off.

We announced portentously that on a certain day the CHUM Walking Man would be at the corner of Yonge and Queen at precisely 12:30 p.m., wearing Black Watch Bermuda shorts and a bowler hat. First person to identify him would win $200. We estimated 50 people would turn up — tops. Slaight, who always had a plan, decided to jazz up this

rather weak ending to our promotion. He directed our announcers to get into their bowlers and Bermudas and jump into four CHUM cruisers. Garry Ferrier was to drive into the intersection from the east at precisely 12:28 p.m. The small crowd would move towards him. After discovering he was not the Walking Man, they'd spot Pete Nordheimer coming up from the south at 12:28:30, then see Mike Darow's cruiser entering the intersection from the west at 12:29 and Al Boliska three seconds later. Then, the real Walking Man would come out of the Stock Exchange Building, move to the designated spot, and be identified, and we'd award $200 to the lucky winner. And a good time would be had by all.

Nope. Naw. Didn't happen. At noon, 30 minutes before the promoted climax, no one could turn left off University onto Queen Street, because it was jammed with cars going nowhere. And there was a good reason. The entire intersection, curb to curb and spilling up onto the sidewalks, was chock-a-block with potential contest winners. This crowd filled the streets up and down Yonge and east and west on Queen. Estimated number — 10,000.

Nothing moved.

Subway trains pulled up, but few people if any got off, because the subway platforms and stairs were thick with people. Traffic was gridlocked four ways for several blocks.

Although some young people rocked the CHUM cruisers, calling out, "How do you like being rocked?" generally it was like a big party. There is always an idiot element, though, and they scared the hell out of our guys. Garry Ferrier asked a cop if he could help us and was told, "You got yourself into this mess, you get yourself out."

Darow, in the cruiser, went into the intersection at 1:20. The prize had been awarded almost on schedule, but our CHUM gang was just getting turned around and headed back to the station. Allan Waters didn't seem overly glad to see us. CHUM apologized on-air to the citizens, police, etc. every 20 minutes for eight hours.

Some staff were secretly pleased with the pulling power of CHUM, but we did not dare express it, particularly as we were sitting in the corner wearing dunce caps.

The only person openly happy with this melee was super salesman Ernie Towndrow of Stephens and Towndrow. He had climbed up on the ledge of a light pole at Yonge and Queen and was yelling to the crowd, "If CHUM can deliver this kind of response for $200, imagine what it could do for your product with a full campaign." Amen, Ernie, amen. But where would we find work?

"MIDDAY MATINEE": TARZAN'S WILDLIFE ADVENTURE

Tarzan's in town! CHUM decided to go wild and have Al Boliska swim against the Ape Man, Gordon Scott, here to promote his latest swing-a-ding-ding Tarzan movie.

We knocked on the door of his cabana on the grounds of Sportsman's Park. Gordon sleepily opened it. Even though he felt terrible, he still looked fabulous compared to us non-vine swingers.

Soon as he knew who we were, his first request was for a quart of jungle juice. Tarzan had been at a bash last night. Our prime primate had an elephant-sized hangover. Sure, we could supply medicinal vodka.

Could we also introduce him to some girls? He'd been away from Jane so long, Cheetah was starting to look good. He was as horny as a single rhinoceros. No, Tarzan. Look at you. Get your own girl, okay?

As for diving into the pool to start the race, it seems the Ape Man had hurt his eardrums in the Fontainebleau pool in Vegas. Tarzan, ever brave, could, and would, wade into the pool. But he who had saved Tantor and wrestled moth-eaten lions hoped the water in the pool wouldn't be too cold. "You know how it is when it hits your nuts," he whispered, using the language of the jungle.

That afternoon, a bronzed, blond giant with two sets of brilliant teeth, loinclothed for the ladies, waded into the pool. Boliska cannonballed, careful not to splash Tarzan. The race, of course, was rigged. A rope was hidden in Boliska's hands. It ran, unseen, under the water, the entire length of the pool. The rope continued to trail over the edge of this outdoor pool, where again out-of-sight CHUM personalities, dressed in old-time bathing suits, held the last 10 feet of line.

The race started. The guys pulled the rope and ran with it, and Boliska tore through the water like a hydroplane, Tarzan coming in a bad second. However, he *was* pleased that he didn't get his hair wet. Umgowa!

BOB LAINE: After the Sportsmen's Show, I'd sworn off water for life. I turned up for this promotion because it was promised I wouldn't get wet. After J.J. interviewed Tarzan, Mr. Muscles walked by me and said, "Me Tarzan. You Laine." Then he pushed me into the pool. It proves you can't trust promotion guys and men who wear loincloths.

Three swingers: J.J. Richards, Tarzan (Gordon Scott), and Neil Thomas

Chapter Nine

THE BIG EVENT

IN THE DUCK DUNG — AND LOVING IT!
THE SPORTSMEN'S SHOW

HAROLD SHIELDS (ex-Sportsmen's Show president): A tiger was the feature attraction of our Sportsmen's Show one year. Al Boliska called me and asked if I could send him some tiger poop. If it had been anyone other than Boliska, I would have asked why. Instead I said, "How much poop?" Al said that a pound or two would be fine. I directed a fellow who handled that end of the tiger to gather some poop, put it in a bag, and send it by cab up to Boliska at CHUM. Al thanked me, but never said what he did with it.

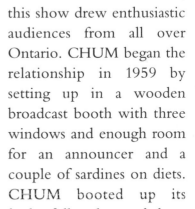

"Tonight! Guaranteed! In a feat that will daze the senses and assault the nostrils, the CHUM Champions will walk on water!"

Our boys were about to race the length of the Coliseum pool wearing enormous Styrofoam shoes called Water Striders. (The pros referred to them affectionately as "Groin Grinders.")

This was just one event in the CHUM Champions contests we staged each year at the Toronto Sportsmen's Show. Sponsored by the Toronto Anglers and Hunters Association, this show drew enthusiastic audiences from all over Ontario. CHUM began the relationship in 1959 by setting up in a wooden broadcast booth with three windows and enough room for an announcer and a couple of sardines on diets. CHUM booted up its activities and launched a full-scale, week-long promotion. For the first time as the CHUM Champions, our announcers entered sporting events where there were professional shows or

Left: "CHUM Chicks at the Ex"; Above: Pete Nordheimer displays championship form at the Sportsmen's Show

demonstrations. Each deejay was rated on his performance in every event. The jock with the greatest number of points would be declared CHUM's Champion of Champions.

Listeners were invited to send in the name of the announcer they felt would win the competition. First correct answer selected would win a fine prize: a boat and motor from Currie Bulmer, with a retail value, then, of about $3,000. The judging was a bit tricky. Often when the CHUM announcers performed on-air or in public, we'd ensure our mercurial morning man, Boliska, would top everyone with some stunt. Here, though, there was an impressive prize at stake, so it was every man for himself.

Log-rolling was one of the highlights. Every year there were a number of sporting events held in a pool set up in the Coliseum on the CNE grounds. For almost every out-of-station event, the fellas were dressed in wild costumes from Malabar. This time they were in old-time bathing suits because we had entered the log-rolling contest. A pro roller, a woman, instead of rolling our would-be loggers off the log, actually tried to help them stay on. Nordheimer remained on for a full five seconds, while a world record of zero seconds was set by Bob Laine — who missed the log entirely. (It's said that record still stands.) One terrific thing about entering

Sportsmen's Show events was that the audiences were very knowledgeable about the contests. As each of our Olympic Hopefuls plunged awkwardly into the putrid water, the crowd had a good laugh. The CHUM Champions had a different slant on it.

JOHN SPRAGGE: There's this filthy pool. First, in go the seals. They crap. In go the ducks. They crap. In go the dogs. They crap. Finally, in go the CHUM announcers. I love these CHUM promotions.

Then there was go-cart racing. Here, a couple of our boys got the crowd's motor revving. Darow always had a heavy foot on the road, and Johnson was a natural speeding freak. Outclassing the rest of the fellas, these two turned it into a side-by-side race, with Johnson winning the champagne as Darow flew off the track. Dave did so well, some fans thought we'd tossed in a pro driver.

As an individual stunt, we asked our guys if they knew anything about scuba diving. Laine knew someone at the diving exhibit, which meant he had impeccable credentials. Our concept was to set an underwater broadcasting record. Laine was given a few scuba lessons and dropped into the tank with a specially-rigged microphone. Bob stayed down there playing giant guppy for the most part of several days as our technical people struggled to clean up the sounds. He even announced part of his show underwater. Unfortunately, it sounded like it, all bubbling and gurgling. He was applauded for his guts, but he of the wrinkled feet didn't appear too impressed.

LAINE: We hated you most for the Sportsmen's Show.
AUTHOR: I thought it was the CNE.
LAINE: It ran a close second.

Dog handling drew a large audience that truly knew its stuff. The crowd was seated in mini-stands only a few feet from the dogs and their handlers. The exercise: handler, with shotgun, stands with dog at his feet, handler fires gun (blanks), a "bird" is tossed over a pond onto a small island, handler signals dog to find the bird, dog swims over to island, locates the bird, points, handler signals, and dog brings bird to handler and sits in his starting position. Yeh. Sure. Right.

The CHUM Champions, nimble Nimrods all, performed variations on a theme of canine chaos, with birds tossed in the water, announcers terrified of dogs, and dogs definitely wary of announcers.

Finally, there was only Mike Darow left. Some character had assigned him an untrained animal, an enormous Labrador named Barney. Darow dutifully fired his gun, scaring the balls off Barney, who turned and, in one move, leapt over a five-foot wall into the audience and onto someone's lap. Bounding Barney then jumped from seat to seat, squashing

people until he disappeared down the corridor. Uncontrollable laughter. Barney was brought back. Mike was told not to fire the gun, but to only clap his hands. He did. He signalled. Barney, in response, strolled over to the stands and had a casual pee. Darow picked

Mike Darow, Pete Nordheimer, Judy Welch, John Spragge, Al Boliska, Bob Laine, and Dave Johnson. Champions all!

up Barney and gently put him in the pond. Barney liked it. He swam back and forth, keeping out of Mike's reach. Darow waded across the pond, found the bird on the island, and with it in his own mouth carried Barney back to their starting place. Sustained applause. We let the dog judges award the points to our handlers. That doggone event wrapped up our first year for the CHUM Champions.

Second year had us back in the Coliseum with archery, judo, canoe-jousting, and high-diving into a massive tank of water. We passed on working with a diving horse when the guys were spotted eyeing me malevolently while fashioning a noose.

Despite a satisfying response to our latest circus-like turns, we were waiting for Boliska to do something spectacular. True, in the bowling competition, he had taken to throwing himself head-first down the alley and landing strikes, but generally he had been rather subdued (for him). Not for long.

Tonight was bait-casting, and we were booked as an introductory competition.

Because the Sportsmen's Show was sponsored by the Anglers and Hunters, bait-casting was a well-publicized centrepiece event that drew excellent crowds. Champion bait-casters of local, national, and international accomplishment were standing by, ready to show off their rather spectacular skills in this sport. But first, the CHUM Champions took a crack at it as part of our Annual Contest.

A long casting pool had been created. A platform stood at one end, facing three plastic circles, each farther off than the last. Dead centre of each circle was a bell. These were the targets for the professional bait-casting competition and demonstration.

The crowd was already falling about laughing. All but one of the CHUM jocks had taken a turn bait-casting, each setting new standards of ineptitude, hitting their feet or heads, breaking or losing the bait in the crowd, becoming tangled in the line, and exibiting other behaviour that tickled the audience. No one was laughing louder than the legitimate champion bait-casters, who could hardly contain themselves.

Bob Laine prepares to prove he can breathe water, encouraged by a CHUM Chick and John Spragge

They'd never seen anything like this.

The last competitor was Al Boliska. Affecting an enormous disdain for the crowd, he mounted the platform regally and, with a cool eye and a cold demeanour, stared haughtily at the audience until they fell silent.

Only then did Al move over to the bait-casting rods. He inspected each one meticulously, as if choosing a foil for a duel. Apparently finding a rod that met his exacting standards, he practised a few fencing thrusts, once stabbing himself in the foot, of course.

finger, then his fly, he simply whipped the rod back once, let go the line, and *whirrrr*, it shot true to its target, in the first ring, hitting the bell: *Boing!*

Generous applause from the audience, cheers from the CHUM gang, and a look of amazement on the faces of the professional bait-casters.

This was vintage Boliska: play the clown, then pull off some impossible stunt. The crowd was a fuel pump for his gassed-up confidence.

In a change of pace, he quickly turned his

Our concept was to set an underwater broadcasting record. Laine was given a few lessons and dropped into the tank with a specially rigged microphone.

Satisfied, he addressed the bait-casting pool.

Putting the rod aside for a moment, Al warmed up. As if he was about to play the piano, he began with finger exercises, then moved on to boxing-ring-style deep knee-bends and ballet leaps. Ending with a bullfighting veronica or two, he again picked up the rod.

As each of his actions brought guffaws from the crowd, Al affected a sneer of disdain, which only brought on more laughter.

After checking the air currents with a wet

back on the pool and snapped off another cast over his shoulder. *Whirr, whirr* went the line, capped off with a *Boing!!* as Al hit the ball situated dead centre in the second ring. A pause from the crowd, then a roar of approval. All of the professional bait-casters had their mouths open like hooked bass, except one who had slumped and was sitting stunned on the floor.

Now was the moment of truth. Would Boliska, who didn't know the word "discretion,"

do as he'd done so often and fumble into an embarrassing anticlimax as he tried to outdo himself? Or would he walk away now, a hero? The answer: neither.

Solemnly, Al called for silence. When all we could hear were our own hearts beating, he again turned his back to the pool. He then carefully placed the plastic bait between his teeth. And, as a final gesture, slowly closed his eyes.

Bending the rod further than before, Al released the line on a high arc. The line went *whirr, whirr, whirr* and climaxed with a decisive *Boing!!!* as the bait hit the bell in the third ring.

The place went mad. Al recognized the applause with cutesy, little-girl curtseys and left the platform. As he reached the floor, he looked over at us apprehensively, and we gave him very deep and sincere bows. He grinned back. Al had just done the impossible. The only people unhappy were the professional bait-casters, who were wondering what they would do for *their* show.

They had discovered that Boliska, like CHUM, was a tough act to follow. Oddly, we felt the same way, coming back year after year.

CHUM CHECKS FROM THE EX: THE CNE

Nowhere did CHUM reflect its patent-medicine show roots as clearly as it did at Toronto's annual Canadian National Exhibition. It fit this venerable whoop-up as snugly as a wiener in a hotdog bun (hold the onions). Part hype, part flim-flam, part personalities, and all hoke, CHUM promotions wrapped themselves tightly in the glitz and glare of the

Ex the way cotton candy sticks to your pinkies.

The CHUM trailer — or Satellite Station, as it was called — sat finned and feisty just inside the Princes' Gates. It was a minor Ex unto itself. Midway cries of "Sno Cones! Sno Cones!" were countered by "CHUM checks from the Ex!" The plaintive call, "Doggie Dooooggie, get yooour Dooooogie" harmonized with our "get yooour CHUM faaaans." And the Hundred Hawker Chorus of the Carnie Chorale exhorting well-heeled, fresh-faced visitors to "step right up, folks, three balls for only a dollar, you can't lose" was matched in allure and zeal by our jocks handing out badges 'n' stuff guaranteed to win the wearers neat-o prizes.

Left: A quiet day for CHUM at the Ex; Above: It's Bobby Curtola Day on CHUM!

And did it pull in the populace! CHUM was a roller coaster and everyone wanted to ride.

DON BUCKLEY (CHUM listener): No matter which gate we entered, we had to head first to CHUM's Satellite Station. We had to have the badges, the fans, see the guys, and get autographs. Everyone I knew did the same thing. Nothing happened until we visited CHUM at the Princes' Gates.

Huge crowds gathered the moment CHUM began to broadcast from the fairgrounds each day, and they were never disappointed. Music: CHUM pumped out the hits over the P.A. Personalities: announcers and newsmen greeted visitors and strutted their stuff in bowlers and Black Watch Bermuda shorts. A listener suggested that CNE should stand for CHUM Nutsy Exhibitionists. (Nobody likes a smart guy.) Entertainment: the small stage at the back of the trailer spot-lighted star after star, kibitzing with the crowd, signing autographs, and shaking hands. And Girls! Girls! Girls! While young people couldn't believe their good fortune in meeting their favourite recording personalities, their dads thought every day was

Father's Day as they gathered in packs back by the trees, checking out the CHUM Chicks.

The latter were exceptional women. Not only were they very attractive (most were ex–Miss Torontos), they were accomplished at representing CHUM well. Like the CHUM personalities, they, too, had to spend long hours handling promotional materials, answering myriads of questions, and generally being pleasant.

The CHUM Chicks were an integral part of our exterior image. It was even suggested by some male visitors at the CNE that our slogan should be altered to read, "CHUM Chicks at the Ex." First to join us in that capacity was Miss Canada Judy Welch, who was to go on to modelling-agency fame. After that we hired mostly Miss Torontos. The gal who was associated with CHUM over the longest haul was a bright, poised, beautiful young woman, Lorna Anderson. At the Ex and other events, she was put in charge of the other gals. We used to refer to her as the "Den Mother," but you'd have to have had real guts to tell her that to her face.

LORNA ANDERSON: We only had one girl who had some weird habits. Although gorgeous and excellent with people at the trailer, she was also in love with animals. She'd spend her breaks in a building with spider-monkeys. I had to talk to her once when she came back with smelly spider-monkey pee all over her blouse. And another time she harboured a snake. It was cuddled between her breasts and it would peek its head out and scare the hell out of everybody. I told her to put the snake in her purse, like any civilized person.

The CHUM Chicks were adroit at warding off the fumblers and feelers, which could include the more ring-a-ding of our merrie men. In reality, the greatest threat to modest behaviour came from a real swinger, Chatter, the CHUM Chimp.

Chatter was handled by Murray Hill out of Chicago.

The gals loved to fuss over Chatter, to the great delight of our CNE crowds. One day, Chatter looked at the audience and, with great aplomb, carefully cupped one of the gal's breasts.

As she removed his hand she said seriously, "He knows what he's doing!"

ANDERSON: Some gals thought the trainer had taught Chatter these games with girls. The trainer was a bit raunchy himself. All I know is that you didn't turn your back on either of them.

Each jock's fans trekked to the Satellite Station to see his or her favourite disc jockey, on-air or out back yakkin' it up. Some loyal listeners bivouacked in the dust for the day, eating guaranteed nutrition-free food and having friends protect their staked-out claim near the trailer while they took a pee break. But, while listeners loved it and station management clocked the thousands upon thousands who visited our miniature musical merry-go-round, there were other slightly dissenting opinions.

GEORGE JONES: The CHUM trailer was a poorly designed, dismally constructed piece of shit. The noisy air-conditioner was located right beside the announcer. Fortunately, this mattered little because it didn't work most of the time. The rear windows were supposedly easily removed and stored. They weren't. There was only one thing wrong with the washroom facilities — being non-functional, no one could use them.

CHUM Chick Lorna Anderson

The centre of the trailer was designated for storage, but served mainly as a place for the announcers to flirt with the CHUM Chicks.

It had been apparent since 1956 with CHUM's first broadcast from the Queen Elizabeth Building during the Ex that the CNE and CHUM were perfect partners for self-promotion. Broadcasting from the old wood-and-glass box was no real hardship for the announcers and technical staff, and the exposure was pretty good. It wasn't until 1959,

when CHUM had really started to cook and a customized trailer was strategically placed just inside the Princes' Gates, that the CNE truly began to take its toll on air staff and others. Fortunately, help was at hand.

For the sweating, overworked, smiling, rictus-faced CHUM personalities, there was one life-enhancing, spirit-lifting element that made the Ex bearable for deejays, guests, and support staff — the Honey Dew Driver!

Smile Police aside, there were increasingly more grins on CHUM jocks' faces. Management put this phenomenon down to firm direction. The true cause had a Russian accent.

One fine, Ex-goin' day, I intercepted two messages at the station from John Spragge, who was on duty at the trailer. One read, "John Spragge needs his shoes." The second note was more desperate: "Bring down my extra-large shoes now!" Puzzled, I volunteered to bring Spragge his shoes. Sure enough, in the announcers' preparation room was a large shoe-box. It felt uncommonly heavy. When opened, it revealed a whacking great bottle of vodka. With some flair and no little over-dramatization, I delivered this potent package to John at the Ex. In thanks and rather shame-facedly, he built me a concoction he had chris-tened a Honey Dew Driver. I sampled it and soon, I, too, was grinning like Chatter the CHUM Chimp. Now, for the first time only,

Chatter sounds de-vine as part of the Chummingbirds

and at great expense to management, John Spragge will reveal his secret and much sought-after recipe for Honey Dew Drivers.

JOHN SPRAGGE: Preparation must be approached with both reverence and resolve.

First, purchase as much vodka as will fit into a CHUM mobile station wagon.

Next, buy a cone (or "carton," to the uninitiated) of Honey Dew. Ask nicely for an extra, empty cone.

Pour half the Honey Dew into the empty cone.

Fill both cones with vodka.

Do not shake or stir. Just slosh them around a bit. (You'll be shaking enough tomorrow.)

Share one with that delicious-looking new friend.

Warning: if you cannot speak, DO NOT PANIC! Simply grin widely and show a lot of tooth.

Music was the name of the game at CHUM, and as stars hit Toronto or appeared in the Grandstand Show their managers would arrange appearances at our Satellite Station.

Most performers knew their public manners and were coached by their managers or the local record rep. Stars referred to our jocks as their old friends and praised CHUM as their favourite radio station. We, of course,

reciprocated by setting them up as the hottest of the hot rockers and personal recording favourites. After one of these love-ins, you had to watch where you stepped, it was piled so deep.

It was mutually understood that they would repeat this palsy performance at other stations and, indeed, across the continent. And further.

Then there was Frankie Valli of the Four Seasons, whose records were riding higher than the Shell Tower. In short, what he did, to perhaps CHUM's biggest crowd to date, was to get them nuts. He kept calling them in for handshakes and autographs and huge hugs. The aroused crowd surged forward, and the trailer lurched, threatening to move off its moorings.

ANDERSON: Our crowd reached all the way to the Automotive Building and across the main street. We signalled for help to the mounted police officers, who tried to use their horses to push back the crowd.

Jocks admonished Valli to cool it. Revved up, he ignored them and started giving out kisses and 45s he'd hidden in his jacket. People at the very front, some of whom had lined up for three hours, were in very real danger of being crushed against the end of the trailer's stage. Guys, gals, everyone from the CHUM side was yelling at Valli to cease and desist (which he ignored) when, suddenly, illusion-like, he disappeared from the stage.

The sharp-eyed might have noticed a huge hand that grasped Valli's neck from behind and whisked him into the trailer.

Hidden from the madding crowd, Valli

chest and head resonance, it had more body and power than Frankie had ever dreamed of.

VALLI (shocked and slack-jawed): Who the hell are you?
DAROW: I'm just one of CHUM's backwater boonie boys. Now, you go back onstage and tell the crowd goodbye. And behave yourself.

Listeners were invited to guess which jock could wash an elephant the fastest.

found himself staring into the broad chest of big Mike Darow, with Laine and Johnson standing nearby, looking angry. This backstage scenario sorta played out like this:

VALLI: What the fuck do you think you're doing?
DAROW: I believe I'm stopping a jackass from having people crushed.
VALLI: Hey! I didn't come all the way to a boondocks backwater like Toronto to be pushed around.
DAROW: So, you came here to have people hurt?
VALLI: Listen, King Kong, when you can do what I do, you get to give me crap.

Darow, pausing a second, took a deep breath and sang in a perfect falsetto, "Sha-a-a-a-ree Bai-ai-bee . . ." Not only was it a spot-on impression of Valli, but with all of Mike's

And he did. Oh yes. Ever wonder why CHUM played his hits, but for years rarely mentioned him again?

After a few years, Allan Waters became more and more aware of the increasing burden we were placing on the backs of the personalities at the Ex: the tough hours broadcasting in that fishbowl (at least, that's the way it smelled), and the very real strain of being up and "on" in that dusty, sweaty, hellish atmosphere, smiling and smiling.

After the CNE, he dropped the boys a small bonus in recognition of the insane hours they racked up.

As if we didn't have enough going on, one year we added an Elephant Washing Contest to our fairground festivities. Listeners were invited to guess which jock could wash an elephant the fastest. Every day for seven days, one announcer would figure out some fun device to speed up the process. Each washing was a crowd-pleaser, but we needed something special for Mac and Boliska. By this time, McAdorey had assumed the role of our number-two zany. So we arranged for a fire truck to come to the trailer at the Ex, and Mac used its hoses on a baby elephant and set a new record in the contest.

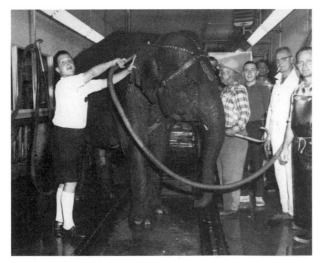

To top this, we had Boliska take an elephant into a car wash. We set up the stunt for a Saturday morning. With a remote play-by-play being broadcast, Al led the elephant into the car wash's exit. This was tricky stuff.

The owner had turned off the water and machinery, leaving cars stopped halfway through the wash. Once the elephant was well into the washing area, the water was turned on. This surprised and scared the hell out of the elephant, who reared up, trumpeted, and butted its head on the pipes. It also did what elephants do when scared. All over the place.

Even more startled was the driver of the nearest car. The machinery had come on with the water, moving the car forward, and the white and shocked face of the driver could be seen through the wet windshield of his car as he spotted a huge elephant rearing just a few feet from his front bumper.

Almost instantly the power was cut again. The agitated elephant was backed out of the car wash and calmed by the trainer. The shaken driver soon emerged, his car adorned with pachyderm poop, giving it a distinctive on-safari look. The driver was not amused. We calmed him down with thanks, an interview on the air, passes, and a special invite for him and his family to visit us at the CNE.

Boliska won the contest. And the elephant tried to forget the whole thing. But in vain.

George: Al, where do you pachyderm? *Al*: In his trunk.

Chapter Ten

THE ADMEN COMETH

SALES TALES: STEPHENS & TOWNDROW

S&T stood for Stephens & Towndrow — Bill Stephens and Ernie Towndrow. They were radio reps on the national level. Their organization influenced advertising agencies to buy radio time and place campaigns on stations they represented. These were usually for large, national companies like Colgate-Palmolive. Bill and Ernie performed this sacred act on a commission basis.

Contracting S&T was a canny move on Waters's part. Actually, like most lasting deals, there was something substantial in it for both parties. S&T made pots of money with CHUM and they were a major factor in CHUM's financial success.

Bill and Ernie were an indefatigable, ruthless, irresistible force. Never mind intimidating agency time-buyers — we found them downright frightening. And sell? They might as well have run a pipeline from agencies to CHUM's Royal Bank account.

Many of the sales revolved around buckshee commercial contests and the attendant freebie promotional plugs. The air reeked with "Free" and "Win" and "Simply buy . . ." Al Slaight was forever tearing his hair out about our cluttered air-sound, even though he collaborated with Bill and Ernie, many times authoring yet another classic, corn-fed contest.

Bill-and-Ernie stories still pop up when old drummers get together over Scotch and arthritis pills. In one classic anecdote, I, alas, feature as the unwitting central figure.

Ernie Towndrow was heading out to an agency. They had a tasty advertising budget for Pillsbury Rolls. They needed a fresh idea. Ernie, as a courtesy, took me along as an observer to give me agency experience. He had already firmly admonished me to "Keep your mouth shut — and watch the master." Green, I was more than happy to sit at the very back of the agency conference room, trying to press my bod further into the woodwork.

The tiger (Lorna Anderson) proves to be a big wheel; McAdorey and Darow approve

Towndrow was at the front, listening to the agency's creative director lay out the challenge to his staff. They threw out what I thought to be rather tepid campaign ideas. This brainstorming session had limped along for about 10 minutes when Ernie, suddenly, leaped to his feet and shouted "No!" He grabbed his soft briefcase and punctuated three more roaring "No's" by smashing it thrice on the desk of the creative director.

Towndrow scanned the room. There wasn't a sound. We'd all heard of people snapping under stress and here was living proof. Ernie's jaw muscles were dancing in his cheeks. A dangerous sign.

Ernie seemed to relax a bit — imagine a tornado relaxing — and said reasonably, "Well, maybe. Could be. Not bad." And then he delivered the following in a rising level of maniacal enthusiasm: "But why settle for 'Not bad' when we can have 'Superb'? Do you not know who's with us here today? A young man whose ideas have set the West on fire! Allen Farrell (pointing at me), TELL THEM WHAT YOU'VE GOT!"

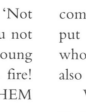

Every agency creative-type turned to stare at me malignantly. They hated me already. I staggered to my feet. And, well, you know, I'd sensed something dangerous about Towndrow earlier . . . and had conceived, for safety's sake, the germ of an idea. I blurted out, "It's called the Pillsbury Bake Out." The agency types still hated me. Ernie nodded encouragingly.

Faking it, my pulse racing, I desperately pulled details out of my mind. It hurt like a dentist's attack on an impacted molar. The concept was that listeners would be encouraged to host a Pillsbury Bake Out for their neighbours. On selected Saturdays, CHUM jocks would visit home after home, allowing people to call in with glowing accounts of how delicious the rolls were, how easy to prepare, etc. These endorsements would be edited into commercials for the campaign. CHUM would put a Pillsbury Chef on the air to keep the whole Bake Out moving. Perhaps there could also be neighbourhood banners and signage.

When I finished babbling, my face was as red as if I had been baked out, too.

Ernie Towndrow

Towndrow, who hadn't said a word during my halting, breathless spiel, took over. "You see?" he said. "You bring in the pros, you get the results."

He then went on to rough up an outline of the Bake Out, complete with a promotional build-up and schedule of commercials, put a ballpark price on it, and walked out with an approval.

When we got in his Cadillac, I was shaking with anger. I told him, "You sonofabitch, I don't care how tough you are, you do that to me again and I'll give you a taste of what I learned in my childhood in East Hastings, Vancouver."

Towndrow observed me mildly, surprised. "What's with you?" he said. "We got the business, didn't we?"

When I stormed into Slaight's office, still frothing as I recounted the story, Al looked at me and said with a kind of rueful smile, "The bastard. He did the same thing to me for Hostess Potato Chips."

S&T went on to book the campaign on the stations they represented, pretty well coast to coast in Canada. They also received a major, glowing, multi-paged article in a trade magazine that outlined the Bake Out and lauded their ingenuity.

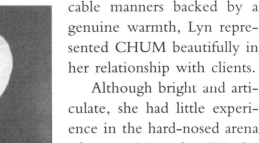

A natural extension of Waters's emphasis on sales was solid presentation support. This important activity was headed up by Lyn Salloum. Always smartly dressed, with impeccable manners backed by a genuine warmth, Lyn represented CHUM beautifully in her relationship with clients.

Although bright and articulate, she had little experience in the hard-nosed arena of competitive sales. "You're not writing for the *Ladies Home Journal*, dammit!" we'd hear Slaight cry, "Write tougher. We're going for the money." Lyn did. Became very polished. First class.

She often called on Ben Wilson, a commercial artist now working full-time at CHUM. With Ben's help, CHUM's written sales presentations were not only crisp, persuasive documents, they also had a professional design.

It was one of these 27-page, persuasive proposals that Bill Stephens toted to Montreal one day in another classic S&T adventure.

Chef John Spragge — a campaign on a hot roll

Stephens had unearthed a major opportunity for CHUM to carry a campaign for Robin Hood Flour. A large meeting room had been set aside in the Montreal agency to accommodate its marketing team, plus the CHUM contingent: Stephens, Slaight, Salloum, and me.

Bill took control of the meeting and made our presentation by thc book. CHUM's written proposals followed classic guidelines and were very detailed. Each contained an Introduction, Background, Creative Solution, Rationale, Extension of Proposition, Timetable, Key Participants, and Costs.

Our proposal was not handed out; instead, a proposal leader would slowly and emphatically read every word of the presentation, providing ad lib expansion and commentary.

Stephens took on this role with energy and conviction, at the same time doing what one does to i's and t's. He finished triumphantly about 40 minutes later.

The creative director, Pierre, and his people praised the presentation. In fact, they were almost too effusive. Then Pierre delivered the bad news. Our presentation had been built on the parameters and objectives we were supplied with. Since then, new, competitive information had come in to Robin Hood, along with some absolutely surprising responses from a very expensive, in-depth survey of heavy users of flour. Therefore, although they applauded our presentation to the last hurrah, it was no longer valid vis-à-vis the new information and the ensuing entire reversal of marketing tactics.

They thanked us again, profusely, and stood up. Many of us stood up with them in a "Well, you can't win them all" attitude. They had given us the perfect excuse to leave with our honour intact. But no contract.

Even as we stood, even as some made a move to exit, Bill Stephens continued to sit, not moving a muscle. He looked up and motioned gently for everyone to sit back down. Although confused, we all did.

He began hesitantly, rather disappointedly, but as if he was explaining something simple to a confused, favourite child.

"We came down here, flew down here, excited, because we thought — no, we knew — we had come up with the answer to your problems, your challenge — and you applauded our efforts." Pierre attempted to interrupt, but Bill softly overrode him. "Pierre here has graciously shown that although we have accomplished what we all worked so hard for — there could be some misunderstanding. I respectfully ask that you graciously rehear what we were so painstakingly careful to prepare, and came down here to Montreal to reveal to you."

Then Stephens read the presentation a second time. This was unprecedented, impossible. He did not paraphrase or skip the details. He reread, carefully, slowly, and with emphasis, every damn word in the 27 page document.

Listeners' faces were pinkish. All our shoulders slumped. We avoided each other's eyes. Finally, he was through. He ended with a ringing "There, you see!"

Into this Kafkaesque scene of unreality, the agency's Pierre once more wearily arose.

"Bill."

"Yes, yes," from Stephens, as if eagerly awaiting an award.

"Bill . . . I did tell you how much we appreciated CHUM's work on Robin Hood's behalf . . ."

"You did, Pierre, and that's what I've been saying."

"However — new research has proven our original strategy to be . . . not wrong — but invalid . . ."

"Precisely," said Stephens, as if he had won a major point.

"But," said Pierre, "unfortunately that means your creative solution is invalid, too." He sat down.

Bill looked as if someone had done something unthinkable to his children. He shook his head as if in disbelief, took a deep breath and said, "You know . . ." and took a pause so long you could drive an objection through it, "Pierre, you sent us some objectives. We took them seriously. [Pierre's head is down. He nods as one might who'd been starved and whipped.] Then, to show our commitment — Pierre — we flew down here in force."

My God, no! But, yes, he was about to read the whole shmear again, from beginning to end.

And he did. Bill did. From page one to page 27. Read the whole thing, the entire, mother-lovin', detailed enchilada for the third time.

Silence. The room reeked of sweat.

Then Stephens went for the sales close. While a tableful of people wished they were somewhere — anywhere — else, Bill quietly asked Allan Slaight if he could put the complete CHUM creative team onto this project. "Because, as Pierre has said so eloquently, there's a lot of work to be done."

Allan, looking more than slightly perplexed, allowed that he could do that.

"So," said Bill, "shall we get to work? When should we bring the rest of our creative team down to meet with your group?"

An exhausted, beaten, dazed, and bemused Pierre conferred with his staff, set a date, and tried once more, saying, "You know, we'll have to start over."

BILL: You made that very clear, Pierre. Beautiful.

PIERRE: And our objectives really have changed.

BILL: No one could have put it more succinctly than you.

PIERRE: And . . . and . . .

BILL: And thank you — and we'll see you next week.

Like boxers who'd just taken an uppercut, the agency staff staggered, rubber-kneed from the room. They were heading towards the nearest bistro.

In the car to the airport, we just stared at Bill. Becoming slightly uneasy, he said, "What? What?" We continued to stare.

"Look," he said, "we flew down here." Crikey, he wouldn't read it for the fourth time! Bill continued unperturbed. "We could either walk away with the business or without the business. If I had thought it would be without the business, I'd have stayed home and put up my storm windows."

S&T served CHUM well for many years. As they added station after station to their masthead, they attracted effective and aggressive sales people to their stable.

S&T was sold to CBS for an extraordinary amount of money. The financial types there scratched their weekly clipped heads and asked themselves, "Why did we spend so much money?"

We could have told them the answer: Ernie & Bill.

GANGWAY! RITES OF PASSAGE

Each morning we hit the ground running. We came to work full of fizz 'n' vinegar, all teeth and blazing guns, looking for trouble, looking for laughs, just frothing to kick our competitors' butts. Man, there must be something or someone we can pulverize today. As we sped upwards on our high-speed elevator, we felt we could take anyone on, lick any kid on the block, do anything. At the core of that confidence was the knowledge of and trust in each other's abilities.

At the nucleus of CHUM was an energized nexus that awaited application. Bombard it with challenges large and small and it would radiate action. CHUM people came to *work*. A modest example:

By 10 a.m., Ernie Towndrow had tromped and romped our halls declaiming that money grew on trees. Advertising dollars demanded to be picked.

The source of this arboreal bonanza — pears!

It seemed that since there were just too

many of them in Ontario that year, they had been hangin' around, doing what bored pears do. Farmers decided to throw them into cans before they could cause trouble. Now, they would be featured in stores and supermarkets for "low, low prices." The ad agency was raking the radio stations, seeking to exploit the situation with a short, but heavy, campaign. Ernie had an appointment to illustrate convincingly how CHUM would pear-a-chute the tins off the shelves and into consumers'

baskets. Oh, the meeting's this afternoon at about 2:30.

Solway fashioned the creative hook and wrote and recorded three commercials worthy of Stan Freeburg's much lauded campaign for peaches.

I knocked out a Pears and Pops Are Tops contest with taped samples.

Ferrier wrote the verse and chorus of an original jingle, recording it with Darow and Mac on backup vocal.

155

Who's minding the store? The CHUM gang in the early '60s

Copywriter Mary-Helen McPhillips designed and voiced 30-second segments called "Preparing Pears" — quick tips on serving the fruit. Ben Wilson gave a graphic look to our approach, incorporating a pear and a catch line. Lyn Salloum and Slaight prepared a written proposal, complete with a rationale for the creative (invented all of 14 seconds before). This was accompanied by a schedule and attendant costs. Lyn gave it a final polish, packaged all the materials, and topped the package with Ben's graphic rendering.

The written and taped segments were presented to Towndrow between 1:30 and 2:00 p.m. Ernie's only comment? "Fantastic!" He then grabbed the package and charged out onto Yonge Street. (Some say he actually walked through a wall, chewing the concrete, but that's probably a myth.)

Ernie barged back in about 4:45, huddled with Waters and Slaight, and then herded our team down the hill to the Bali Hai room to celebrate.

As for the tinned fruit, it promptly dis-a-pear-ed off the shelves before the campaign was over.

When CHUM ganged up on a project, it transcended teamwork. Unfortunately, it also led to glitches in our personal journeys, teaching us erroneously that all employment — and employers — were F-U-N. Not!

WHAT A GREAT, GREAT FEELING: THE TIGER IN THE TANK CAMPAIGN

Six suits sat on one side of the boardroom table. I sat on the other. Each suit sported a puffed handkerchief and a rather darling tie. Allan Waters had introduced them as people from McLaren's Advertising Agency who worked on the Imperial Oil gasoline account. Allan said they had a rather thorny problem and he would like me (us) to help them if we could. Right-o, sir.

We stared at each other a while. Then, one of them, a sort of spokessuit, spoke.

He said that Imperial Oil in Canada had decided to adopt the "Put a Tiger in Your Tank" campaign. It was believed that the "Tiger" concept began in Britain, jumped to France as "Mettez un Tigre dans Votre Moteur," and then ranged all over Europe and, finally, the U.S.A. Wherever the Tiger had roared, it had been an outstanding success at the pumps. Now, it was to raven across Canada.

"So, what's the problem?"

"Our agency has been asked to introduce it to the dealers."

"So, what's the 'thorny' bit?"

"We . . . uh . . . don't know how to do it."

"And you want CHUM to . . . ?"

"Please."

For those of us who have not studied destructive distillation of petroleum and the marketing of its by-products, perhaps a little expansion of information would be in order.

The service stations were operated, for the most part, by independent dealers. In order for any petroleum promotion to be effective, there had to be a high percentage of participation. Why wouldn't the dealers participate? First of all, it would cost them money. They had to pay for the tiger tails, pump-toppers, station signage, and materials connected with prizes. Of equal importance, the dealers and their staffs, including jockeys who only pumped gas (*especially* them as front-line customer contact), must be extra — excuse me — pumped up.

When asked why the dealers didn't see the obvious benefits of a major promotion like this that would almost certainly draw a flood of extra traffic, the suits sneered that the aver-age service-station worker had only about grade eight education. And many of them hated and mistrusted Imperial Oil. Relationships were very strained.

The answer to the question of how dealer introductions to earlier promotions had been handled was illuminating. With almost a touch of defiance, the suits replied that Imperial threw dealer meetings in some local (read "cheap") hall, at an ungodly hour (read "inconvenient"), outlined the promotion briefly (read "unprepared," "arrogant"), kicked their collective asses for previous lack of enthusiasm (read "jerks"), served them a coffee (read "Boy, that'll thrill someone who has already downed six coffees that day"), and only charged them a few bucks to attend (read, "Has anyone checked Imperial's profits?").

We sat staring at each other for the longest time. Finally, I said, "OK, I feel Mr. Waters would want me to commit CHUM to this task. [Sighs of relief.] But there are some non-negotiable conditions. [Gasps of apprehension.] CHUM has total control of the event. Sure, we'll run a script past Imperial, but no interference from some agency creative director. Without getting ahead of ourselves, we will make it convenient for the dealers and staffs to attend. CHUM will probably perform two or more presentations. We will not hold it at the

Skunk Works, but rather in pleasant surroundings. Although coffee, soft drinks, and a light snack will be made available, dealers and staff will also be offered a beer or two before the show. No one, *no one!* will kick them in the ass. Instead, we'll develop fun invitations and, at the event, treat them like the important team members that they are. Oh, by the way, we'll write and produce our own radio commercials."

delivered, the heads of the six suits would turn inward towards the IOL exec. If he laughed, they all laughed. When he chuckled, they'd dutifully chuckle. Or when he downright guffawed, the suits fairly fell over themselves in the helpless laughter department. But on the few occasions when he frowned or looked puzzled, they scribbled hurriedly in their notebooks and stared woefully at the stage.

Spoofing the upcoming "Tiger" concept, he laid out a series of slogans, including "Put a Pussy in Your Petrol," "Place an Ass in Your Gas," "Put a Skunk in Your Trunk," and "Force a Horsche in Your Porsche."

A deal was struck. The suits swore on their Great God of Paranoia and we shook hands.

Now, to write it.

Dress rehearsal. For us, the performance in the audience was almost as funny as the show on the stage. An Imperial Oil exec sat front-row centre. Beside him perched six agency suits, three to the left and three to the right.

As each humorous line or comedy bit was

Dress rehearsal over, the exec stood immediately, beaming and clapping, followed instantly by the six suits who manfully attempted to stare at the exec, face the stage, and beam and clap, all at the same time. Verdict? Wonderful! Perfect — except for three gags that he found questionable. Would we expunge them from the script? We could. And did — only to replace them before the show.

Like Mike Darow, the Tiger in the Tank campaign was a gas

Show time next afternoon at the Park Plaza Hotel. Full turnout of invited dealers and staff. Met by our guys, they were steered cheerily over to the bar for a free brewskie.

The show was an absolute rubber-burner from its opening lines. All the fellas did well. Jungle Jay outdid himself as a nervous ad-agency type presenting promotional ideas to IOL people. Spoofing the upcoming "Tiger" concept, he laid out a series of slogans, including "Put a Pussy in Your Petrol," "Place an Ass in Your Gas," "Put a Skunk in Your Trunk," and "Force a Horsche in Your Porsche."

Mike Darow, in full hockey outfit, killed the dealers with his impersonation of "Tank" Mahovlich as a First Star winner on *Hockey Night in Canada*. Naturally, Mr. Happy Motoring himself, Murray Westgate, set up our commercials. Dealers were astounded to see Murray in the flesh. The show finale was our version of the Imperial Oil jingle so familiar across Canada. Our guys took bows to clapping, whistling, and foot-stomping.

Now we sprang our surprise (to Imperial, to McLaren's, to everyone). John Spragge stepped forward from our cast of crazies and delivered a powerful message. The gist of it was that we, at CHUM, thought this Tiger promotion had the potential to truly bring in customers, but only with the wholehearted enthusiasm and co-operation of the people in the room. He talked about the success of CHUM as a team, how Imperial had done its part, McLaren's its part (sure), but that the ultimate success rested on the shoulders of the dealers and their employees. Then, a first: we invited them to sign up right then and there. With that, the CHUM cast began a kind of conga line, picking up dealers and leading them to tables at the back of the room, where personnel waited to take their applications. And they signed up. Almost every one of them. The Imperial people were flabbergasted. This was unprecedented.

CHUM staged two shows the first day and went on to perform a series of others. Scripts were packaged along with photos, tapes, commercials, and extra comedy bits and sent to radio stations across the country.

There they copied, adapted, and personalized the show for their listeners, English- or French-speaking. (In Quebec, "Put a Tiger in Your Tank" became "Mettez-y du Tigre.") Each station delivered and earned a similar, positive response from earlier hostile dealers. They, too, enjoyed record sign-ups for participation.

What makes this unusual, off-air activity worthy of mention in detail is that a handful of CHUM personnel accomplished what one of Canada's largest companies and one of the biggest agencies could not. We took on an adversarial situation between an oil company and its dealers and turned out a highly charged team. In Canada, "Tiger in Your Tank" became not only one of the most memorable national marketing events but also the most successful petroleum promotion in the industry's history, both in measurable results — at the pumps — and in increased service work. "Tiger" rules!

Footnote to this chest-thumping occurred at a celebratory party when the campaign had proven an unqualified, unheard-of success. CHUM's cast and participants were invited, much to the dismay of McLaren's.

At one point, a rather conservative Imperial exec, glass in hand, said, rather grandly, "I salute all you CHUM lads. I admit, to my embarrassment, that to this date I have not been a CHUM listener. But, if you'll pardon a small joke, after seeing you in action — and the results — I may change my *tune*." Here, he paused for the expected chortles. "So, picking up on your Imperial 'Team' theme, I feel you've earned the right to be privy to our dirty little secret." He paused dramatically for effect. Olivier, move over. "Our stalwart agency here, McLaren's, didn't like the 'Tiger in Your Tank' concept — and advised us against it. What truly made it work was CHUM." Suitable chagrined looks from McLaren's types. "Now, tonight, I intend to spend some time with CHUM people here and learn more about your remarkable station." He reflected and smiled. "'Put a Pussy in Your Petrol,' eh? Droll, indeed. Droll."

Chapter Eleven
MUSIC, MUSIC, MUSIC

MUSING ON MUSIC: NOW LISTEN HERE

Rock music was the honey that attracted listeners to CHUM the way pollen invites a bee's French kiss. Yeah, one might keep on listening because of the fun, the foolin', and the fellas. But first discovery and tune-in was inevitably because of the music.

PAUL WINER (CHUM listener): For me, it was always the music. It was our life. We were tuned to CHUM day and night. Even lying in bed. We listened so intently that, 35 years later, I hear the opening bars of a song from that time, and bang — I know the title, the artists, and the words. Scary.

Music was CHUM's fuel, CHUM's engine, and CHUM's energy all plugged into one high-voltage electrical grid marked 1050. And what music, man! Music that *doo-ahhed, shoop-shooped, oop-ooped, sha-boomed, mmmmmmmmed, rat-tada-taded, belenka-blonked, rama-lama-ding-donged* and *la-laaded* mightily. Not to mention *dood-a-langed* and *bomp-ba ba-bomped.*

Blues, gospel, doo-wop, and country slipped into bed together, and their intimacy produced a bouncin' baby — rock. This fruitful conjunction was applauded by rockabilly and plain old eight-to-the-bar boogie-woogie, kissin' cousins who wanted to get in on the action. And sometimes did.

The musical mélange was often wonderfully warped in the studio — echoed and reverbed, multi-tracked, sped up, slowed down, or played sideways.

As for lyrics, they were up, happy, peppy — even when the topic was serious. There'd be teens bemoaning the fact that a boyfriend/girlfriend was lost, that a boyfriend/girlfriend was back, that their angst was caused by large zits, that someone had been killed in a car accident, or that their daddy was such a meanie that he threatened to take the T-Bird away. The minor musical mystery was that no matter how serious or tragic the record's

163

Let's see. Is it Dave Johnson on the left and Fabian on the right, or . . . ?

theme might be, it still bopped and drove dancers up onto the floor to make moves that would distress mom and dad. Rock music was fun. And sexy.

White girls discovered what their black sisters had known all along — they had hips. And how they began to move them! They put a wiggle in their walk doing the Stroll, the Monkey, the Hully Gully, the Watusi, and the undisputed champion of dances, the Twist. And when the girls got up to dance, the boys were sure to follow.

PAUL WINER: The music in that period marked our generation. It was fun, sometimes nonsensical, but also innocent and free of cynicism.

And if you couldn't get enough of a tune — even on CHUM — you could buy the 45.

SAM (THE RECORD MAN) SNIDERMAN: CHUM had a tremendous impact on the record business. If you go way, way back, selling records was a viable enterprise. But the introduction of radio almost wiped out the record industry. Records became a sideline and generally you could only find them tucked in the dusty corners of a few stores. Everyone wondered why they bothered.

Then came CHUM, and rock and the whole shebang exploded. Stores opened, ded-

icated to records, followed by competition and discounting. 45s became big business and we sold them for 66 cents plus 3 cents tax. Oh, we loved rock!

ALCHEMY OF A HIT: THE PLAY LIST

CHUM's Play List detailed which records would be played, when, by whom, and how often. Excluding the financial balance sheet, there was simply no other document at CHUM that matched its importance. Its creation could be deeply intimidating.

BOB MCADOREY: When 10 — or more — new records a week would sing out for attention, sometimes we felt like examining the entrails of animals for guidance, in the manner of ancient Romans.

The music library was our first destination of the day, a gathering place to gab and grouse over a cup of coffee. The only time its doors were shut — tight! — was when the blessed Play List was being prepared each week. Slaight was part of this musical meeting of the minds as was McAdorey, the music director.

Muttering "Double, double, toil and trouble" our CHUM charmers would drop many

items and considerations into the programming pot: the current Play List, the best of the new records, and trends from *Cash Box*, *Billboard*, and *Record World* magazines along with the Gavin Report. Other indicators would be stirred into our witches' brew: results of CHUM's Battle of the Bands, votes from Spragge's Housewives' Hit Parade, and the CHUM-Dinger. Our concoction was further augmented by listeners' calls, jock gossip from dances and remotes, and hot tips from someone's hard-drinkin' Uncle Harry. We paid particular attention to talented young artists and often gave them their break. Ask Gordon Lightfoot.

MCADOREY: Our gals ran the music department on a day-to-day basis — first Millie Moriak and Scoob McInnis, then Sheila Conner and Barb Sterino. As music librarians, they were the most knowledgeable people in the station as far as music was concerned. Immersed in it every day, they had their ears to the gramophone and were front-line contributors to the formulation of the Play List.

The whole magical mess was shaken, not stirred, and somehow the next week's Play List would emerge, steaming and smelling of vinyl and sweat.

"I WOULDN'T HYPE YOU ON A DOG, BABY": RECORD REPS

SPRAGGE: If you're doing a chapter on record reps, you should talk to Ronnie Newman.
AUTHOR: John, I believe he's dead.
SPRAGGE: Well, knowing Ronnie, he might still have something to say.
AUTHOR: OK, I'll give it a shot.

You could hear his strange noises in the hallway before Switchboard Betty would warn the record library with "Look out, Ronnie's on his way."

MCADOREY: Newman would be dancing before he hit the library. He'd get the girls up, shake his bootie, and have them shaking theirs. Short, chubby, he was not exactly a dance master, but in waltz-like moves, he'd dip the girl, slip a new record onto the player, and have it playing before you could say "Fred Astaire." Or "Get out!"

You couldn't help lovin' this guy. When bringing in a new record, his favourite expression was "I wouldn't hype you on a dog, baby." Then he'd do precisely that: sing, dance, and generally extol the virtues of a record so doggy you could catch mange just from listening to it.

Newman was working for Phonodisk and was the clown prince of record reps, those hard-working guys who chaperoned recording artists from station to station to plug their latest offerings, or simply brought in the 45s or albums and bent your ear and your arm to give them a spin. They included Gord Edwards (from RCA), Charlie Cameleri (Columbia), Al Meyer (Attic Records), and Billy Kerns (Quality Records). This was a tough job, and by and large the gals in the library gave them time to make their spiels.

MILLIE MORIAK (ex-CHUM librarian): I felt the library was the heart and soul of the station. It was a centre of constant activity with all our deejays popping in to hear the latest discs and a steady stream of record-promotion people and visiting artists. The perks were incredible. Invitations to anything musical came our way — plus a constant round of cocktail parties for artists. They were all part of our workaday world. Who wouldn't love it?

The record reps were personable and took their jobs seriously. Gord Edwards, for example, was a pro and straight as an arrow. When Harry Belafonte, who was on his label, was appearing at the O'Keefe Centre, Gord put together a promotion with CHUM. There would be a reception first and Gord,

aware of our guys' reputation for buffoonery, was a bit nervous. In his own decent way, he sort of quietly cautioned us to be cool when we met Belafonte, because Harry was serious and a class act. We gave our best Boy Scout and Girl Guide pledges to behave.

At the cocktail affair, we hit it off well with Belafonte. This was partly because we introduced the topic of Harry's early work as a jazz singer. Darow was particularly well informed, and we soon shared a big laugh with Belafonte.

Gord, hearing the laugh and fearing the worst, forced his way like a fullback through the throng of tipplers, arrived red-faced and sweating beside our group, and asked rather frantically if everything was all right. Belafonte assured him it was, and it would have been if Gord, nervous we might make a gaffe, hadn't dropped his drink, which splashed all over Belafonte's shoes and tight pants. As Gord, ashen-faced, horrified by what he had done, apologized, we winked at Belafonte and gave him a "You can't take these record reps anywhere" look.

BARB STERINO (Ex-CHUM librarian): Newman was in a frenzy. Bob McAdorey had just told him his new record was such a bow-wow it had flea powder on it. The 45 he was plugging was a strange instrumental. It went

Duh . . . duh duh . . . duh duh duh . . . duh duh duh. Not rock. Not a CHUM sound. Kind of . . . nothing. Go away, Ronnie.

Newman, with froth on his lips, jumped onto Scoob's desk. There, his fingers on his pants' zipper, he threatened to expose himself if we didn't play the record. As this would not exactly make our day, we looked over at Mac.

MCADOREY: I stepped in then, but before I could haul Ronnie off Scooby's desk, the gals hit him with these shrivellers along the lines of "Excuse me while I find my magnifying glass" and "You've met the man, now meet his namesake" and "Remember a song called 'Inchworm'?"

Ronnie decided to keep his privates in his pants and left muttering about not being

through yet. And he wasn't. Not by a long shot. Newman headed down to Sam the Record Man's. Again, he was told no! Who wanted to hear a funky instrumental? Sam wouldn't stock it.

Ronnie left, only to return with a card table, a player, a speaker, and a pile of his 45s. He set them up on the sidewalk in front of Sam's, turned on the player, and as the record *Duh . . . duh duhed*, Newman danced up a storm on the street. In minutes, he was selling the 45s like they featured a new Elvis release. Sniderman watched as Ronnie sold the second pile of records and pocketed the coin. He finally said, "OK, I'll stock it. No sense letting you have all the money."

As for that doggy record, it was "Wheels" by the String-a-longs. It became such a hit that it sat on the CHUM Chart for 13 weeks and reached the number two position. And did Ronnie let us forget that?

PRESSING THE FLESH: OUR LIFE WITH THE STARS

In the early '60s, rock was out of the crucible stage and definitely Hot! Hot! Hot! Hardly a city in North America was without a rockin' radio station. Or two. Or three.

Record companies and promoters, their

Mary (Scooby) McInnes, Harry Belafonte, and Millie Moriak. Day-o!

heads spinning with dreams of Elvis-like El Dorados, toured their performers mercilessly, pitching and plugging their newest stars or releases. Their carrot? The cocktail party.

At these get-togethers, recording company representatives or the performer's manager would keep the artist circling the room like a goldfish in a bowl, stopping only to be introduced to newspaper, radio, and TV types. Pictures would be taken, mutual admiration expressed, interview dates set, and hands shaken. At least twice.

The whole experience became a blur, a musical montage of miles and miles of smiles and smiles from literally hundreds of performers with hits. We popped till we dropped.

This misty vision included a broad spectrum of memories from the early days. Guy Mitchell, cowboy-outfitted with six-guns. Frankie Laine, his head-rug loose and slightly north-by-northwest, approaching everyone (sometimes twice) and asking shyly if he had shaken their hand. Earl Garner, meeting no one, but smiling at everyone as he performed exquisite, impossible jazz riffs on the 88s. Glenn Gould, gloved and glowering (we were told not to offer to shake hands). Percy Faith, outgoing, gabbing, a gas. Phil and Don Everly, somehow managing a tired laugh as the 5,000th person asked how to tell them apart.

CHUM personalities pretty well gladhanded every notable in our quadrant of the showbiz firmament: we showcased them all, and shared them with listeners. But when it comes to recalling the long scroll of their names, that tower of talent melts into an amorphous mass.

When pressed, CHUM veterans parade out the obvious: Elvis, the Beach Boys, the Supremes (and the whole Motown mob), the Beatles, the Stones, and the British Blitz (perhaps an unhappy choice of phrase). Top o' the mind, too, are artists such as Roy Orbison, Ricky Nelson, Jerry Lee Lewis, Ronnie Hawkins, Buddy Holly, Bobby Darin.

Canadians remain in the foreground of memory: Gordon Lightfoot, Bobby Curtola, Paul Anka, and David Clayton-Thomas.

169

Brian Skinner framed by the Everly Brothers

Then all them C&W good ol' boys: Marty Robbins, Stonewall Jackson, George Jones, Jimmy Dean, and Conway Twitty.

When further queried about which stars they met, many deejays will simply say, "Ask us who we *haven't* met rather than who we have."

Obviously, some encounters with celebrities were not all sugar and spice. Some stars left a very bitter taste. One was Jerry Lewis.

Yet another promotion. CHUM would sponsor a preview of *The Nutty Professor*. Jerry Lewis would appear live at the showing, do some bits, then go out and buy more hand mirrors. Everything was progressing smoothly until we mentioned to Lewis's manager that we planned to have Al Boliska open the preview and introduce Jerry. His answer was a firm "No. Jerry hates amateurs working before him."

We explained that Boliska was loved and respected by the audience, that he'd keep it short, sharp, and professional and do a crisp job of setting up Jerry. No. Still no.

Then we explained, if that were not the case, we'd cancel the preview, go on the air, decry Lewis's peevishness and lack of respect for CHUM's morning man, and make suggestive comments about why Jerry kept his hands in his pockets. Okay, okay — but . . . keep it short.

Hello, Buddy Holly!

On the afternoon of the preview, Al, having been briefed, strode onto the stage of the movie theatre to a nice ovation, performed about 90 seconds of humorous material that went over well, and concluded with a solid introduction that was so lavish it would have made Charlie Chaplin blush. Ending with "Now here is my favourite entertainer, and

Lewis waltzed through old material he'd honed with Dean Martin. It went over pretty well, and the movie was not bad.

Then there was Johnny Cash at Massey Hall in 1961. The impatient crowds had started rhythmic clapping. Emcee Bob McAdorey, usually unflappable, was definitely flapping. Lips

When pressed, CHUM veterans parade out the obvious: Elvis, the Beach Boys, the Supremes (and the whole Motown mob), the Beatles, the Stones, and the British Blitz (perhaps an unhappy choice of phrase). Top o' the mind, too, are artists such as Roy Orbison, Ricky Nelson, Jerry Lee Lewis, Ronnie Hawkins, Buddy Holly, Bobby Darin.

perhaps the funniest man in the world — Jerry Lewis!"

Lewis walked on. Boliska, on his way off, offered his hand to Lewis, who deliberately snubbed Al, slapping his hand away. Boliska quickly made a joke of it, signalling to the audience, "Funny ol' Jerry."

We in the wings were livid. The manager, embarrassed, spouted "Sorry."

and arms. Our star attraction, Johnny Cash, hadn't shown.

The CHUM gang were generally nuts about Cash's records and jumped at the chance to sponsor him in concert as part of the United Appeal's fundraising drive. But where in the name of the Nine Naughty Nuns of Nashville was he?

Country & western performers had set

171

such sky-high standards in unreliability that it took rock stars ages to attain — or surpass — them. This was long before Johnny embraced salvation and the healing balm of June Carter and the love of a good woman. John Cash was currently taking on drugs and alcoholic fuel like a southern tanker-trunk sucking up gator milk. We knew his reputation, but our little ol' station thrived on optimism.

The crowd was getting nasty and was on the verge of shouting things not approved by the PTA. The opening groups had done their schtick, we'd stretched the intermission, and it was time for that craggy-faced, barrel-chested, lived-in body to stride world-wearily into the spotlight. But nope. No.

Just as Mac headed reluctantly towards the stage to make an announcement about Johnny's "illness" — he had a bad case of Scotch — in reeled the man in black himself.

Lurching about, Cash refused all advice about cancelling. He looked shocked at the thought. He took charge. Demanding a stool be set centre stage, he then threw one arm around Mac and one around me and slurred, "No introduction. Just get me out there, amigos."

To enormous applause, we three staggered on stage, Mac and I bent under Cash's bulk. With some difficulty, we sat Johnny on the stool. He fumbled with the mike and said,

"You may wonder who these fellas are. These good ol' boys and I go away back — and are a couple of my best friends. You probably know them. Their names are [looking at me as I whispered "Allen Farrell"] Alex Varrell [small polite applause] and . . . [looking at Mac, who said, sotto voce, "Bob McAdorey"] Bob McAlorey [triumphantly]. Nice applause for Mr. McAlorey." We waved at the audience and made the thumbs-up gesture to Johnny, who returned the signal, nearly sliding off the stool. We hurriedly left the stage to Mr. Cash.

It would be pleasurable to report that John pulled himself together and tore up the place, country-style. Alas, no. Only rabid fans would call what he did a performance. He was just too stoned. Fizzle comes to mind. Flop, too.

Next morning his manager called and said John wanted to return his fee of $25,000 to the United Appeal. And would we accept an apology? We accepted both. The manager made one proviso. We must never tell anyone Johnny had refunded the . . . oh, well . . . cash.

One fine day Polish Prince Bobby Vinton was stomping around the CHUM music library when he decided upon a career change. Those were the days before he was a hit vocalist. Bobby was promoting his latest big-band album.

Johnny Cash, later, in fine form

When he asked if CHUM played his records, the gals answered with the old, crystal-clear standard, "Yes and No." No, we didn't play them on the air; and yes, we used them as background for promotional announcements.

"That does it!" said Vinton. "I'm hearing the same thing from stations stateside, too. You've helped me make up my mind. I'm going solo as a singer." "You're a singer?" our girls chorused. Vinton rolled up his eyes and his promotional materials and left.

Sooner than you could say "smash record," our deejays were wrapping their trembling tonsils around "Now, a musical bouquet from Bobby Vinton, 'Roses Are Red (My Love).'"

Another day, in 1962, Chubby Checker's plane was twisting its way towards Toronto. CHUM had already committed to this cyclonic dance craze, previewing the Peppermint Lounge movie for listeners and performing twist sessions featuring CHUM jocks and CHUM Chicks at company parties. Included in our lessons was live instruction by New York dance instructor "Killer" Joe Piro. Now it was Chubby Checker's time, and he had just landed.

The record rep, hand on Chubby's elbow, steered him directly into the waiting CHUM cruiser, which had been permitted to drive onto the tarmac. Fans screamed and reached out from behind barricades. Tolerant RCMP grinned beneath their broad-brimmed skimmers. Imagine Prince Philip arriving as a rockin', swingin' dude.

After picking up a crescendo or two of crowd craziness for ambiance, Dave Johnson broadcast his exclusive interview with the chubby one live from the CHUM cruiser. It was still early enough in Mr. Twist's career for him to enjoy it. Johnson finished his chat with Chubby just as we pulled into an airport-strip hotel. There, the other radio and TV stations, plus the press, elbowed and kneed each other for their piece of the Chubster.

After the scrum, Chubby graciously gave them a free master-class in twisting. To see this gang of cynical reporters studiously putting their toes down — oh, so genteelly — while determinedly waving their ample rear ends — it was to laugh.

CHUM was already laughing. We had scooped them all again and made sure our audience knew it. However, even the CHUM types were heard to boast they'd had a twist lesson from Chubby himself.

Under Slaight, we had learned to give our competition nothing. Nothing but abuse. He insisted we listen, watch, and read — and when we sniffed anything that could interest (or impress) our listeners, we were to snatch it for CHUM and guard it like we were German shepherds. If we couldn't hoard it or deny 'EY access, we at least must have it first. This was particularly true of anything to do with our music.

CHUM's listeners enjoyed our battle, lauded our victories, and shared in our triumphs. Mrs. Miller comes to mind.

Mrs. Miller had recorded a cover of Petula Clark's "How Gentle Is the Rain." When this classical-cum-folk tune was rendered by Mrs. Miller, it became a novelty hit, as sharp as it was flat. Mrs Miller was middle-aged, stout, bespectacled, and on the plain side. But her voice, oh, her voice — questionable. Hers was a tremulous soprano, a songbird of a voice that flitted between notes, never quite knowing where to perch. No wonder every pop station in North America wanted a piece of her.

Slaight drove us mercilessly to interview her. At one point CHUM had assigned seven people to do practically nothing but find Mrs. Miller. For three days the phone lines burned.

We inquired, begged, threatened, and considered offering bribes to anyone who could help us set up an interview with Mrs. Miller. Local news ground to a halt. Commercials were read live, not recorded. The audience was spared yet another contest. We were issued "Double-0" credentials, licence to kill anyone who got in our path of taping she-of-the-not-quite-notes.

Finally, through fasting, cold baths, and iron discipline, we reached and taped Mrs. Miller by phone. She, of course, was a perfectly nice woman. Although she was dazed with the grasping attention of a thousand rabid radio stations, bewildered, and wondering what the fuss was all about, her interview was still a quiet one, a comfy parlour sort of chat, redolent of sachet bags, lavender, and home cooking.

We thanked this nice woman, aired the interview a few times, and continued to play her record for a very short while. Mere months later, Mrs. Miller had sunk into the plush cushions of Novelty Heaven. It was definitely over when the fat lady sang.

CHUM
MAC meets
MRS. MILLER.
CHART

Mac swings while Mrs. Miller sings

TREMBLING TONSILS: *TALENT IN TORONTO*

Like many rockers in Canada, CHUM origi- nally created some programs as a sop to the BBG or CRTC. Unlike some stations, and this is not a criticism, CHUM broke its back to make these programs fun and palatable to its regular audience. *Talent in Toronto*, CHUM's live talent program and competi- tion, was a prime, meaty, Grade A example.

"It will be a live program," said Waters, "which will feature vocal talent in Toronto." With a smirk on my face and my tongue firmly tucked in my cheek, I said, "How about calling it *Talent in Toronto*?" As I looked smugly around for any laugh from the hip- sters, Waters said, "I like it." Would you believe it? Immediately, *I* liked it, too.

GARRY FERRIER: Phil Stone managed *Talent in Toronto*. He auditioned vocalists and we had them sing live on the program Sunday nights. I emceed, and an excellent trio backed the hopefuls. It was composed of Lou Snyder on piano, Mickey Shannon on drums, and Murray Lauder on bass. The show originated from CHUM's studio A, Sunday nights, 11 till midnight. To be candid — and hopefully not cruel — it was tough to keep a straight face when someone sank "Anchors Aweigh" or a budding Maria Callas sang an aria from *La Traviata* in the key of Q. That is not to say there weren't many excellent singers with outstanding voices.

We chose the best of the best, and each year CHUM staged a concert and competi- tion at the Eaton Auditorium (part of the for- mer Eaton's store at College and Yonge) to sold-out crowds. The whole event was given serious and first-class treatment. A top-line professional entertainment panel judged the performers and prizes were awarded to the best three singers. The show was broadcast live with Phil Stone as emcee.

One year — I believe it was our third annual Concert of Canadian Talent in 1961 — Mike Darow sang. Mike's powerful version of "The Battle Hymn of the Republic," with a special arrangement by Lou Snyder, fractured the audience, and, even though CHUM per- sonnel weren't competing, Mike left the judges mentally holding up sixes. I seem to remember one judge who staged the CNE Grandstand Show saying, "Wow! Where the hell did *he* come from?"

Over the years we were pleased to hear from some participants and finalists who made singing their profession or avocation. For the most part, however, CHUM received little credit for this feature. (Except in the awards that overflowed the glass display cases.) Then, to our astonishment, CFRB's Gordon Sinclair — who certainly spoke his mind — wrote in the Toronto *Star*: "CHUM is the only radio or TV station in this area giving a break to aspiring Canadian talent."

Thanks, Gordon; we always thought you looked great in your kilt.

J.J. STEPS IN: CHUM STEPS OUT

From 1958 to 1965, J.J. Richards pretty well did it all at CHUM, from deejay, newsman, talk show host, and companion to the CHUM Witch to acting as a merchandising door-knocker and Mr. 1050 at the CNE.

As a special correspondent for CHUM, J.J. covered race riots in the southern U.S.A., plane crashes in New York, the John Glenn ticker-tape parade, and the Martin Luther King march on Washington. But for danger, excitement, and sheer adventure, nothing matched the challenge of being chosen as host of "CHUM Steps Out," our live broadcasts from Toronto's night spots.

J.J. RICHARDS: Each night, Monday through Friday, CHUM would broadcast live from a different Toronto club or room. Some of the spots were fairly tough and held wise guys (literally) and others who either hated CHUM or loved simply to heckle the host. With my comedy background (for years I had played what Lenny Bruce called "the toilets"), I welcomed hecklers. I'd tie the broadcast and P.A. mikes together and work centre stage. When the audience heckled the guy from the "little rock 'n' roll radio station," I'd bury them à la Don Rickles.

The clubs we aired Monday through Friday sort of ranged from the subslime to the meticulous.

Monday nights, the owner of a club on Dundas East would kick out the hookers and the pimps and bring in Mike White's Dixieland Jazz group. After several weeks, phone reaction indicated we'd begun to build an audience for live music.

Tuesday nights we played the Town Tavern,

Allan Slaight, J.J. Richards, Paul McCartney, Dave Johnson, and Jack Kusch

with entertainers the calibre of Carmen McRae. And always attending, of course, were the boys, the guys with the twisted noses who talk out of the sides of their mouths.

Wednesday nights were split. One week at the Park Plaza to the music of Peter Appleyard and his group to a mostly college crowd. They would attack me from the moment I walked on stage with my huge CHUM sign. (College boys full of beer were no match for the announcer who soon was going to be known as "The Arabian Fabian," or "The Sneak of Araby," or "The Used Camel Dealer." Danny Thomas and I had the same background. Lebanese parents. [Author: And the same gall.]) Alternating Wednesdays were at a small hotel on Front Street called the Indigo Room. They had a maitre d' who was a smooth, good-looking Italian kid who was a character out of *The Godfather*. The boys would be there every night with their ladies. But when they brought their wives, the maitre d' would say, "Tony, where have you been? Mrs. Tony, you have to get him out more often, we haven't seen him in months." Everyone went home smiling.

Thursday night was really different: the first honky tonk club in Canada. They brought in Bob Darch, who could play ragtime music like no one I ever heard. For perhaps the first time, Pierre Berton, a regular, approved of CHUM.

Friday night was from the Imperial Room of the Royal York Hotel, with Moxie Whitney. I arranged it so I wouldn't arrive until there were about five seconds left. I would race across the dance floor and leap to the stage, braying, "Live from the Royal York Hotel." Moxie would hit the down-beat: bump . . . bump . . . bump. "From the beautiful Imperial Room in downtown Toronto, it's Moxie Whitney and his Orchestra . . . as CHUM Steps Out!" The crowd would go ape.

The live shows every night of the week did a lot for my social life. Remember, I was single. It was Harem-Scarem for the Arabian Fabian until the Beatles came to town. I was handing out Jungle Jay sweat shirts to those in line buying concert tickets. A tiny red-headed Greek kid came up to me and said, "You forgot me. Give me my sweatshirt." I threw one at her

178

and said, "Beat it, kid." She said, "I'll get even with you for this." And she has. We've been married for 30 years and she gets even every day.

WHAT'S IN A NAME? THE CHUMMINGBIRDS

When Jack Q'Part and partners chose CHUM as their station name, it proved not only to be warm, folksy, and memorable but also a useful platform for promotion.

Starting with CHUM News, CHUM Sports, and CHUM Time, it expanded into single words: CHUMidity, CHUMometer, and when it was raining — the CHUMbrella. Announcers had to but glance up to see a long list of CHUMisms pinned to the wall of the announce studio. Corny? Right. But corn that popped.

Our deejay sports teams — hockey and basketball — and our much vaunted Sportsmen's Show heroes all were named CHUM Champions. (We played soccer as the CHUM No-Stars.) We ran a CHUM Bug Club, and the CHUM Chart sported a CHUMdinger. Our fellas lip-synched Beatles records as the Cheatles.

Those CHUMmonikers — and others — served the station well, particularly from '58 to the lateish 60s. But the name that gained the greatest recognition — and flew highest — was the Chummingbirds.

GARRY FERRIER: Folk was very big, with "Tom Dooley," "Green, Green," and all the rest. Farrell had approached Slaight with an idea. Why not have the jocks form a folk singing-group and perform in public — particularly at the Ex? His name: The Chummingbirds. He went to Slaight for permission because, if this idea proved feasible, it could affect air-shifts. Slaight called Mac, Spragge, and me together and told us he wanted us to do this insane thing — be sort of a Kingston Trio. Mac played a 12-string guitar, I played ukulele-banjo, and John went out and bought a bass drum. Even though we had radio voices and could hold a tune, something was missing. That something was Mike Darow, who had a wonderful voice. And he knew his harmonies. He could sing "If I Had a Hammer" as well as the record. Now with Mike, unlike Tom Dooley, we could appear in public without hanging our heads.

One of the aces the Chummingbirds held initially was that no one expected them to be good. And they were more than that. They were excellent — and fun — with Spragge bangin' that big ol' drum. Garry did spot-on impressions of Diefenbaker, Pearson, and Ed

Sullivan, adding voices of his own. Mac cracked wise and Darow, tappin' a tambourine, delivered in the vocal department.

Just how good they were can be heard on their record, *The Brotherhood of Man*. Garry Ferrier wrote it and the Chummingbirds recorded it. CHUM's general audience, many of whom hadn't seen the group, appreciated their sound, and their requests proved it. The Chummingbirds appeared at many events around town, and on television a number of times, and were guest performers on "On the Scene" when Al Boliska hosted it.

Most folks, however, remembered them from the CNE. In the half gloom of approaching night, with a crowd stretching as far as the eye could see towards the Midway — an audience often bigger than the Grandstand Show's — their voices would float on the evening air. Their show energy and damn-it-to-hell antics cut through the dust and tawdriness and the pain of just plain sore feet.

Tonight — The Chummingbirds perform! Applause, applause.

THE LIVERPOOL LADS: BEATLEMANIA

Even as the first strains of "She loves you, yeah, yeah, yeah" were soaring out on 1050's airwaves, CHUM out-of-station promotion had begun. We invented the Cheatles. Dressed in mod clothes and wearing outlandish Eton schoolboy-type wigs, our fellas prepared to hit the high schools and any place that would book them. They took a few days to memorize and practise hot Beatles songs. We added some simple choreography, and 'allo, 'allo, 'allo, here were the Cheatles, lip-synching Beatles songs all over Toronto. Introduced as Bob "Pomp-Adorey," "Jumbled" Jay, Brian "Bangs" Skinner, and David "Sheepdog" Johnson, they wowed the crowds. In cold fact, they were pretty rough and far from slick. Didn't matter a "brolly in your trolley" — Beatlemania had just begun and it carried their credibility. The Cheatles hitchhiked their 20-minute performance onto regularly scheduled events of many kinds as a "Special,

Surprise, Attraction." For us, the surprise was how well our Bobbed Boys went over and how audiences didn't want to let them go. Ours was the Lyrical Liverpool Lads in fright wigs.

CHUM's music library was jammed. Everyone wanted to hear what the over 'ome and over-the-foam fuss was all about. "Are you sure it's not spelled 'Beetles'? You know, like the bugs?"

The Capitol record rep hustled in with the *Hard Day's Night* album. Hurriedly, he played several cuts. Silence. There was definitely something there, but . . .

Slaight took the safe route. We promoted the heck out of the cuts and played them first on the Johnson show, asking listeners what they thought. The cacophony of ringing phones could have challenged Big Ben. That did it. The Beatles were hyped. Their records played and replayed. CHUM became Pick-a-dilly Circus and Jolly Roger Hockey Sticks, don't-chew-know? Simultaneously, as the Bard might say, we slipped the dogs of war. With Slaight giving us "a touch of the cat," we strained to hobble the competition and make the Beatles our own. We used the CHUM Chart to feature photos of the Beatles (and the Cheatles). CHUM added contests and a Beatles concert promotion.

BARRIE FARRELL (CHUM brat): With my dad being the promotion guy, I'd get a CHUM Chart before they hit the record stores. When I brought the first chart featuring the Beatles to school, about 20 girls crowded around me, screaming. At least a dozen of them jumped on me. Unfortunately, I wasn't old enough to take advantage of it.

On-air, it was "Win this" and "Win that." Win their album. WIN TICKETS TO THE BEATLES CONCERT! Each night at 8 p.m., Dave Johnson had guest host Trudy Medcalf — president of the only official Beatles Fan Club affiliated with the International Fan Club. Thirty minutes of Beatles news and music. (We labelled it the Paunch & Trudy Show — we just couldn't leave Johnson's weight alone.) "Join the club and receive a Beatles Newsletter and wallet-sized membership card and photo of the Beatles!"

CLARA PACITTI (CHUM listener): We were mad for the Beatles. I still have a

Some talented fellas, trying to make good

Beatles Fan Club Newsletter signed by Trudy Medcalf. That year my girlfriend won Beatles tickets from CHUM. We had great seats in the centre, but we couldn't see a thing. We waved our sweaters throughout the show. It was fabulous.

Stan Obodiak, who, instead of sealing our usual handshake contract, asked if we could come down there to talk to Ballard. Harold was infamous as a self-styled bastard, so this was equivalent to being invited to the finals of a Mexican farting contest. But Slaight and I went.

Friday nights, Johnson had an additional guest, John Horan. English, and expert in British groups and performers, he styled himself the Principal of the Liverpool School and included the Beatles' doings in his musical news and information. Beatlemania found a welcome home in the CHUM asylum.

Central to hogging the Banged Boys all to our greedy, pinched chests was officially presenting their concert at Maple Leaf Gardens. Because of our long history and tight relationship with the Carlton Street Coliseum, this should have been a done deal. Then came the phone call. It was our Gardens contact,

Ballard curtly, and with the charm of a badger with its balls in a trap, informed us that CHUM would not be presenting the Beatles. Why? Because he didn't need us. They could sell the show out three times without our help. So you helped us out before? So what?

Slaight paused for a moment, then said mildly, "Harold, can you hear it?" "Hear what?" snapped Ballard. "The silence," said Slaight. The silence," he continued, "in an empty arena when you bring in all those rock groups you've booked — particularly the lemon no-names and downright ratshit Cavalcades of Has-beens. The silence," continued Al, "because CHUM won't be sponsoring those

"Hey! Does anyone want free tickets to the Beatles?"

shows either. They'll never be mentioned on the air, we'll forget the artists' names and lose their records. This jumbo joint will be empty. But there'll be plenty of room for you to stick your finger in your ear."

With that, Al motioned me to leave with him. Ballard said, matter of factly, "Hold it.

You've got it. CHUM presents the Beatles." "Fine" was our only answer. Adding, "Only this time, put it on paper!"

When I asked Slaight what that was all about, he said, "It's about Harold being a mean son-of-a-bitch whenever he thinks he can get away with it. It'll probably catch up with him someday."

The night of the Beatles' first Toronto concert has been documented many times. Outside, the CHUM Satellite Station and the CKEY trailer sat broadcasting. CHUM had five times the crowd around it. It seems some sleazy promotion-type had raided CHUM's lockers of giveaways, products, T-shirts, badges, and the like and was giving them away — and also providing soft drinks to teens and hot coffee to adults in line. So we bought affection. So?

Inside, the Beatles were on stage and no one could hear a thing. Non-stop screaming seemed to ride on the waves of light from flashing cameras. Many CHUM listeners were there. Quite a few for free. It was boss and beautiful.

183

Trudy Medcalf and Dave Johnson

Chapter Twelve

AFTER HOURS

MAGICAL MYSTERY TOUR: CHUM'S TORONTO

Listen up, folks. Everyone here? In just one minute we will all seat ourselves in the Nifty Ten-Fifty Tour du Jour bus. But because we have assembled on the sidewalk at 1331 Yonge Street, you might want to take a peek through the window blinds and wave at the CHUM newspeople and announcers. Sure, tap on the glass. They *love* that.

No, Mrs. McNulty, I don't know what the tall, angry man said. Could it have been "fuddle duddle"?

All aboard, everybody. Remember to show your CHUM Bug card and the tour is free, courtesy of Radio One. Soon as you're settled, we will begin our visit to the haunts and hide-outs habituated by CHUM folks and their associates. Feel free to take pictures. Or thumb your nose. And awaaaaay we go!

We are heading north up Yonge Street and on the right is Senior's Restaurant. Most days you can catch CHUM people in there scarfing truly fine smoked meat. See? There's host Eddy serving Spragge and Millie. Give 'em a wave, folks.

Same to you, John.

We are passing Swiss Chalet, another CHUM lunch spot in this area, along with Fran Deck's. As we come up to St. Clair, look at the northwest corner for the building that houses CFRB. You probably won't spot any 'RB announcers, though. I believe it's their nap time.

Of course I'm kidding, Mrs. McNulty. Their nap time is much later in the afternoon.

Quickly check out the barber shop on your right on St. Clair. That's Allan Waters getting his usual brush cut. The younger man in the next chair is having his hair cut the same way. Probably sucking up to the boss. I think his name is Pharaoh.

Here, above St. Clair, on your left is Christopher Beacom's, where many of the CHUM on-air personalities have their hair done. Chris brought men's hairstyling to Canada from Scotland and was the first to introduce unisex cuts, which really caught on with the CHUM gang. A raconteur, Chris supplied humorous stories for many of the CHUM deejays. Most of the gags were great, but some made Boliska's World's Worst Jokes on-air.

We'll make a U-ey by the cemetery and head back down Yonge. I'll slow as we drive by the Ports O'Call, formerly known as the Northgate. The liquor store's just below us near Summerhill, a major supply depot and resting spot for CHUM types recovering from the day's travails with a vital, liquid food group.

If you wanna dance . . . the Masonic Hall's on our right at Davenport. Promoter Norm Muir runs dances there with live bands and singers. Entertainers like David Clayton-Thomas often appear. He's managed by Duff Roman. Bob McAdorey is a popular emcee. Ike and Tina Turner? Sure, they performed there. The Supremes? You know it! A blast!

The Carlton Street area is coming up and that means the Westbury Hotel. It's in the Westbury that the CHUM Champions usually warm up before some strenuous event in Maple Leaf Gardens. The meticulous discipline employed as CHUM's latter-day jousters build up their stamina and courage with sets of elbow lifts at the bar is a sight to behold and a thing of legend.

For the fashion-conscious, allow your eyes to glide to the right to Warren-Evans Men's Wear. Look carefully and you can see J.J. Richards and Mike Darow in there, smiling.

No, Mrs. McNulty, they're not having their inside seams measured.

Now, without tilting the bus, look to the left side of Yonge and Cy Mann's. Garry Ferrier is being outfitted by Bill Williams so he can cut a dashing figure in his Jaguar. All those three need now is a hat from Sammy Taft on Spadina, and they'll be knockin' over the gals like Johnny-Be-Good.

If music be the food of love . . . and CHUM . . . keep peering to the left for Sam the Record Man. Sam is catching up to A&A Records and it's predicted he could become the dominant force in record sales in Canada. If you visit him, look for the enormous CHUM Chart blow-up over the top-50 records display.

Now we're moving into the blocks o' rock as we enter the Yonge Street Strip. Here, the more nocturnal CHUM specimens can be spotted late at night grooving off Bo Diddley in the Zanzibar or watching Jerry Lee Lewis tear up the place as he pounds out "Great Balls of Fire" on his standup piano.

But most evenings you're more likely to catch CHUM night crawlers slaking their thirst at Le Coq d'Or. By 10 p.m. the place is batshit. Go-go girls in cages tossing it at ya. The place shakin'. On stage, leerin' and steerin' pretty young thangs wrong, is Mr. Forty Days, rockin' Ronnie Hawkins.

Hey, hey, here's luck! There's Ronnie himself come out of rehearsal to wave at our bus.

No, Mrs. McNulty, I don't know what he's waving. Maybe it's his Mojo. What? No, I don't have his phone number.

As we put the bus in gear, here's a 1050 Tip. Hawkins' drummer Levon Helm is thinking of breaking away with a band of his own. Wonder how they'll make out.

This detour takes us west along Queen Street. Nights when Moose Latreck has a hankerin' for hurtin' music, why, he wrangles up a pa'cel of us good ol' boys and gals and herds us into C&W country, where the twang's the thang.

No, Mrs. McNulty, Moose did not go on the air and say, "May the good lord shit on ya sideways." However, at one cocktail party for C&W stars . . .

People, people, anybody hungry? Radsville! Let's head back up Yonge. If it was suppertime there'd be every good chance that CHUM gourmands would be woofin' down wine, garlic pickles, and a rare filet at Harry Barberian's on Elm. But since this is lunch-time, we'll turn up our nose at the Côtes de Beaune and head back to CHUM. Then we'll ankle up to Senior's for some lean pastrami. And if you

really want the inside info on CHUM types, just ask Eddy or his wife.

What do you mean, Al, that I'm giving Senior's free plugs? I know taking gifts is taboo. But a corned beef on rye?

Ladies and gentlemen, you've just experienced A Day in the Life of CHUM People. All tips are gratefully received by your genial driver.

No, Mrs. McNulty, I can't change a quarter.

DON'T BEND DOWN, THERE'S AN ELF IN TOWN: CHRISTMAS AT CHUM

The holiday season at CHUM was rum-punch rich and Drambuie delicious. It was Ho-Ho à Go-Go. Cheers!

Christmas at CHUM meant abundance — a time to welcome a profit-sharing cheque from the Super Chief. And a Happy Holiday to you, sir.

Christmas at CHUM was music — and the annual fretting about how many Christmassy tunes we should play, when they should start, and when we should return to regular programming. CHUM always feared it would carol listeners to death.

Popular with listeners was our airing of the choirs of the Toronto and District Public Schools. CHUM recorded them and played them as an integral part of its holiday music.

Christmas at CHUM meant a personal touch — like Garry Ferrier writing and recording "Ringo Deer," a cheery, novelty seasonal tune.

Christmas at CHUM was our annual staff blowout. Everyone would arrive for the party all gussied up and ready to kiss and hug fellow employees whom they had not seen for at least four hours. Wives and husbands, single gals and fellas boogied till midnight. They then sashayed back to the Waters's home for a nightcap and more CHUMerriment. (Sorry, old habits die hard.)

One year, at the height of the "named" dance craze — the Twist, the Stroll, and similar chiropractor-loved gyrations — we created a dance based on one of the senior staff's mannerisms. With a wailing rock band backing him, Jungle Jay was a grooving machine as he belted out the song, demonstrated the steps, and generally got down in a bluesy, blackish rendition that had everyone on the floor, high-steppin' and stompin'. When it was revealed that the name of this daffy dance was "The Slaight," Al's wife threatened serious harm to the sensitive body bits of its creator.

Christmas at CHUM sparkled and sparked warmth. We felt extraordinarily close to our listeners, and joined them in a Dickensian flurry of fun and kids and caring.

In this spirit, we built a promotion around

bringing a better Christmas to a family that was having it rough. CHUM jocks and other personnel would arrive carrying a tree and the trappings for the great day. We would spend a few hours with the family, stock shelves with groceries, put away an immense turkey Tiny

Tim would approve of, help trim the tree and, under it, place a present for each member of the family.

After three years, we gave it up. Even though the families were grateful, it still proved to be embarrassing for both them and us. So we dropped it, confident in the knowledge that

Santa (Mike Darow) helps the Salvation Army keep their bells ringing

our hearts were in the right place and that eventually CHUM would come up with an attractive idea that involved our listeners. How about CHUM's Christmas Wish?

Christmas at CHUM meant double duty as we prepared a snowstorm of fresh sounds and ideas. They would ring in the New Year and proclaim that CHUM and the world were making a brand new start. And that our listeners could, too.

Christmas included Christmas Eve — when we created specially recorded Santa's Sleigh Spottings, beginning with the RCAF picking up unidentified blips on their radar screens. Approximately three times per hour, starting at about 4:30 p.m., we would feature these reports, which tracked Santa on his way to Toronto. Our last report cautioned that it was time for bed. Many parents told us they relied on it to get their kids to put the lights out.

One Christmas Eve, we introduced a young Rich Little, airing his inventive and comedic version of *A Christmas Carol*. Rich played all the parts as celebrities, including Jack Benny as Scrooge and Fred MacMurray as Bob Cratchit. For many, "God bless us, every one" got it exactly right.

The Holiday Season at CHUM was hectic — but not on Christmas Day. The music was seasonal and what commercials there were mostly took the form of thanks from sponsors, expressing best wishes and, perhaps, a Happy Hanukkah.

Allan Waters and his family would come in and visit with the operators and announcers. Actually, many of us — often with our families — made a visit to the station a part of our Christmas ritual. We would relax in the announce booth for about an hour, sometimes slipping the on-air guy a lightly rummed eggnog for the last hour of his shift. A lot of smiling went on — especially by the jocks who had had three or four eggnog visits.

Everyone knew that tomorrow would be business as usual. But on this special holiday, it was smooth sleddin' all the way.

Have Yourself a Merry Little Christmas.

Chapter Thirteen
THE SPORTS CONNECTION

COURT JESTERS:
THE CHUM BASKETBALL TEAM

Annette Funicello, former Mouseketeer, was livid. Having parlayed her popularity into roles in "horny and corny" beach movies with Frankie Avalon and pals, riding the crest of stardom, she (in her mind) had sunk to the lowest depths possible: cheerleader for the CHUM Champions basketball team in a Toronto high school.

Like a hundred other CHUM promotions, we had arranged to air a contest, run a preview screening for our listeners, and generally promote her new flick. The film company had agreed, in return, to provide one of its stars, Annette, to go out on a promotion with us to a high school. Problem was, they had not warned Signorina Funicello.

To rub more sand into the crotch of this beachy-keen scenario, no one recognized Miss Funicello as she ran out onto the basketball court. When we gave her a great big

introduction, there was little reaction: the crowd simply did not believe us. Wasn't this another of CHUM's stunts? As the introduction was shouted down good-naturedly by the school kids, Annette sat, seething, and was literally ignored. At the first opportunity, she stormed out of the gym and into the waiting limo of the publicist.

When we got back to the station, we were greeted by the first words Slaight always used after an out-of-station event: "So, how'd it go?" We could not resist. With our hands held up like ears, we sang in ragged harmony: "M-I-C-K-E-Y M-O-U-S-E."

Earlier, our spies had whispered to us that CKEY was seriously fielding (or should it be "flooring") a basketball team. We had to act. Immediately, on the air, the station trumpeted that CHUM now had a hot squad of basketball players made up of CHUM personalities. High schools were invited to challenge our Champions to a game. They could charge a fee, with proceeds going to a worthy cause of

Flo de Leaf, Mabel Leaf, and Chicken Wing: the three witches from McCHUM. They loved the Maple Leafs.

their choosing. This was done, of course, before 'EY could make an announcement.

While games were being booked, behind the scenes we were busy fitting uniforms, writing a playbook of comedy bits, and holding a few practices.

Soon as we had confirmed our first game for November 5, 1962, we stepped up our on-air bull roar, discussed the depth of our team, took tips from coaches, and encouraged our listeners to advise us on diets, training programs, and mental attitude. It was a beautiful thing to watch as CHUM listeners responded. They caught exactly the right tone, somewhere between being serious and knowing that CHUM was shovelling it again. And at some tonnage.

Game day, we would promote the contest vigorously, with even our sports announcers giving the event a plug. After the game, one of the jocks would get on the horn and call in with an analysis in the form of a two-way conversation with the drive-home announcer. It was often "a hard-fought battle with CHUM squeaking out a victory over a heroic but disappointed high school team . . ." or some version of that theme.

Our squad included the following: forwards — Al Boliska, Peter Dickens, and John Spragge; centre — Mike Darow; guards — Bob Laine, Bob McAdorey, Just Plain George;

rover — Moose Latreck. (This was a position that we borrowed from lacrosse and adapted to our comic playbook.) Later, future deejays Jay Nelson and Brian Skinner would serve as our fab forwards. Also in attendance were Lorna Anderson and another of our CHUM Chicks as cheerleaders, and station extras dressed in medical emergency whites.

Toughest job of all was briefing the school team that this was only a gag. They knew in their hearts that we could not be beating all those hot high schools. Yet they had grown up with the legend of our Champions pulling off some seemingly impossible stunts. What about CHUM's athletic record at the Sportsmen's Show? So our first job at each game was to convince a fired-up high school team that we were not hotshot hoopsters. Rather, we were overweight, out-of-shape radio jocks.

Next chore was to make it perfectly clear that there was room for only one funny team out there — and that was the CHUM Champions. The school team must be straight men for our gags.

What might those gags be? Us paying off the referee with money in plain sight of the crowd, putting boxing gloves on their team, and (they loved this one) having our gorgeous cheerleaders distract their star players, flirting with them, sitting on their knees, cuddling up

. . . while CHUM pumped in basket after basket. We placed ladders and mini-trampolines by our opponents' basket and introduced about 25 other surprises we would spring during the game. The school's players were great, going along with gags and looking suitably frustrated. One fact the CHUM guys all agreed on was that we met a lot of fine young people in those schools.

We would open with a comic warm-up, a sort of floor play. As you might expect, the games themselves were freewheeling affairs, with laughs every minute. They all began officially with six-foot-five Mike Darow as centre taking the toss-up, aided by Moose Latreck, who scooted out at the last minute and climbed on Mike's shoulders. The two caught the opening ball, ran down the court, and Moose dropped the ball into the net. CHUM Champions, 2 points.

For two full seasons, the team played to capacity crowds in pretty well every high school in the Toronto area. CHUM's Travelling Hoop Troop was a big hit at every game, and there was good reason for it: solid preparation and a commitment to entertaining no matter what it took. In truth, these games were a real pain and a strain on the guys and the resources of the station. To play a 4:00 p.m. game, we would have to head out about 2:30 to accommodate traffic, find the school, get into the

locker room, change, and run through a pre-game review. This meant messing with our air-shifts. Jocks who had been up at 4:00 that morning were asked to play basketball when they should have been sleeping. Others had to shower and rush back to go on-air. Or try to work in a nap before an all-nite shift, for example.

Moreover, not only were these announcers expected to play basketball, they also had to be cheerful, funny, professional clowns. As with all CHUM non-commercial promotions, no one received a dime for their extra effort, nor much — if any — praise for their sacrifices. It was inconvenient, tiring, and felt like a major penalty. The payoff? A personal, powerful impression in every high school in Toronto, a growing audience, listener loyalty, and fortification of the CHUM image.

Sometimes the fellas' sacrifices went beyond the call of duty. The Champions were in a hot 'n' heavy, hilarious game at West Hill Collegiate. Mike Darow went up to intercept a pass. He was bumped, and fell, off balance. His foot was seriously dislocated at the ankle and was sticking out at an obscene angle. The play went on, but the crowd's attention was on Mike, who was lying on the floor, writhing in pain. This was obviously funny-old-CHUM, and the crowd was howling louder than Darow. Even some of our players thought it was a gag — especially Boliska. Al, his comic antennae twitching, knew an opportunity for laughs when he saw one. He pounced on Mike and, trainer-like, began chopping him up and down the leg as if relieving a cramp. When Al chopped him right on his dislocated ankle, Mike screamed in agony, much to the delight of the crowd. This spurred Boliska on to greater heights of invention, actually attempting to pull Mike by his injured foot. To prevent this, Laine tackled Boliska, and in seconds the entire team was pushing, wrestling, and arguing with each other. The audience went wild. This was the CHUM they had come to see.

Even when we stopped the play and announced that Mike was hurt, even when we carried him off the floor on a stretcher usually reserved for comic bits, even when it was obvious the game was over, some members of the crowd did not believe us. They sat in the bleachers laughing and waiting for us to come back on the floor. We rushed Mike to the hospital, where a young doctor pulled Darow's foot out and reset it into his ankle. By this time we all felt a bit sick. This called for medicinal alcohol for the team. Mike got plastered. But only his ankle.

Because we focused on the major high schools in Metro Toronto, schools in surrounding towns and cities wanted us, and put

pressure on the team to show up. We decided to take some action. Our plan was to choose one school reasonably close to Toronto and make a big on-air splash by staging an extra-special game with more bells and whistles. Our decision was to play a school east of Toronto. We would charter a bus to carry the team and add in extra entertainment, plus coaching and management types.

We had only one concern: demon drink. However, shades of the Walking Man, Slaight concocted a timing plan, which he laid out as follows: "Let's see, the bus could leave CHUM at 4:30 p.m. Even in rush hour it can't take us more than 30 minutes to hit the 401. Then it's a clear run east to the town. Let's be generous and say we'll hit the school in 75 to 90 minutes. All right, so we're in the dressing room by 6:00 and on the gym floor by 6:30. Now, if we figure our guys will drink one beer every 30 minutes or so on the bus, it'll average out to about two or two and one-half beers per person. Knowing their capacity, they can handle that easily. Sounds like a plan to me. You'll have to teetotal, Farrell, and keep the guys in check."

As a plan, it wasn't a bad one. In practice, it was a disaster. Two things happened, one of them partly my fault. My father was in town from Vancouver, and he introduced me to a drink called a Dog's Nose. You take a Pilsener glass, pour a shot of vodka in the bottom, and fill the glass with beer. This drink is guaranteed to have you rolling over and barking at the moon. Having loaded only beer aboard the bus, I felt free to tell our merrie men about this drink and suggest they try it some time when they had vodka. What fool, I. There was only a slight pause, then a round of smirks. You see, the CHUM Champions might have travelled without high-level sports skills, they might have sallied forth without superb discipline, but they never travelled without vodka. To be fair, it was always for after the basketball game. Not this trip. Out came the ruin of Russia. Snap went the top. And down the hatch went Dog's Noses all around.

I said two things happened. Just as our bus turned onto the 401, one of our hoopsters looked at the window and said, "Boy, that Dog's Nose must really have a kick. I'd swear it was foggy." It was. Pea-soup thick, I-can't-see-a-damn-thing foggy. Traffic was at a standstill.

There were a lot of long faces on the highway, but not in the CHUM Champions bus. No sir, it was party time. The fog socked in. The traffic inched along. And the Dog's Noses were definitely cool, wet, and I am not so sure about healthy. To make a long story short, we arrived at the high school at 8 p.m.,

three and a half hours after we had left CHUM. The bus door opened and out spilled the CHUM Champions, many howling, and, yes, barking.

The school gym was packed. The students had waited hours for this event, and the shouting and laughing heard from the CHUM Champions' dressing room built anticipation even higher. Not as high as our guys, but . . .

Changed and charged, and totally monstered, the CHUM Champions hit the court like a hurricane. The game was pure slapstick, with our boys improvising, leaping into the audience, tying up the officials, and generally acting like lunatics, much to the crowd's delight. This loosely bonded madness boiled on without incident until one of our stalwarts slipped, hit the deck, and shouted, "Fuck-a-duck!" The F-word being strictly taboo, its echoes signalled time to begin to wrap up the game. It was like trying to capture a greased pig in a plastic sheet. Finally, through gentle persuasion, threats, screaming, and other subtle pressures, the fellas finished up a fun-filled finale to this farrago, sometimes even sticking to the script. The crowd could not get enough of it.

As our champs staggered towards the dressing room, it was clear that although the game might be over, the festivities were not. The showers resonated with a spirited version of

Bobby Darin's hit, "Splish, Splash, I Was Taking a Bath." This was complemented by a chorus of high-pitched female shrieks as a couple of our likely lads decided to go public with their privates and ran nude in the girls' changing room.

When all our court jesters had been rounded up and prodded like cattle into the bus, we began our trail drive back to Toronto. Singing, shouting, and slugging back Dog's Noses were interrupted only to drop off each player or cheerleader at his or her door, handed over to the gentle ministrations of their families.

A few of us went all the way back to the station. Al Slaight and I sat down on the floor in the lobby in our overcoats, sipping a last beer. After a moment of contemplative silence, Al said to me, "You know, Farrell, all things considered, I thought that went rather well."

PASS THE LINIMENT: MAPLE LEAF GARDENS

Defeat does not rest lightly on their shoulders.
— *Slogan in Gardens' Maple Leafs' dressing room*

The CHUM/Gardens connection goes way, way back.

BILLY HARRIS (ex–Toronto Maple Leaf): In 1946, Ed Fitkin was public relations assistant at the Gardens. He was also sports director for CHUM. He ran a contest and welcomed listeners to guess the final score of an upcoming Boston-Toronto game. I guessed 6–3 for the Leafs. The actual score was 7–2, but since I was closest, I won. I was a guest of CHUM's Ed Fitkin for the Leaf–Chicago game, March 2, 1946.

Our first venture into that venerable sweatshop was when we had Al Boliska wrestle Whipper Billy Watson. It was an unqualified success. Being from the "If you've got a hot idea, flog it to death" school of promotion, we followed up with a tag-team match, pairing Al Boliska with Whipper Watson versus Mike Darow and Gene Kiniski. This drew an even larger crowd and helped cement CHUM's relationship with the Gardens.

Coincidentally, I created and recorded an original, on-air comedy piece entitled "The Maple Leafs Forever." It was a mock hockey game that used short record-clips from our Play List as punchlines. "Calling" the game was Faster Foster (Billy Hewitt) and Faster Foster's father (Foster Hewitt). It set a long-time record for positive audience response and we created a new version each year. Second year, Garry Ferrier joined me on the voices.

Garry's impression of Foster was outstanding. From its first exposure, we received calls from Maple Leafs players asking for copies. We were happy to oblige.

Next, having parked our brains in the puck-freezing fridge, we conceived the idea of playing hockey against the Toronto Argonauts football team. The fellas did their usual boasting on the air about how we'd put the Argos on ice, wrap them in our net, and generally show who were the best athletes out there.

Then we secretly watched an Argo hockey practice outdoors at the De La Salle high school rink. To our dismay, we saw huge hulks of men gleefully throw themselves on top of each other, wrestle the goalie, and generally act like grizzly bears having a fun free-for-all. This inspired a legitimate case of nerves and a checking of life insurance policies before the game.

The main event in the Gardens was the High School Hockey Championships. It featured a preliminary match between the Old Timers. As they came off, they smiled at us and wished us good luck from toothless mouths and faces that boasted 100 or so scars. We assumed they'd all been in commercial radio.

Next up was CHUM versus the Argos, and much gulping could be heard from our side.

As part of our comedy bits, we'd had huge, special hockey sticks made: one with blades on both ends, one with a net that would hold a puck, one with two blades and a puck trap. We found that two others of the giant sticks had already been broken by the Leafs players who had used them that afternoon in a practice. Among the other comedy props, the black yo-yo used at the faceoffs was particularly popular.

The game was to start. First, we introduced Just Plain George (who actually played hockey in an industrial league). George was goalie, and he skated on with confidence and a special stick that covered the entire goal mouth.

Next, newsman Peter Dickens. Pete was a rabid Leafs fan, and stepping onto the ice at the Gardens was to be the biggest thrill of his life. Unhappily, as he put his skate on a Band-Aid on the ice, his feet flew up, and Pete went ass over teakettle in a sensational slapstick fall. The stands exploded. Boy, those CHUM guys are sure wild and crazy, huh? Even the newsmen.

Rest of the team were CHUM personalities plus a couple of pretty good players from our sales staff. (Later ex-Leaf Danny Lewicki was to join CHUM. We could have used him that night.)

So it went on. Each personality with his

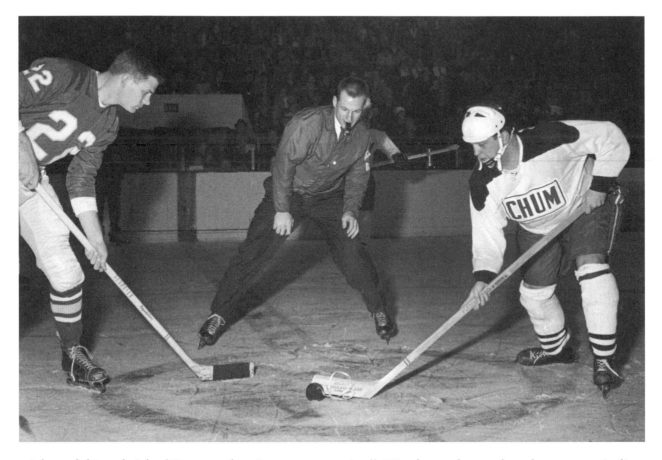

stick and his schtick. 'Course, the Argos got huge applause, too.

The game was just one laugh after another, with CHUM using every hoary old gag we could find. We'd asked former Leafs player and hockey's clown, Eddie Shack, to referee. Though popular with the crowd, Eddie drove us crazy because he'd get so caught up with the comedy, he'd forget to call the "penal-

ties." We shouted ourselves hoarse reminding him. The game ended in a tie.

CHUM, bears for punishment in the Gardens (or having been punished by bears), went on to further sports glory, playing more hockey, taking on the policewomen in broomball, and demonstrating our blazing blades in a race against figure skaters as part of the Ice Capades.

Argonaut star Dick Shatto, "referee" Eddie Shack, and CHUM forward Al Boliska

Sports, of course, was only one part of the CHUM/Gardens relationship. Perhaps the more visible activity was the sponsorship of singers, groups, and musical rock shows.

As part of our policy of being King of the Mountain and giving 'EY nothing but seal breath, we greedily grabbed pretty well every pop music show at the Gardens.

CHUM would present the Beach Boys, for example, promoting the appearance, running a contest or two, giving away tickets,

embarrassed man, followed by an irate young singer in her unmentionables. It seemed that, to pay the rent, these girls were turning tricks on the side (or some other position). "Hooking" had long been a penalty call in Maple Leaf Gardens, but we'd never heard it applied before to a singing group.

On occasion, we teamed up with the *Telegram*'s After Four section for a joint sponsorship. Our plan was to stay very close to all pop performances — be they in Massey Hall,

Though popular with the crowd, Eddie drove us crazy because he'd get so caught up with the comedy, he'd forget to call the "penalties."

and emceeing the show. This treatment would apply to each Gardens attraction, including some of the more tawdry ones. These shows would be made up mainly of acts with one hit or two and often on the slippery slope to oblivion. Most were paid very little and this tour was an act of desperation for them.

With 50 acts — count 'em, 50 — our staff was kept busy assisting in calling performers for their turn on stage. As we tapped on the dressing room door of one particular Detroit three-gal act, out popped a half-dressed,

the Royal Alex, the Bathurst Street Sub-Sewer Saloon, or the Gardens, CHUM would be there. This paid off when the British Invasion attacked Toronto in non-army-issue haircuts and CHUM presented almost anyone of note.

The Dave Clark Five appearance leads us to a Gardens sidebar story. Executives of the Musicians' Union had time on their hands. They'd left their Dinky toys at home, had examined their earwax, and, therefore, had nothing to do. So, they decided to bug

CHUM. They called and demanded we hire a so-called standby band for the Dave Clark Five appearance.

Their tactic was based on two points of argument. One, what would we do if the group didn't show? And two, they claimed we were putting Toronto musicians out of work. Both arguments were indefensible, of course.

If Dave and his gang didn't show up, money would have to be refunded to ticket holders who sure wouldn't want to hear some local musicians play, professional as they might be. Also, we weren't putting musicians out of work, because they weren't singers and international recording stars.

The hoary rules they were citing were

CHUM Champions teach Boliska some of the finer points of ice dancing

based on the antediluvian times when bands, often travelling by bus, didn't make their gigs because of bad weather, or because they were broke or drunk. Or all three. So, to guarantee patrons an evening of dancing, for example, one hired standby musicians. Remember, these union execs were the same ones who thought records would soon go away after five or six decades of existence. They did have one card to play: their alleged book of rules and regulations. Thought to have been brought down from the mount, it was rumoured to still have these outdated directives in hard print. So, they invoked them — saying it wasn't their idea, and that we should blame it on the book.

What made this practice such a scabrous scam was that the standby band rarely, if ever, showed up. Better still, they often took another playing job when they were supposed to be standing by. This was featherbedding at its most flagrant.

To avoid any confrontation or negative publicity, whoever booked the band often agreed to pay a standby band scale, plus double for leader. So did we. (Even though CHUM had no obligation here, as the station not only did not book the group, it also had no financial interest in it whatsoever.)

Since the English sense of fair play oozed like treacle in our veins — and, besides, we owed them one — we made a number of demands in return.

One: the standby band would show up at the Gardens. Over their spluttering and splattering and spitting, we told them we found we could invoke that action as per an article in their rules and regulations.

Two: the band would wear formal evening wear.

Three: they would come — and play — at a rehearsal in the afternoon.

Four: they would play that night during the show when we decreed.

Pouring honey into the phone, we told them that it wasn't our fault — it's in the book.

It is said that revenge is a dish best served cold.

So it came to pass that a pitfull of snarling musicians played pop tunes for our entertainment at lunch while we munched down our salads with Cokes. Our request to "Play 'Melancholy Baby'" met with a hostility usually seen only in naughty vicars caught wearing the widow's knickers.

But it was that night that we enjoyed more tickling than leaping naked into a flower box of furry caterpillars. John Spragge, who had been in on this caper from the beginning, was emceeing. The opening bands had finished, and John ran on and said with great glee, "The Dave Clark Five will be on right

after this break. However, a super surprise. Give it up for Toronto's own Clem Clap and the Clappers!"

He signalled the standby band and they started to play the Lawrence Welk–type boom-chang music we'd demanded. Silence. Then a chorus of booing and catcalls from the audience, followed by a rain of paper and programs. It was here Spragge gave the leader the "cut" signal and the band stopped playing.

As they packed up, furious, we told them we had nothing against unions. It simply was not fair to blame CHUM or the Gardens. They should blame their own chiefs who put them through all this. And never was heard a sour note again.

CHUM went on to present nearly every pop music show imaginable in the Gardens and elsewhere with nary a peep from the union. Mind you, it's tough to talk with your head firmly up your brass.

As a coda, I'd like to give credit to entertainment impresario Hugh Pickett from Vancouver, whom I watched invent this ploy and execute it molto bene and con brio!

Corporately, and as individuals, we felt privileged and honoured to be permitted to ply our craft in the House That Smythe Built. Personally, I grew up with a large poster of Charlie Conacher over my bed. Later, skater.

MABEL LEAF FOREVER: THE CHUM WITCH

What began quietly as a CHUM newsman's inspired kicker to his 'cast was picked up by an ever-ravenous promotion pusher; coddled and cared for by nature's gift to women; made corporeal by a high-spirited entertainer; evolved from a one-off, on-air black arts novelty into a major listener entertainment that included four-city involvement; had Punch Imlach screaming, tickled the Smythes, and even made Harold Ballard chuckle; and morphed into a mystical force that seemed to confound the Toronto Maple Leafs' opponents, helped inspire them to a Stanley Cup, and received thanks from the great Johnny Bower himself on national radio and television. I speak of Mabel Leaf, the CHUM Witch.

Vancouver has the natural beauty, Calgary the pride, Montreal the style, and the East Coast the wonderful people. Toronto? Well, it has great hockey fans, arguably the most knowledgeable on the continent, and certainly the most faithful.

It was natural for CHUM's morning newscaster, Peter Dickens, a fierce Leafs fan himself, to make a comment about the then failing Leafs. We were well into the 1963–64 season and the Leafs were flat, faltering. Peter had said something along the lines of "Well,

Toronto greets Dick Clark

the Leafs lost another one. A few more like that and they won't make the playoffs. Maybe they need a CHUM Witch to put a hex on the opposition." Then he signed off.

It was just coming up to 9 a.m. I heard this comment in my car, slammed on the brakes, left the vehicle parked illegally, and ran into CHUM's newsroom. I asked Pete to tell me all about it. He could see I was excited but he didn't know what I was talking about. "The witch, the CHUM Witch." Pete said that that was just a kicker. I gave him an are-you-kidding look . . . and went on to say I thought it was the hottest idea we'd had in years. Leaving Pete to ponder my alleged sanity, I charged upstairs and hit Slaight with the concept.

His "If you like it that much . . . go, go, go!" was following me as I sped downstairs. Within minutes, Ferrier and Solway were writing hexes, Moose was finding music and sound effects for their production, and I was seeking out our VP of Oddball Assignments, J.J. Richards. Since the witch was a woman, who better to handle her than CHUM's

official expert on things female? J.J. assured me he was up to the rigours of the task. He chose Phyllis Shea, whose outgoing personality and experience in London and Paris as a nightclub entertainer provided the chutzpah the role demanded. He couldn't have made a better choice.

With cackling, gurgling, and screams rending the air, shrieking out hexes, we gave it the full treatment. The CHUM Witch would attend that night's game in Maple Leaf Gardens and put the whammy on the Leafs' opponents.

That fatal night of February 15, 1964, the CHUM Witch, garbed in her costume, stirred a boiling cauldron outside Maple Leaf Gardens. Her face was made up green and gruesome after the wicked witch in the *Wizard of Oz*. (Later, we'd drop this and the witch would become quite glamorous.) That night the CHUM Witch entered the Gardens, sat in CHUM's seats in the Blues, hurled hexes at the opposition, and waved her wand magically at the Leafs. Toronto won 4–1. Before that the Leafs had won only four games out

Mabel Leaf spells it out to CHUM newsman Hap Parnaby

of 12. We had accomplished what we had come to do. So, Mabel Leaf, the CHUM Witch, could go back to appearing in productions of The Scottish Play. It was a terrific one-time promotion.

You must be joking. When the Leafs lost the next game, the calls poured in from listeners. And from the Gardens. Punch Imlach, who was superstitious, had left a message that he expected to see Mabel at the next game. We sent her. The Leafs won. Now there was no turning back. We were in this promotion up to our charmpits.

We'd never experienced such a frenzy surrounding an out-of-station event. It took on a life of its own. Sports, led by Dickens, was frantically working out appearance strategies. Creative kept the air a-cracklin'.

Mabel had become popular with the Gardens' ushers and they welcomed her in. The coach and some of the players seemed more confident when she attended games. Harold Ballard was heard to say, "We were on a plane, and Punch Imlach said he wished that the CHUM Witch was aboard so he'd be sure the thing wouldn't go down. He's a

very superstitious guy, you know."

Did we ever know. After the Leafs lost a game that Mabel didn't attend, Punch called and reamed me out. Why wasn't the CHUM Witch at the game? I explained that she sometimes got tired. I even threw in a little gag line to lighten the moment. "After all," I said, "when you're 500 years old, you're not 21 any more." Punch ignored the quip. He snapped, "Listen, you, I don't accept limp excuses from my players and I'll sure as hell not take it from some damn witch. You tell her to get her bony ass down to the next game!"

She did. The Leafs won again. Punch flashed her an "I told you so" smile.

With Mabel in attendance, the Leafs won 11, lost two and tied one.

J.J. RICHARDS: When the Leafs lost, the fans wanted to know what happened to her mysterious powers, not what happened to the Leafs players. We always had a ready answer for our news or sportscasts: that her potion wasn't strong enough, or she was "hex-austed." We knew we had to do something, though.

Huh? We knew *we* had to do something? That's the way everyone was thinking. We'd fallen under Mabel's — say it, say it! — spell. And no wonder. In the dying seconds of one game, the Leafs losing 3–2, I said to Mabel (Phyllis), "Do something!" Convinced I'd lost it, she still leaped up, charged down the stairs to the glass, and pointed her wand at a Leafs player who had circled behind the net. He was now at the point. She screamed, "Shoot!!" He did. The puck went into the upper corner of the net, the light went on, the buzzer sounded. Leafs had tied the game and went on to win in overtime. Moments like that made believers of more than one person in the stands.

Richards accompanied Mabel to New York's Madison Square Garden, the Olympia in Detroit, and the Montreal Forum (J.J. passed on the broomstick and insisted they fly by plane). He'd report back with results and the fans' reaction to the witch.

The CHUM Witch was held in reserve when the Stanley Cup semifinals opened in Montreal. Leafs lost the first game 2–0. Mabel flew to Montreal. Leafs won the second game 2–1.

The series became tied at three games apiece, with the deciding game to be played in Montreal. CHUM conjured up some help.

RICHARDS: We had a CHUM sales secretary, Shirley Hart, dressed in a different witch's costume. She was presented as Flo de Leaf, Mabel's sister. While Mabel was to charm the Leafs, Flo's job was to put a hex on the Montreal team.

The power of these sinister sisters was potent. Montreal didn't have a ghost of a chance. Toronto won that seventh game 3–1 and prepared to take on Detroit in the finals. Mabel graciously gave full credit to her beloved team, the Leafs, and said that now it was up to them to win the cup.

Three of the first five games went to the Red Wings. Mabel and Flo had to repack their spells and ply their witchcraft. Once more they headed to Detroit for this must-win game for the Leafs.

RICHARDS: Getting into the spirit of the thing, the Olympia dreamed up a sort of wizard, a hex-ecutive in the black arts, who was charged with neutralizing our demonic duo. Toronto won 4–3 in overtime. The wizard failed, and he left with his wand drooping.

SHIRLEY HART: Not all the Detroit fans succumbed to our charms. Outside the Olympia, a half-dozen tough-looking characters chased Phyllis and me, calling us something that sounded like "witch." Just then, J.J. stepped in, and with his growly voice chilled them right out.

Next game was a must. We decided to form a power line by adding one more witch. She was Mary McInnes (Scooby) from our library. Garbed in costume with black cloak and mask, she was transfigured into Chicken Wing, Mabel and Flo's mother.

At each game the witches carried signs on poles with slogans along the line of "CHUM Witch Hates the Hawks" and "Mabel Leaf Stabs the Habs." That night, the final match saw "Flo de Leaf Stings the Wings," "Chicken Wing Hexes Old Man Howe," and "Mabel Leaf — It's Punch Bowl Time."

On the ice were Red Kelly, playing with torn knee ligaments, and Bobby Baun, who had scored the overtime goal in the sixth game in Detroit. Baun had broken a bone in his lower leg and should have been in plaster. Instead both he and Red, taped and full of Novocaine, played their hearts out.

RICHARDS: We had our own lineup of supernatural superstars, each with her role in the game: Flo de Leaf would slow down the Detroit players; Chicken Wing, as Mabel's mother, would hex older players such as Gordie Howe; and our leading scorer, Mabel Leaf, would surround the Toronto team with charm and charms.

To the delight of a crazed crowd, Toronto won the game, 4–0. The Maple Leafs were the Stanley Cup champions!

In front of a coast-to-coast television audience, Johnny Bower, who had played so brilliantly, said, "And I want to thank the CHUM Witch, Mabel Leaf, for being here!"

Perhaps she should take the final bow.

PHYLLIS SHEA: This is one of the most satisfying jobs I've ever had. I'll always be ready to help if the Leafs get into trouble.

Maybe they should give her a call.

CHUM's
Double
Contes

WIN
AN ADMIRAL TWIN
STEREOPHONIC CON.
Furniture
380 FLEET St.

If you resemble a fa
personality from show b
politics... sport... or one
CHUM's announcers ...

Enter CHUM's
'Double' Contest

Send your photograph with
the name of the personality you
resemble, to...

'DOUBLE' CHUM
TORONTO

Chapter Fourteen

THE KING IS DEAD, LONG LIVE THE KING

LOOK, MA, NO NET: BOLISKA BAILS OUT

Imagine, if you will, a celebrity charity hockey game at the George Bell Arena. The date, November 19, 1963. Imagine, too, that all the players are in shadow, except two, each one in a spotlight's beam. Representing one team, the mayor of Toronto, David Sommerville; on the other side, Toronto's Morning Mayor (as he was called), CHUM's Al Boliska. As Mayor Sommerville's stick touches the puck, he is bumped gently by Boliska and falls. He stands up easily. Both he and Al are laughing.

A few minutes later, Sommerville, again, drops to the ice. He has suffered a heart attack. Mayor David Sommerville, born in Toronto in 1915, is dead.

SHEILA BOLISKA (ex-wife): After Sommerville's death, Al didn't know whether to blame himself or not. He cloistered himself at home for five days. Al ate almost nothing, and slept hardly at all. He wouldn't respond to me, the kids, or his best friends, who tried hard to communicate with him. The station called and asked when he would be back at work. He wouldn't even form a reply. This seemed to me to be a turning point for Al. Always shy, now he was darkly withdrawn.

There never was so much as a hint of correlation or accusation regarding Boliska's bump and the mayor's heart attack. This was a fun game and everyone had been horsing around a bit. Any blame existed in Al's mind only. He confused coincidental with causal.

Lest we do the same, attributing that fatal incident with Al's increasingly thin skin towards comment or commentary on that fatal incident, we should remember that his downslide was already in progress. Did Sommerville's death speed up the process? Maybe.

At announcers' meetings, where the jocks' air-checks were played and criticism levelled along with horseplay from their peers, Al had

Al Boliska sees double

shown zero tolerance for any advice. Twice, when his tapes were chosen, he'd lost his voice, stomped upstairs, and croaked his resignation to Allan Slaight. Slaight would kid him out of it, we'd all fool with him a bit, and life would go on as normally as it ever did at CHUM. Till the next meeting.

We should have known something was in the wind when Al voluntarily spoke to us about quitting. He said that he might — only *might* — quit, but, "I'll swear on my Hungarian family honour — I'll *never* go to CKEY. Believe me, please, friends."

Less than one week later he quit. To go to CKEY. As their morning man.

I called Al Slaight in Ottawa. In the room with him were Allan Waters and Fred Sherratt.

When they were convinced he'd truly made the break and gone to our hated competition, Slaight said, "Let him go, then. It's obviously over. And Farrell . . . you know what to do."

NOW YOU SEE HIM, NOW YOU DON'T: SMOKESCREEN

CKEY, our compliments! You've finally done it. One-upped CHUM and sent us riding around in a 1928 Tizzy.

CKEY would happily honk 'n' hoot, blaring about the fact that Al Boliska had joined their staff. They had an excellent talking point, a legitimate sales message, and we had no doubt they'd make the most of it. Of course, we couldn't let that happen.

First, we consulted our dog-eared copy of the *Farmer's Almanac* and sought direction through ancient maxims. Ignoring "A stitch in time saves nine," we settled on "When you have a lemon, make lemonade."

The following strategy has been jealously guarded up to now by Harvard Business School profs, who use it as an acid test for those MBAs who choose a career testing acid. Now, it can be yours.

All CHUM on-air people — and support staff — were directed to deliver some version of the following:

Day One: "Al Boliska is gone. We had some great times. We wish him good luck. We'll miss him."

Day Two: "Al Boliska left us. He made a contribution — and the station did lots for him. Wonder who'll take his place?"

Day Three: "Al Boliska was part of a very tight team here. Candidly, although he'll be missed, he *did* go to a competing station. Sort of disappointed in him. Many of the guys are. Anyway, CHUM will probably come up with a great replacement."

Day Four: "Well, the search has begun to fill the position of the most important morning show in Canadian radio. [Stations across the country are writhing at this statement.] Since Al deserted — left — his friends and the CHUM team, we'll have to top him."

Day Five: "The contest is on — we're hearing from fantastic people who'd love to fill this important post. Here's the hot question in town: Who will be CHUM's new morning man?"

That was the strategy. Reinforce the importance of the CHUM morning position. Do it in such a way that it smothers or diminishes the fact Boliska is gone and is over at 'EY.

The CHUM radio personalities ostensibly asked for a shot at the position (some seriously). Each one, publicized round the clock, took over the morning show for one or more days. Those of you who don't miss a damn thing will have smugly noticed that this gave CHUM a terrific chance to feature all its people before the morning audience. They all grabbed the helm and navigated through the shoals of the a.m. mayhem.

We also auditioned outsiders for the job, including Phil Givens, Pierre Berton, and Whipper Billy Watson, who hosted the show.

Then we explored another angle. Why not employ the technique and expertise CHUM had learned in creating the simulated Dick Clark show? If performers couldn't come to us, why didn't we . . . you know?

We began with Conway Twitty, who was playing in Buffalo. After all, it was Conway who'd talked our good buddy Ronnie Hawkins into coming to Canada.

The Pres, C&W deejay Moose Latreck, and I worked all night preparing a script for Twitty. The simulated Dick Clark show had indeed broken us in. It also taught us that assembling some amateur production that might melt their pants in Peoria was a far cry from convincing a Toronto audience that the person was actually on CHUM, live, and auditioning for the morning show.

On two hours' sleep, we drove to Buffalo. By suppertime, we were taping the segments, leaving space to cut in Hawkins's comments.

Moose and Twitty sat on a bed in Conway's hotel room and, with scripts before them, let loose. Dang me, but they sounded good.

Pres and Moose slept in the rear seat of the CHUM cruiser on the way back that night. I drove. Just as we approached the Seaway Hotel on the Queen Elizabeth Way, I fell asleep and the car hit a median. Fortunately, we only lost a hubcap and suffered a flat tire. Tire changed, and now wide awake, we continued home.

Claude Deschamps applied his mixing magic, Hawkins added gags and colour, and the audience was treated to a very entertaining audition for CHUM's Morning Man position by Conway.

Slaight liked it so much he said he'd decided to send me to Hollywood, California, to enlist some big guns.

Hollywood! My eyes shone. Flying first class. Throwing back the free champagne and orange juice. Being discovered in the Top Hat Café with Lana Turner. Borrowing her sweater. Fame and fortune. Starlets everywhere. Streets paved with mattresses.

Then . . . POP! . . . Al was still speaking. His directive went something like this: "Dick Clark is the biggest rock-related personality there is. Get Dick to audition. Connie Francis is currently the number-one pop singing star in the world. Get Connie. Now, to top it off, *The Beverly Hillbillies* and *Bonanza* are North America's top-rated shows. Get one or more of the principals — say, Granny (Irene Ryan), or Pa Cartwright (Lorne Greene) — to audition. *Dr. Kildare* is huge, too. See what you can do with, say, Richard Chamberlain. And if you can pick up another movie or TV star or two, good. You can fly out to Los Angeles Sunday night, be back by Friday, and we'll have them on the air by the next week."

What went unsaid was that it usually took up to three months to arrange any kind of taping from first-line TV or movie stars.

The longest item they'd tape (for the few who agreed) was about 10 seconds — and only for American charities or other not-for-profit organizations. So, here I was about to muddle into Hollywood, swanning around with long scripts and my request for stars to record for a radio station (not TV), in Canada (not the U.S.A.), for a profitable business (not a charity), this week — preferably tomorrow (not three months from now) — and — *are you kidding me?* — for a recording duration of at least an hour (not 10 seconds). For free, of course.

For the trip I bought a sharp new suit, shoes, watch, and briefcase. Lookin' good. The first-class flight allowed me — not to drink free champagne — but enough room for my portable typewriter. By the time we landed in L.A., I'd polished off two scripts — one for Doris Day and one for Rock Hudson (I'd promised John Spragge) — plus enough straight orange juice to float a football parade.

My glamour-gilded days were festooned with such rounds of licentious pleasure as rising at 6 a.m., sitting at my typewriter in my underwear to keep my clothes pressed, phoning agents and agencies and networks, and lying through my freshly brushed teeth about the tri-city TV and radio promotion we were preparing — Toronto, Buffalo, and Cleveland — and why I had to have this or that star do a little recording. Terrified I'd miss a message telling me to waltz my Wollensak over and tape Elizabeth Taylor, who was hungering to meet and please me, I ate all my meals in my room. After two days, I overheard a room service clerk refer to me as "the guy in the boxers who phones actors and eats BLTs."

My first returned calls stated "Doris Day cannot see you," "Rock Hudson might see you, but later," and "Dick Clark will see you tomorrow afternoon at his home."

Next day, having churned out more scripts, eaten my BLT, sporting new boxers, and wearing my freshly laundered clothes, I cabbed it over to Clark's.

I skipped up the stairs to Dick's Hollywood apartment — if you can call it skipping while lugging a briefcase and a Wollensak tape recorder. His wife invited me in. Dick isn't home yet. Cup of coffee. Sit and talk. She's from Toronto. Could I watch her baby? Sure.

Clark arrives. He's red-faced angry. Who are you and where's my wife? As I awkwardly explain that I'm a writer and part-time babysitter, she appears from the other room. Clark is pissed off. Oh, not at us. It seems someone bashed into his new car on the freeway. He's forgotten our appointment. He's

guesting on a medical TV show and the cast is coming over to rehearse. Do I mind waiting? Of course not. I settle down in an anteroom to amuse the baby.

The cast arrives. I'm introduced as the babysitter. Funny old Dick. Good as his word, though, each time the rehearsal takes a break, Dick scurries over and tapes a part of the script.

The cast went home and Clark finished up the long task of taping the segments of the three-hour show. As we were wrapping, about 7:30 p.m., Clark said, "It's coming back to me now. CHUM, of course. You've got that guy there who keeps bugging me for more clips for the Dick Clark show on CHUM."

"As a matter of fact, Dick . . ." and I pulled out a new list Claude had slipped me just as I was heading out. Clark, his eyes rolling back in his head, taped the clips.

As I left, offering profuse thanks, he said, "I know you think I say this to all the stations carrying my show, but you can tell that Clod guy [Claude Deschamps] his production is in a class by itself." (Dick was so impressed he tried to hire Claude away from CHUM. Immigration red tape prevented the move.)

I had my first tape. Gold. I returned to my hotel, first picking up my phone messages: "Tony Curtis cannot see you," "Rock

Hudson cannot see you," "Cary Grant will not see you," and "Connie Francis *will* see you at the studio tomorrow at 1 p.m." Yahoo!

I gave my clothes to the hotel valet for cleaning and freshening, sat in my underwear, tore up the Curtis and Hudson scripts, and worked till 1 a.m. on an audition script for Johnny Weismuller (Tarzan). I sipped a hot chocolate.

I slept well. I trust the Clark baby did, too.

Next day, after a morning of writing scripts for Richard Chamberlain, Lorne Greene, and Lucille Ball, I presented myself at the front gates of MGM.

There I was led in and sort of stuffed into a crowd of singers and dancers from another film. They'd just wandered over to see Connie work.

The set is sparkling: a balcony, a bower overlooking a spectacular lake at sunset. Out of camera view is Connie Francis, her very Italian mother and even more Italian female hairstylist — a sort of rogue volcano.

The music track starts up, and Connie, exquisitely gowned, walks into the shot, looks adoringly towards her (off-camera) movie lover, and sings along with herself on the track. Oops. A technical difficulty. "Twenty minutes, Miss Francis." She beckons me into her trailer, we chit-chat, I show her a picture of Dave Johnson and herself. She remembers. (Remember that she liked Dave Johnson and always asked for him in interviews when she was in Toronto.)

Her mother and her fire-breathing hairstylist are in the trailer with us. As she begins to record the script, the hairstylist insists on not only talking, but also fussing with Connie's hair. A knock on the door: "Miss Francis." Tape ruined.

Connie begins again, looks longingly, starts to sing . . . and another technical difficulty. This really pisses off the hairstylist, and I pick up some Italian phrases not taught at Berlitz.

We begin taping once more. Again the fire-breather futzes with Connie's frizz. Again, we're interrupted. "Miss Francis." Tape section buggered up. Nice.

This time Connie doesn't even get to sing, as a piece of scenery falls over in the opening bars of the song.

Fire-spouting dragon hairstylist wigs out. She quits. Spits out some Latin lingo and stomps off the set. Mamma, too, is doing her Italian hand-thing.

Connie and I try again. She just begins when the trailer lights go out. No sweat, though; the glow from her Mamma's eyes and cheeks could light up an avenue.

And so it went all afternoon. It was 17

botched efforts before Connie was allowed a clean take. Cut. Finally, it's a wrap. I had arrived at 1:00. It was now close to 6:00.

So, now it was just ol' angry Connie and ol' nervous Allen. Connie never spoke to me again. She pointed at the trailer. Because of the interruptions, Connie had to begin again with line one, which she did. She read, she acted, she performed the entire script.

As I set a new record in speed for check-

was Canadian, asked me if we had taxis where I lived. I assured him cabs were becoming more commonplace, but the dog team was the preferred transportation in Toronto in winter, especially in polar-bear season.

Two targeted tapes down. Oh boy, how I rewarded myself in the fleshpots of Tinseltown. The rainbow-hued neon signage. The hypnotic, Latin rhythm of the taxi meter, the thrilling elevator ride two storeys to my

Connie begins again, looks longingly, starts to sing . . . and another technical difficulty. This really pisses off the hairstylist, and I pick up some Italian phrases not taught at Berlitz.

ing the tape, "Many thanks, Miss Francis." (Silence.) "So good of you, particularly in light of . . ." (Cold.) "I mean, I'll give your best to Dave Johnson . . ." (Frigid.) ". . . and the best of success with your movie." (Mount Rushmore.)

Once off the set, I boogied on towards the taxi stand, singing, "Ma-maah!" My spirits had definitely picked up. I didn't really mind when the L.A. cab driver, discovering I

floor, the sensual stripping to my boxers, the taste-tempting BLT, and, most of all, messages to moisten my palms. "Kirk Douglas cannot see you." "Lucille Ball will see you — next week — in New York. Call this number." And "Johnny Weismuller needs more information, but would consider seeing you. When could you fly to his home in Acapulco?" Certainly not today, Tarz.

That evening it was writing scripts for Pa

Cartwright in *Bonanza* and Granny in *The Beverly Hillbillies*. And bed.

Friday morning proved exhilarating. More messages arrived with my breakfast. The room service clerk had become used to seeing me in my shorts and he came all the way into the room.

One message read, "Richard Chamberlain will see you next week." But, Dick, I'll be home by then. Physician, heal thyself.

Now for the biggie. One more score would give me a Hollywood hat trick.

I'd talked to the publicist of *The Beverly Hillbillies*. He was a kindred soul (promotion) and said he'd do his best. He was at the studio. When I tried to contact the *Bonanza* bunch, iron gates clanged in my face. Within a half hour, I was talking to the director of *Bonanza* on the set. He asked me how I got the phone number. I told him I'd phoned the studio and told them I was his brother. After he expelled his breath with a "Jeez," he wrapped up our conversation in the following way.

"Let me get this straight. You don't carry *Bonanza*, you're not even a television station, you're a radio station in bloody Canada, and you want the superstar of America's top-rated show to record for — what was it — an hour? And for nothing?!"

I told him he'd pretty well summed it up.

He asked if anyone had taken me up on my kind offer. When I said Dick Clark and Connie Francis, that both Lucille Ball and Richard Chamberlain had agreed to meet me . . . and that I was probably seeing Irene Ryan today, he answered, "I believe you." Then he added, "You've gone to all this trouble, so let me give you some free advice. Lorne and the guys don't fart for less than $25,000, for about 15 seconds of their time. I suggest you finish up seeing those other folks and I wish you luck. Actually, you'd probably do very well down here. Now, fuck off, and don't call me again . . . brother." I said "Thanks" and "Adios." He grunted goodbye.

Then the waiting game began. If I was turned down by Granny, I'd have to stay over and focus on Richard Chamberlain and others in high-rated TV shows.

The phone rang. The label on my shorts jumped. Bad news. The publicist had done his best. (I knew he had.) There was just no way. Sorry.

Perhaps it was my experience with Bill and Ernie; perhaps I feared facing Slaight without the real goods; perhaps it was because I'd asked many shy CHUM announcers to let it all hang out in public — to perform, with aplomb — feats they feared. Now that it was my turn, I didn't give up.

Between all the scriptwriting and having

Author Allen Farrell with Irene Ryan

suits pressed, I had written a little fall-back piece. It began with my saying I couldn't go back without the Granny interview. Then I rhymed off all the things I'd be willing to do: "Repair their old car." "Fight Jethro." "Babysit the raccoon." "Work on their oil rigs." "Clean the swimming pool." And on and on. The publicist laughed and told me to hang tight. Once more he'd ask, but please don't rely on it.

About an hour later, just enough time to bite my toenails off, the phone rang. It was the publicist. He said, "Remember what you said about the swimming pool? Well, the pump has clogged temporarily. Come now and I'll meet with you in the front office with Granny."

They arrived, Irene in costume and make-up. The publicist said, "The pool could be fixed in five minutes or it could be 20. Good luck."

Ms. Ryan turned out to be as gracious and sweet as anyone I've ever met. She said she knew Toronto and had played the Royal Alex much earlier. I handed her a page of the script. She read it wonderfully as Granny. I handed her another page. Then another. After about seven pages she took to peering at me impishly over her glasses. She knew precisely what this meant to me.

The pool mercifully stayed clogged for about an hour. She read every line on every page with professional emphasis and feeling. When she was finished, and I had practically kissed the hem of her dress, she said, "I bet you'd like to meet Elly Mae." I agreed with alacrity. She took me on the set, introduced me to the cast, and allowed me to watch the shoot. Later, she (and the publicist) arranged to have us photographed together. I had a great tape. Thank you, Irene, and thank you, Mr. Publicist. Thank you, thank you, thank you, thank you.

Early that evening, I arrived back at CHUM, looking for someone I could crow to. The response was mild. "Oh, you got the tapes? Good." They told the on-air jock, "Farrell got Granny." "Hey, that's good, man." Then they told me what had taken place on the air. "Good," I said, "real good." "So," said someone at CHUM, "that's good then."

Agreeing it was good, I headed home for a bite of supper. No damn BLT, you can bank on it. Life was . . . oh well . . . good.

IT'S A JUNGLE IN HERE: JAY NELSON

CHUM was in dire need of a topper. By God, we had to have a sensational climax to our on-air commotion. Boliska had decamped.

We'd all but obliterated the news of his turn-coat trek to 'EY with the most intense misdirection in the history of radio (or magic). All our efforts — and our audience — were intensely focused on who would be the next morning personality on CHUM. Listener vibes hinted that our surprise had better bloody well be good. We talked a good fight on the air but, if the truth be known, we were fast running out of viable contenders.

Then, out of the mouths of babes (in a way) came the best idea yet. Allan Waters's young daughter, Sheryl, brought it to her father.

SHERYL WATERS BOURNE: My girlfriend Nancy Smith Fairweather and I were watching Jungle Jay on Buffalo TV, just as we did every day. Nancy said, "Wouldn't it be great if Jungle could come to CHUM and take that job?" I said I thought he'd be perfect. Soon as Dad came home I told him Nancy's idea.

Reaction to this recommendation at the station ran from "Great!" to "Genius!" Jay and his wife were wined, dined, and wooed by CHUM. Like most Americans, they knew diddly about Canada. Management answered their questions and hung out an attractive pay packet.

Jay signed on the dotted line.

When it was announced that the new CHUM Morning Man was Jungle Jay Nelson, it struck a perfect chord. Jay, an American, from television, was considered a star in the bigger leagues. CHUM had done it again.

Our promotion machine leaped into high gear: interviews, photos, the CHUM Chart, the whole nine yards. Jay's on-air debut on CHUM was much ballyhooed, and he lived up to his advance notices. Jungle was funny, a bit irreverent, did voices and impressions, and fit CHUM like handcrafted shoes. Astoundingly, after only a week, it felt like he was an old CHUM hand.

Nelson, after a nip or two, would often-times sing out, "I'm Jungle Jay from Scranton, PA." In truth, he was born Frank Cox. (His name change came about at WBNY, New York, where he first became Frank Jay, then Jay Nelson.) At 16, he had already developed some acting fundamentals, particularly in comedy. Since Pennsylvania wasn't exactly famous for its Shakespearean companies, Frank turned to — oh, such a surprise — radio.

TERRY COX (son): Dad had a legendary story built around him when he was just 16. He approached someone at radio station WARM in Scranton and asked to do the overnight show. He said he thought the current all-nite

jock, Lou Dobbs, was no good. He was given an audition. He won the job. Frank then wanted to thank the guy who provided the audition and asked him his name. "I'm Lou Dobbs," he said.

Jay became known — and popular — with Toronto people with his afternoon show on WKBW TV, where he showed Tarzan and Sheena movies. He wore his pith helmet, styled himself "Jungle Jay" and created other characters such as Professor Smart. The pie in the face became his trademark. When Jay joined CHUM, we gained yet another comic performer.

For years, a feature entitled "Hello Toronto" was Jay's best chance to show off his talents daily. It was a genuine copycat of "Hello Buffalo" from Jay's former TV show. Original, it wasn't. Funny, it was.

The concept was simple. Jay would phone someone cold with an idea that ranged from slightly off-kilter to absolutely ludicrous. He'd keep on phoning until he hit a nerve and elicited a strong reaction. Jay would then identify himself and ask permission to play it on the air. The listener could hear him- or herself at 6:45, 7:45, and 8:45 the next morning.

We had a three-person team producing this feature. My job was to come up with zany ideas. I had plenty of help. We had a "Hello Toronto" idea box that the staff dropped their concepts into.

The second member of the team was Claude Deschamps. He'd edit the phone calls, stress the humour, tighten them up, and keep them punchy. Many a time, Claude's clever editing turned a so-so call into something genuinely funny.

But it was Jay who made the feature sizzle. He had the guts of a hockey goalie. No matter how outrageous the idea, Nelson would get on the phone and give a performance. He'd slip in and out of characters and voices like a chameleon. It was damned hard work, turning out a new call five days a week. (It could easily take 20 calls to find a winner.)

To encourage Jay to stay on the phone (after a three-hour air-shift that began at 6 a.m.), Claude and I would keep him company in the studio, encouraging him, laughing at reactions, and generally cheerleading, but by the second year of the feature he was losing interest. At one point, I began scripting every call, writing in gags and absurd lead-ins. If he couldn't uncover a willing victim, he could always fall back on the script. "Hello Toronto" was a signature feature for Jungle, who churned out this hard-won humour month in and month out. It was easy to criticize when his patience and stamina wore thin, but I can't think of anyone else who could have accomplished

Jungle Jay Nelson left no one hanging on "Hello Toronto"

what he did over the long haul.

Al Boliska was often prodded by pitch-forked devils, and Jay Nelson had his own dirty dozen demons. Meet Boliska for the first time and he would be shy, awkward, but unfailingly polite. Nelson covered his insecurity in sandpaper-abrasive tactics. Introduce him to someone (often someone in awe of Jay) and he might do any of the following:

1. **Reach out, then snatch his hand back before it made contact.**
2. **Shake hands, pick up on your name, and say, "Let me wish you luck. All bad."**
3. **Much as above, adding, "Never heard of you. Why are you wasting my time?"**
4. **Go into high-speed schtick, running impressions into dialects into one-liners.**

The effect of any of these actions was rude in the extreme. Just as the visitor paled and pulled back, Nelson would sort of collapse his body, beam a huge smile, turn on the warmth, and call the person "pal," "buddy," or "friend." "See, pally, it's just funny ol' Jungle Jay havin' some fun. Okay?"

Jay saved much of his charm for the air, and today Jay was excited. His guest was Frank Fontaine, an old-time vaudeville-style comic, who had recently had his career elevated on *The Jackie Gleason Show*.

Frank had a stock character, Crazy Guggenheim, who did a bit on *Jackie Gleason* each week. Jackie, in a touch of genius, also showcased the other side of Craz', his creator, Frank Fontaine, as a ballad singer, with a tearjerker tune aimed to make Mother McCree sob. The Great One made Craz' a regular. Today, he was a guest on Jungle's show. In five minutes he would push the plunger that would make the CHUM phone lines catch fire, take years off the life of Switchboard Betty, and leave Jay's followers wondering if he'd tripped on a vine.

To the casual listener, Jay had asked Frank about how he balanced a personal life with a showbiz career. Frank had replied something about a combination of spiritual guidance and the support of his spouse. Here, inexplicably, Jungle exploded into helpless laughter, couldn't stop, and had to rely on his operator to

222

TV's Johnny Crawford (from *The Rifleman*) sets Jungle Jay a difficult "tusk" save him with commercials and music.

Outraged listeners called in and demanded to know what Nelson found so damn funny about spiritual guidance and marital support.

Shall we sneak into the studio and back up the interview a bit? Before we replay Jay's interview, please note that every announce studio has a cut-off button. The announcer uses this if he has to cough, for example, or between times when he's actually talking on air. Frank Fontaine, veteran of a thousand

it's easy. We both look to the good Lord for guidance and spiritual and marital harmony . . . [Here, Frank pressed the cut-off button so the listeners couldn't hear, and said quickly to Jay in Crazy's voice] . . . and I've got an eight-inch dick and a ten-pound tongue! [Frank snapped the button back to "on" and CHUM listeners heard Nelson losing it.]

The interview was in a shambles. When it was over, Jay said to him, "Now I know why

It was easy to criticize when his patience and stamina wore thin, but I can't think of anyone else who could have accomplished what he did over the long haul.

interviews, was well aware of this button. Ssh, ssh, they're going to replay that interview.

JUNGLE: Frank, with your television schedule and club appearances and publicity tours like this, do you have any personal life?
FRANK: Jay, I try to balance my career with a solid marriage.
JUNGLE: You'll agree that many people try to accomplish that . . . but few succeed. To what do you attribute your marital success?
FRANK (seriously, solemnly, sentimentally): Jay,

they call you 'Crazy.'" As for Frank Fontaine, he said Nelson's was the best reaction he'd had to that gag in ten years.

Jay might well have been an actor himself. If he had had the discipline and could have put aside his ego, he might have enjoyed a career as a stage performer. His voice was flexible, he enjoyed creating characters, and he knew intuitively how to build a scene.

DOUG THOMPSON (producer): Jay could be incredibly kind when he felt someone

223

needed — and *wanted* — his help. Brian Skinner was working incredibly hard (too hard) to establish himself as a regular member of the CHUM on-air team. Jay would finish his Saturday morning shift . . . and then go live on Brian's *Grooveyard* show, creating characters and voices. Skinner was perhaps the best audience of any-one at CHUM, and that egged Jay on to greater comedy efforts. Conversely, if you were operating for him and you didn't laugh big at his gags, he'd intro the record, slam down his earphones, and stalk out of the studio, scowling.

Jungle was at his best when he was doing schtick with two or three people he knew and felt comfortable with. For those few minutes he'd be generous with his laughter (the man loved to laugh), and he'd share the improvised scenario with his fellow funny men, even doing set-ups and acting as a straight man. (Garry Ferrier's character, Mysterious Minerva, used to murder him.) Let Jay feel upstaged or threatened, though, and he could engage in unprofessional behaviour.

Rich Little had been contracted by CHUM to play a series of characters who were supposed to be the real celebrities. It was mandatory that everyone play this straight if the audio illusion was to ring true.

All went well until Rich appeared on Nelson's morning show as John Wayne. Jay couldn't bear it. He began doing voices and impres-sions of Ed Sullivan and Bing Crosby.

Rich, a major cut above Jungle in doing impressions, did his best to keep things going, praising Jay (as Wayne) on his talent — all the while looking through the studio glass for help. We arrived, signalled Nelson to cut it, and Rich Little covered and saved the day.

Nelson was furious. The dressing-down he received after this shift started with "Of all the jealous, amateur, peevish, show-off, bush-league, stupid stunts . . ." and then it got nasty.

This lapse of judgement was unusual for Jay. Like Boliska, he kept it professional on the air, providing an entertaining, high-energy show. Most times, too, he would take this

Jay Nelson shows his chops with a great axe

professionalism with him on stage in personal appearances. (CHUM deejays were in their listeners' faces and lives as often as we could manage it.)

When Jungle strutted onstage, say, as emcee of a Beatles concert, he never disappointed. Upbeat and professional, he seemed aware of whom the audience had paid to see and didn't try to upstage them.

BOB MCADOREY: I really liked working on stage with Jay. We'd be out doing some emceeing job and the two of us would sort of turn on comically. We'd anticipate each other. He'd finish my lines and I'd finish his. The result could be pretty funny, with the audience hooting.

Jungle Jay deserves his place in the CHUM Hall of Fame.

FOUL SHOT: BOLISKA DROPS THE BALL

The Harlem Globetrotters were enormously popular. They mixed high-calibre basketball with trick shots and comedy turns. (Sort of giant black CHUM Champions who could actually play basketball.) Their appearances filled arenas around the world. They travelled with another pro-level team. Their games were exciting, but their comedy capers were number one.

Phone call to CHUM: Would we care to have our basketball team play the Globetrotters in a short preliminary game?

This was CHUM's meat. Ballyhoo the game on the air, give status to our basketball team, run a contest for free tickets, promote it on the chart, and make another strong, out-of-station impression. Perfect!

We turned them down.

Made excuses. Really sorry to miss this opportunity. Breaks our heart. Have another game that day we can't get out of. Just a thought. Hate to help the competition, but maybe CKEY's team could be available. Suggest you make like they were your first choice. Again, really feel bad about missing this golden opportunity. Please think of us next time. Good luck.

CKEY jumped at the chance to play the Globetrotters the way a steelhead strikes a fly. They crowed on the air that it was the CKEY team who'd been chosen. With Al Boliska captaining their squad, this would be a game to remember. Yes. Yes! They'd beaten those CHUM bastards at what they generally did best. 'EY was to play the Harlem Globetrotters. CHUM, put that in your pope and smike it!

There were people within the CHUM

organization who quietly asked me why the decision was made. Thoughtful questions like "What the hell are you doing, you lunatic? Have you finally lost all the peas in your sports whistle?"

Our reason for turning down the game was simple: there is room for only one comedy team on the floor. With the Globetrotters, it surely wasn't going to be us. Play this world-renowned team and we'd come out looking like monkeys.

Game day, a group of us headed down to the arena and were soon hot-dogged and huddled in the stands. We had come with our souls full of scorn, which we planned to pour onto Boliska. When the 'EY team was announced, it received a fair applause from the station's fans who had come out to support them. That wiped the grins off our faces and we began to have doubts about the decision to pass on the game. Surprisingly, too, the 'EY team had a few good players, backed by jocks doing their best to clown it up. Al got a nice hand as he deked and did a lay-up, right out of the CHUM team's handbook.

The Globetrotters' theme song, "Sweet Georgia Brown," cut in and their team hit the floor to great applause. Boliska was dribbling a ball around, trying to hang on to some attention. As a Globetrotters player passed Al, he effortlessly snatched Boliska's ball away and

casually tossed it into the basket. Al, still game, went into his "I've-been-cheated" routine. The Globetrotter responded by handing the ball back to Al. Just as Al took it, the player grabbed the ball back. He dribbled the ball around Al, daring him to take it. Boliska tried. And tried. His smile was strained.

The huge player taunted him, signalling to the laughing crowd, "Why won't this boy take the ball?" Now the player bounced the ball to Al, only to have it fired back into his hands because of the powerful spin he'd given it. Most of the action had stopped and the entire focus was on this debacle. The Globetrotter was making Boliska look like a hapless fool. Al was seething. Finally, the player rolled the ball to Al, the way one would to a little child. Al, in a cold rage, took one look at the 'EY players standing helplessly around, heard the derisive laughter from the crowd, picked up the ball, fired it at the Globetrotters' bench as hard as he could, and stomped off the floor. He didn't return.

The game started and the 'EY guys did their best to make a match against a highly skilled trickster team. It just sort of fizzled out and soon the radio squad followed Al to the showers. The audience was in a downer until the real opposing team ran on and the game began.

It wasn't funny; it was pitiable. We all came to gloat and left feeling rotten.

BREAKING UP IS HARD TO DO: CONTRACTS

Boliska had taken years of CHUM's time and effort to promote him into a premium household radio name and, with his departure, made a gift of it to our traditional rival. It may sound naive, but this defection really shook Allan Waters. A decision was made to sign all the jocks to contracts. Slaight told Waters, "I think I can sign most of the guys, but I sense I'll have some trouble with Spragge. You talk to him."

JOHN SPRAGGE: I said to Waters, "Allan, what you want is my reassurance that I will never do what Boliska did — go across the street. Why don't we shake hands, and I'll vow that I will never, never go across the street, and go on-air on a Toronto radio station — unless CFRB offers me the *Wally Crouter Show*, in which case I'll give you, maybe, 20 minutes' notice." Waters laughed, we shook hands, and I never signed a contract, although the others did. For some time after that, Waters would pass me in the hall and say, "John, there's a message for you from 'RB at the switchboard." And then he'd laugh.

As was soon proven by other stations' jocks, most of those contracts weren't worth jack, and the courts upheld a person's right to work. As for Spragge, I saw him as a rebel without a clause.

Chapter Fifteen
ON-AIR TALENT III

THE PRES: BRIAN SKINNER

The CHUM Bug Club was an anomaly. Usually, we'd think of an idea, and have it on the air that day, with all stops pulled. However, in this case, we pulled a slow one. Whenever pop stars or other celebrities visited the station, we'd have them record station idents and the like. For more than two years we'd asked top showbiz people to record, "Hi, my name is _____, and I'm a CHUM Bug. Are you?"

What particularly diddled our juvenile minds was that Southerners sounded like "Hi, Ah'm Carl Perkins. Ah'm a CHUM Bugger you." Easily amused or no, by the time we introduced the CHUM Bug concept, we had recordings of several hundred major entertainers of all styles, boasting

that they were CHUM Bugs. We considered it a throwaway, until the thousands of requests for cards flowed in.

In response to CHUM's hot on-air lineup, CKEY had thrown out a cross-Canada net, hoping they'd catch some rare and exotic fish. They landed a keeper in CKY, Winnipeg — not a goldeye, but a large-jawed specimen known as Brian Skinner the Chinner Spinner. Brian was hooked, and soon did double-duty at 'EY: an early evening shift on-air and assisting in promotion during the daytime. Skinner had a spout of ideas; the problem was turning him off. When Westinghouse bought 'EY, Brian was unhappy, talked to Slaight, and soon was performing on-air weekends on CHUM.

Brian was wonderfully imaginative. He

Left: Moose, Mac, Millie, and Jimmy Dean jaw awhile; Above: Skinner flashes the peace sign, even as we war with CKEY

believed in extra-terrestrials among us and ESP, and was enamoured of the afterlife. Being off-kilter, he fit in perfectly with our mad mob.

DOUG THOMPSON: Skinner loved alien-spotting as much as he did the occult. I can't think how many evenings he dragged me up on some hill to search the skies for UFOs.

Brian had the usual rock deejay traits — high energy, a sharpish, cut-through voice, and a driving sound. He also had a love affair with phantasmagoria. Brian called his show *The Grooveyard*, and filled the air with ghouls, ghosts, vampires, mummies, and that whole grisly group who reek of the grave.

The Pres — so called because he was president of the CHUM Bug Club — shanghaied staff in the halls and dragged in outsiders, and turned them all — taped or live — into bony-fingered horrors, witch doctors, warlocks, and zombies. Featured were tarot cards, palm and teacup readings, seances, and exorcisms of studio demons. To be heard, the Top Forty, the Pick Hit, and the CHUMdinger had to fight through a sea of ectoplasm. It was said that if you liked exhumations you'd love *The Grooveyard*.

Dave Johnson left CHUM in late October '65, and Skinner took over the 7-to-10 p.m. slot. By now the Pres had perhaps the most wickedly wacky, overproduced show in radio. He was running amok, tying up studios to create ghastly and ghostly pun-based intros to songs and mad ways to set up the news and sports, and formulating gagging gags to fire in between commercials.

News spread of his nightly horror-filled happenings, and Brian was invited to create and perform a *Grooveyard* sketch live on CFTO teen dance show *High Time* with host Bob McAdorey. It began with Skinner, made up as Dracula, in a coffin. As his mad doctor, Eye-gore, I was hidden behind the casket. The sketch was to begin with eerie music and fog rolling in. One teensy problem: the little pea-brained special-effects people did not use the accepted dry-ice machine to create the fog. No, to save money, they instead sprayed a noxious pesticide. Somewhere in the cellars of CFTO is footage of two CHUM people coughing and gasping their guts out. When we ran off to vomit, they decided to switch the cameras back to the dance party. Ironically, the last line of our sketch had Brian saying, "Is that you, coffin?"

Meanwhile, back at CHUM, Slaight had heard one graveyard gag too many, and had Brian cut his monster mayhem back to a simple wild and weird party.

Brian, in his search for another megillah,

pretended his show was being broadcast from what he termed the bowels of the building. (And no, for a change, I won't touch that phrase.)

BRIAN SKINNER: Doug Thompson made it sound like I was giving my show from inside CHUM's air-conditioning duct. Went over quite well. So we stepped up to the real thing. Our FM tower was on CHUM's roof, so up I climbed with a microphone and binoculars. I reported traffic, weather, and some hot 'n' heavy goings-on in a nearby apartment. We stopped lots of traffic on Yonge. I was just about to ascend to the very top, when someone yelled "Stop." I did. And was informed that the antenna was hot and if I'd climbed up just one more foot, I would have been frizzled Brian Burger.

THE TWANG'S THE THANG: MOOSE LATRECK

The career of country & western performer Jimmy Dean was flagging and falling dangerously near the hole in the little house out back with the moon on the door. In a desperate move, he wrote a song during a flight to Nashville and recorded it. This flight of fancy turned out to be an immense crossover hit and revived Dean's status as a first-line star.

The song? "Big, Bad John." Now, as part of his new promotional tour, he was about to be interviewed by Moose Latreck on CHUM.

CHUM's chief operator, Fred Snyder, was plumb crazy about country music, or what he might call hurtin' tunes. "Man, this music's gotta moan," he'd cry, while accompanying Hank Williams on an imaginary guitar.

After years of lobbying Slaight to add a touch of fresh country air to CHUM, Al relented, comfortable with the station's ratings which were "as high as an elephant's eye," and programmed a half-hour of country & western each Friday at 10:30 p.m., with Fred as the host.

But, shucks, what would we call the program? *Fred's Favourites*? *Snyder's Riders*? *Boots and Seidels*? Besides, what kind of handle was "Fred" for a country boy? It should be "Slim" or "Tex" or . . . ? What to do? What to do . . . uh . . . podner?

Fred already had a bit of Saskatchewan chaff in his throat, aging and adding vocal character. He'd been affecting a touch of hayseed for years, so, together, the voice and sound would be accepted. But the name?

"How about Moose Latreck?" I said. The silence that followed could be likened to a funeral on Boot Hill. I applied my Sherlockian logic. Fred is a part-time artist and is not tall. Think of Toulouse Lautrec. In country lingo,

it's Latreck. And wouldn't it be CHUM-like to make the host sound big on the air? So, rhyming with Toulouse, came "Moose." And because of Fred's rough 'n' rural vocal prairie hangover, we'd add "Old" and "Big" before Moose much of the time. There, you see? Perfectly logical. Moose Latreck and I shook hands.

We went on to add signature phrases and a standard closing that kind of went like this: "This is the Ol' Moose, signin' off, and sayin' be good to your mama, and if drivin', stay off the moose juice, or you'll end up in the moosegow."

The Moose Latreck Show was popular with country fans, and even those who preferred

An elephant and a Moose moanin' a hurtin' tune

rock tuned in to hear Moose's over-the-top, homespun homilies when he introduced the hurtin' music he obviously loved.

Moose was added to our gang of bad on-air hombres and went out as his character with the CHUM Champions, playing basketball and raisin' Cain, if not money for good causes.

Jimmy Dean, you say? We warned him he was about to be Moose's first celebrity interview, and that Fred was tighter than a guitar string. Things started well, however, with Moose giving Dean a nice intro. Then, about 30 seconds into the discussion, Moose froze. Dried up. Sat staring at his guest.

After a pause of only a second or two,

233

It's a grin-grin situation as Moose raises funds — literally

Dean, spotting the problem, leaned into the mike and said, "Pardon me for interrupting you, old buddy, but I was just thinking about some of the questions you asked me when we were shootin' the breeze earlier. Would you like me just to talk a spell about the record and tour and my life?"

Dean settled back, and, with warmth and charm and an aw-shucks accent you could cut with a spur went on yakkin' and jawin' about life in country music. He was entertaining. He was terrific. He worked in compliments to CHUM on playing country music and subtly brought Moose back into the interview with well-placed questions. This was a touching example of a pro being generous and givin' a hand up to a tenderfoot in the business.

Afterward, Moose and everyone in the control room thanked Dean profusely, which he waved off in a friendly, modest manner. The station gave him a colourful Mexican vest, which he seemed to receive with honest appreciation.

Two weeks later, Jimmy Dean appeared on *The Tonight Show* wearing the Mexican vest. Johnny Carson commented favourably on it and asked where he bought it. Dean replied, "Actually, it was given to me by some good ol' boys at CHUM Radio in Toronto."

Jimmy Dean, y'all come back now, y'hear. Ya'll come back anytime.

THE ROMAN CANDLE: DUFF ROMAN

DUFF ROMAN: In the summer of '55, I was working in construction. I received a letter from CHAT in Medicine Hat, where I had taken an audition. It read, "We are prepared to take you on for training as an announcer. Please report in two weeks." When I told the construction boss why I was quitting, he said, "Are you crazy? What do you know about fixing radios?"

Duff grew up David Mostoway in a whistle stop just outside Swift Current, Saskatchewan. Graduating from high school at 16, he was already radio crazy. His father worked for the railway. Duff could get day passes, and he took auditions in Swift Current, Moose Jaw, Regina, Medicine Hat, North Battleford, Lloydminster, and Saskatoon. Once he got aboard CHAT in the Hat, he felt his dream had begun to come true.

ROMAN: If you lived in the Prairies, you could get radio signals from all over the place. A great memory is sitting with other rock jocks on top of the hill in Medicine Hat listening to the *All Night House Party* from San Bernardino, California, sponsored by Shaky's Pizza Parlour. Or the Southern stations like the famous WWVA, Wheeling, West Virginia.

One of their ads went like this, "Friends, put your hand on the radio as a point of contact. Then send $25 for your genuine plastic replica of our Lord and Saviour Jesus Christ . . . with a match scratcher on the back. That's Jesus Christ and the match scratcher, WWVA, Wheeling, West Virginia. Bless ya."

Once lit, Duff's career took off like a rocket. He moved from station to station, radio and TV, and in one seven-and-a-half-month period hopped, skipped, and jumped from a 250-watt station in Swift Current to CHED, Edmonton, and to the mighty CKEY in Toronto in November of '59. He was 21. Duff went on the air 9 p.m. to midnight on 'EY as Digger Dave Mostoway.

Owner Jack Kent Cooke hated the name Dave Mostoway. "Duff Roman" was chosen and, on the next shift, Duff Roman it was.

Many jocks across the country augmented their salaries by emceeing record hops. Often they'd have their own gear — turntables, amplifier, big speakers, and maybe a van. Like most things he did, Duff decided to go the whole nine yards. Duff teamed up with booking agent Ron Scribner to rent Dunn's Pavilion in Bala in the Muskokas. This was a particularly tricky manoeuvre because earlier rock concerts had attracted motorcycle gangs and trouble. Duff and Ron ran a first-class dance and a very tight ship. Still, he and Ron had to meet the town council each week to receive the go-ahead for the next week's dance. All went well, with Ron booking in Richie Knight and the Midnights, Little Caesar and the Consols, Sonny Thomas (soon to be called David Clayton-Thomas) and the fabulous Shays.

Duff had the power of publicity from the station behind him. He was now doing the *Rolling Home* show on 'EY. It seemed cool to the listeners that the smooth guy they'd just seen emceeing the dance was now talking to them as they returned from Bala, Lake Joseph, and Rousseau. (Talking, yes, and plugging next week's dance.)

PETER BRUCE (CHUM listener): In the summer months we'd all go to dances, especially in Bala. Duff Roman used to host. I remember

Duff Roman points the way to a fast-rising career

him at the pavilion wearing cool-looking suits . . . and the girls would swoon after him.

It might have simply sounded like a couple of young guys having fun, but they already had the moves of solid businessmen.

ROMAN: We took over or developed dances at Port Carling and a number of other towns. I made enough money to finance a small record company.

Duff had watched Canadian performers go to the States to be recorded, solid talent like Paul Anka and The Four Lads. He decided to give recording a shot. His company produced "Boom Boom," with the driving sound of David Clayton-Thomas, "Walk That Walk," "Take Me Back," "Out of the Sunshine," and, finally, "Brainwashed," with The Bossmen. Each record made the CHUM Chart, with "Brainwashed" outselling the Beatles locally.

ROMAN: CHUM not only listed those records, they played them. Even with me working at 'EY.

Duff produced records with a number of partners and under several labels, but all did well. Even though Duff was a popular personality and was bringing in extra revenue with his hops and recording, he kept one eye on CHUM.

ROMAN: It was obvious that CHUM was crazier than 'EY on the air — a sort of controlled mirthquake. The sense that I had was that CHUM was not just good, but relentless. They never gave us any breathing space. CHUM kept beating us up, with no detail too small to go after. That's why I really wanted to go over. I could see that we at CKEY were just marking time.

As Duff looked for an opening to join CHUM, we were watching him carefully, too. We thought that Duff sounded like he'd work well with the CHUM sound — and would bring his ambition, business sense, and knowledge of the recording scene with him.

Duff left CKEY to focus on his recording career. Slaight picked him up to cover shifts

236

on CHUM. This worked out perfectly because it left him plenty of time to promote his artists.

Meanwhile, it was unanimous that Duff fit the CHUM style, and he was offered a full-time on-air position. He accepted, began by working weekends, and soon had his own 1 to 4 p.m. shift. This was 1966.

CHUM's promotion people picked up on the obvious, and soon Duff could be seen on billboards wearing full Roman legion regalia and brandishing a sword. It was Duff as tough stuff. Duff was popular with the CHUM guys and often could be heard regaling them with tales of Jack Kent Cooke in a bang-on impersonation. Duff was a keeper.

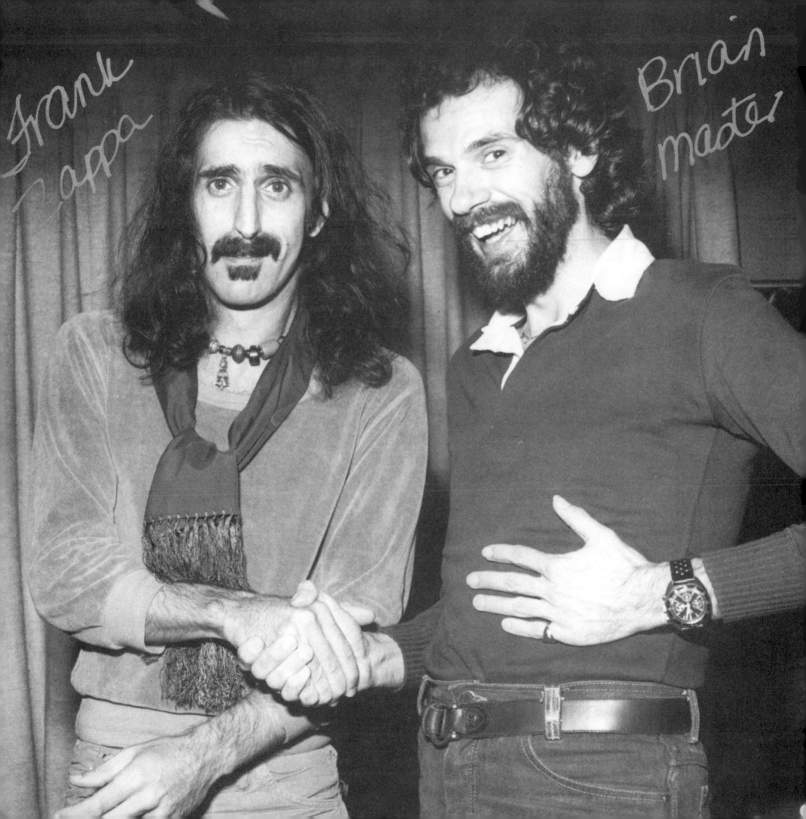

Frank Zappa

Brian Master

Chapter Sixteen
THE TIMES THEY ARE A-CHANGIN'

"PROBABLY JUST ANOTHER FAD": CHUM-FM

One can but speculate how benumbed the CHUM announcers were as they heard the Storz-style tape in '57 and were told to emulate it. Now Waters was about to take his staff into shock city again.

When Allan started and startled our meeting with the announcement that CHUM was going after an FM licence, many swore on a stack of CHUM Charts that the strains of "They're comin' to take me away, ha-ha, ho-ho . . ." were playing in the background.

FM? What FM? The only FM receivers extant rested and rusted in a few cars, plus those in the large, burled-oak cabinets of crazed, frothing-at-the-ear sound nuts. FM was the precious, petit purview of those audio fanatics who, early in life, had surely whoofed their tweeters or tweetered their woofs. Or both. And you know how that smarts. There were next to no FM receivers around to program to.

There was very little FM action on American (and Canadian) radio stations. In fact, it was rumoured that Westinghouse, a major player in American AM radio, had sold its string of FM signals for one dollar each! Ouch!

Despite nothing but negative indicators and dire predictions for FM's demise, Rogers (CHFI) promoted FM radios and Waters, as always, saw his plan quietly through.

After a beautifully crafted audio FM application by Larry Solway, voiced exquisitely by Richard Thomas, CHUM received its FM licence in 1963 and went on the air in 1964 at 104.5 on the dial. Perhaps not too strangely, there was no fireworks salute.

CHUM-FM, true to its promises for a licence, played mostly classical music, a little opera, a touch of jazz, and, on special occasions, plays ranging from Shakespeare to modern American and European avant-garde. By the blasted beard of the Bard, CHUM-FM fairly reeked of breeding, culture, and tone.

239

Shades of things to come — Frank Zappa and Brian Master

AL SLAIGHT: When CHUM-FM went on the air, it was already sold out commercially for a year. True, we weren't charging the moon, but this revenue was just above paying the bills. Typically, our FM announcer did a long, but not too demanding, shift. We were able to attract a competent staff of professionals, including Richard Thomas, Shef Frenkin, Don Denova, and a brilliant librarian, Rosemary Short.

CHUM-AM and CHUM-FM shared the same building. When you walked down the long hall between the two operations, you had rock on one side and Bach on the other. And for some years to come.

With the sprinkling of FM receivers out there, this was true one-on-one radio: one commercial, one listener.

What was the result of all the effort from the first movement to the coda of our labours? CHUM-FM pretty well locked up an audience of at least a subway-carful of people. (Stats available to those who should get a life.)

In ad-agency argot, CHUM-FM owned — *owned!* — vertical markets of librarians, grammarians, vegetarians, and octogenarians. Whoopee!

From a profit standpoint, it was agreed FM radio promised the golden goodies of marrying a rich widow (the woman has needs!)

— only to find yourself hitched to a faithless frail who steals your wallet, pinches your poke, yanks your shank, and slips off into the night mixing your metaphors and squeezing you dry.

FM's initials had many interpretations. Techies, and others with anodes in their thingmus, insisted FM meant "frequency modulation." (Now, *that* clears it up.) Station owners secretly thought FM stood for "foolish man," "fritterin' money," or "effin' maniac." Once more, a sales-savvy Waters and his team bucked and beat the odds. But only just.

MUCH SLAIGHTER: THE CHIEF MOVES ON

By May 1966, Al Slaight had pretty well accomplished it all. He was now vice-president and general manager of CHUM. Al had done Waters proud, spearheading a relentless pace that drove the ratings up and ever up. Bash of the year was the 42.5 percent party hosted by Al. (Our long-time goal had been 40 percent of the listeners in Toronto.)

CHUM had been showered with honours and industry awards. The station was making money and there was beer in the fridge.

He continued to hound us all, ever cautioning against complacency or smugness, right up until that June day in 1966 when he quit. You're surprised? We were shocked. Slaight was the last person we thought would leave CHUM.

Al had seen a potential opportunity in England with the pirate stations. There was no commercial broadcasting, per se, over 'ome, but there was rumour there could be. Rock 'n' roll and pop programming was broadcast only from illegal pirate ships, anchored offshore.

Al and his partner, Terry Bates, had a chance to work with Radio Caroline, a pirate station named after Caroline Kennedy.

The industry threw a farewell party for Al, with people attending from many stations, ad agencies, and other allied industries, like radio reps. Peopled by many of Toronto's zanies, it really took off.

Garry Ferrier wrote and recorded a terrific comedy piece that had Slaight taking over Buckingham Palace as a radio station. Queen Elizabeth was a disc jockey talking to Slaight on the phone saying, "But Al, I *am* socking in the hits!"

At the fete's conclusion, as Al stood there in a dustman's outfit, soaking wet (the jocks had been busy), he made a small speech of thanks. He concluded by saying that his only regret was that his creative people didn't get enough credit or financial rewards. Hmm. Wonder if he still feels the same.

THE REAL SKINNY: ALLAN WATERS

AUTHOR: Slaight, is it true that Allan Waters is a risk-taker?

SLAIGHT: It must be. He hired you and me.

The portion of the CHUM tale that kicked off with rock 'n' roll and brought us up to the late '60s begins and ends with Allan Waters. As certain key members of the team who were prominent during those explosive-success years left the organization, it became evident that no one was indispensable — no matter how great his or her contribution — except Waters himself. (He'd demur and deny this, but, happily, he's wrong.) The '60s had been fads 'n' furious. By '67, every department was in excellent shape, and the station was deep in talent and skills. On top of that, there was enormous momentum. CHUM bopped. Ratings rode high on the horse. Sales were singing. In addition to CHUM-AM and CHUM-FM, CHUM Limited wholly owned CFRA and CFMO Ottawa, had a 50-percent interest in CKPT Peterborough and CJCH Halifax, and had a one-third interest in CKVR TV Barrie.

So what about this Waters person anyway? We know he played squash and liked to walk to work. He and his wife Marjorie have lived in the same rather modest home for about

40 years. As parents, they stressed to their children the message that they were nothing special and must never put on airs. That message was well taught. And lived.

But as this book is not about the life of a saint, Allan's friends, employees, business acquaintances, and family were invited to let it all hang out about "what Allan Waters is really like." Here, for the first time, we tell all. I'll lead off.

Allan Waters is known to be conservative. And he is. Also to be low-keyed. And he is. But . . . just as you have him pigeonholed as some downright, upright, forthright, foursquare square, he'll make a leap of faith and take a risk that'll leave you breathless.

SAM SNIDERMAN: I never heard anyone say anything against Allan Waters. Actually, he always stayed in the background, out of the limelight.

Joyce Davidson, Allan Waters, and director Daryl Duke plan *On the Scene* telecast from (and about) CHUM

SHERYL WATERS BOURNE: Once Dad came home very excited. He had a new record by Chubby Checker. He taught us to do the Twist. But when he twisted, his hips stayed rigid and his whole body moved. This was hard to do. [Author: Now we know why he didn't dance much at CHUM Christmas parties.]

FRED SHERRATT: Allan is what his reputation is — a man of integrity. He can be tough, but he's fair and honest — qualities he demands from those who work for him.

FRANK BUCKLEY (of Buckley's Cough Syrup fame): I always think about Waters and CHUM in relationship to ourselves. In both instances, we had a unique product. Like Buckley's, when Allan introduced rock music to Toronto, many people gagged on it. But he stuck by his product, and, again like Buckley's, it sure worked.

JIM WATERS: Dad arranged fourth-row tickets for my sister and me to see Elvis in '57. Sheryl claims it was awesome and that her heart went pit-a-pat. Unfortunately, on one of the rare occasions where we received preferential treatment, I missed the concert. Mom says I fell asleep.

AL BOLISKA (in an earlier interview): When I'm asked what Allan Waters is really like, I answer, "He really likes business, water-skiing, and tutti-frutti ice cream."

SLAIGHT: Waters was great. We had a sensational relationship. He left us alone to do our thing. And he was cheery and supportive. I have nothing but good things to say about him.

MARGE WATERS: When Allan comes home from work, he often sits around in his underwear shirt. [Author: Now we're getting to the bare truth.]

RON WATERS: It's been said many times. One of Dad's key strengths was to hire the best people and let them do their job. We still do that today.

MARGE WATERS: Allan does not like to be told he's wrong. If you can prove you're right, he'll accept it and take appropriate action. But he won't like it much.

MOSES ZNAIMER (City-TV's co-founder, president, and executive producer): Allan likes to say that he's not creative. He means it sincerely. I smile when he says it, because, of course, he's built this astonishing company.

And he only could have done that because he *is* creative. But in a way that common language doesn't normally describe. Common language says that if you're daubing paint on a canvas, you're a creative person, but if you're running a business, you're not. Creative is not *what* you're doing, it's how you're *doing* it. Just because you're slapping images on celluloid, it doesn't make you creative. We've seen a lot of sliced salami in the movies, right? Equally, just because you are a business person doesn't make you not creative. Innovation is CHUM's (and City's) contribution to the scene. I don't believe a non-creative guy can make a creative company. Including the decent and genuinely self-effacing Allan Waters.

HONEST ED MIRVISH: One ingredient in running a successful business is foresight, or the ability to anticipate trends. Now, if you can serve the public by riding those trends with products or services, you can end up a winner. My impression of Allan Waters is that he's very good at that.

Perhaps the following incident will shine more light on the Super Chief.

Allan Slaight was away. I was summoned to Allan Waters's office: a rare occurrence (he always came to you). Waters, sitting rather uncomfortably behind his desk, motioned me towards a chair to sit. Considering my activities, I was wondering what I'd done and how long I would have my job.

Judging from Waters's mien, however, he didn't seem about to fire me. Instead, he asked me how the station was going from a promotional perspective. I reckoned it was going okey-dokey. He then congratulated me on the newest piece of promotion to hit the airwaves. I blushed prettily, and thanked him. There was an awkward pause. But Waters kept smiling. I noticed that his hand had drifted towards a drawer in his desk. He opened it. He brought forth not the .44 magnum my fevered imagination had conjured up but, rather, an early CHUM Chart, which I could see sported the cat, "Clementine," on the

Above: Waters and George Jones celebrate CHUM's increase to 50,000 watts; Right: Waters and Gordon Lightfoot

Mr. Allan Waters

Gordon Lightfoot

Gordon Lightfoot

cover. Before I could babble out an abject apology for having changed the cat — now obviously his *favourite* cat — to a kangaroo, Waters pulled out a bottle of marbles. "He's going to tell me I've lost my marbles," I panicked, and was about to lurch to my feet, when he said softly, "I was involved only peripherally in our early promotions. The CHUM Chart for one."

I was desperately forming phrases in my mind to the effect that the CHUM Chart was, indeed, a dynamite promotion device, when he continued: "At one time we put a bottle of marbles in the window and asked listeners to count them. Closest answer won a prize." I was nonplussed. What did he want to hear? Gambling everything, I said, "You want me to rerun 'count the marbles in the jar' . . . and . . ."

"No, no," he said, sensing my rising anxiety, "not those promotions — but *like* them, *similar* to them, the *spirit* of them." He stood. The discussion was over. His secretary, Lee, loomed in the doorway, making little pitbull noises, and I was ushered out.

This interview happened again, the following year. This time, I related it to Slaight, who assured me he would not have stood for it. Sure. Nothing of this scenario was ever mentioned again. But several years later, as Waters, Slaight, and I arrived at the CNE for first inspection of the Satellite Station, there, on top of the trailer, stood a giant, clear plastic container holding ping-pong balls that bounced and blew in the air. Below it sat a sign that asked viewers to count the ping-pong balls and win a wizard prize.

Waters, surprised, beamed. Slaight pulled me aside and whispered, "Farrell, you are a suck."

"You bet," I replied and oiled my bod over to stand beside Waters. And as the ping-pong balls perked and danced merrily, Allan Waters and I beamed together.

THE SECOND TSUNAMI: UNDERGROUND ROCK

Hush. Just listen. Whispers, chimerical shadows of things to come.

Underground rock. When you go to San Francisco, be sure to wear some flowers in your hair. The Doors. Woodstock. Psychedelic soul. *Hair. Sgt. Pepper's Lonely Hearts Club Band.* Diana Ross to leave the Supremes. Yoko Ono. The Rolling Stones launch their own record label. "Let It Be" — The Beatles' final top-10 entry as a group. Janis Joplin overdoses. George Harrison's concert for Bangladesh. Kent State. Make love, not war. Jim Morrison dead in Paris. *Jesus*

Christ Superstar. Progressive Rock.

The pace of change accelerated during the 20th century. Change picked up speed, doubled, tripled, quadrupled its velocity, and raged towards the new millennium, reckless, breakneck, and with some mad god at the wheel.

The first tsunami that was Top Forty music was pretty well spent by '66 or '67. As it very slowly ebbed, it would leave a legacy of AM rockers, transistor radios, sock hops, going steady, deejays, 45s, platters, albums, charts, clothes, cherry Cokes, record requests, and dedications. Potential collectors, take note.

Top Forty music would continue to endure for some years, but in an ever-diminishing capacity. There was a huge vested interest in its continuance, and recording companies, artists, and (mainly) AM radio stations fought for its survival. Already there were convincing indicators that its place would be taken by a new, trillion-ton tidal wave — a concerned, agitated kind of music. Its protracted birth from San Francisco was heralded not by a primal scream, but rather a relieved sigh of some force released. Unleashed. Finally free, man. Since we name newborns, it was called Underground Rock.

You may wonder how anyone can make a claim that Top Forty music peaked about '66 or '67 when thumpin', great, high-quality hits kept making and topping the charts? If Top Forty was fizzling, how do we explain, even as John Lennon was saying "The Beatles are probably bigger than Jesus" . . .

1966. "Good Vibrations." "You Can't Hurry Love." "When a Man Loves a Woman." "Summer in the City."

Or these babies from 1967 . . . "Light My Fire." "Daydream Believer." "A Whiter Shade of Pale."

Or from the charts of '68 . . . "Hey, Jude." "I Heard It Through the Grapevine." "This Guy's in Love with You."

1969 provided air time for these pop hits . . . "Proud Mary." "Bad Moon Risin'." "Wichita Lineman."

And, all through the '70s, as rock jocks love to say, those hits just kept on comin'! "My Sweet Lord," "Gypsies, Tramps and Thieves," "American Pie," "Tie a Yellow Ribbon Round the Old Oak Tree," "Bad, Bad Leroy Brown," "The Way We Were," "Benny and the Jets," "Feelings," "I Write the Songs," "You Light Up My Life," "Don't It Make My Brown Eyes Blue," "Y.M.C.A.," and "I'll Never Love This Way Again."

Still, into the '80s and '90s — and beyond — Top Forty-type tunes would be churned out. Many stations — more and more AM ones only — continued to play this music — and prosper. So why all this fuss about change? Because underground rock, joined at the hip with changes in social attitudes and behaviour, was coming on strong — much more powerfully than those clinging to the status quo of Top Forty.

After a period of adjustment, another generation of outstanding personnel would put their stamp on CHUM 1050 as part of an ongoing renewal process.

CHUM would go on, playing out its hand with upbeat on-air personalities, inventive contests, great stunts, and fun. The formula that Allan Waters initiated in 1957 would continue to be viable and successfully draw audiences for many years. However, the opportunities that Waters was so eagle-eyed at sussing out and exploiting would focus more and more on television. And FM.

This wave, this culture would grow — buoyed by the music of young people. Sides would be chosen. Either you smoked dope or you didn't.

Its monumental shadow would eclipse Top Forty music and its trappings long before it picked up express-train speed and thundered down on our senses and perceptions.

Underground music would become accepted, almost gentrified as progressive rock. This enigmatic study in contrasts — an eclectic, fierce, cooler, impassioned, indifferent, caring, as often under-rehearsed as over-produced phenomenon — disdained and deplored Top Forty's comfy AM residence. AM was too restraining, too unhip. Even hip was unhip. Besides, in the new vernacular, the AM sound . . . sucked. Progressive rock would choose FM. Or, contrariwise, FM would pal up to this new kid on the rock. Ultimately, it was the sound-conscious listeners who called the shots. They preferred — *demanded* — the better fidelity, the higher-quality sound of FM.

This new tsunami — this second tidal wave titled progressive rock — would become mainstream. And CHUM-FM would wallow in it.

DO WE HAVE ANY BUSINESS IN FM? SNEAK PREVIEW

May 27, 1957, was considered a day of infamy by people who could barely remember Pearl Harbor. (The attack was applauded by those who hated Hawaiian guitar music.) As any musicologist with a Ph.D. in backbeat will tell you, it was the day Allan Waters brought rock to a tepid Toronto.

Not satisfied with owning one date, Allan decided to put his stamp on another: July 2, 1968. On this cool, man, cool day, CHUM traded its classical conductor's baton for a

long-stemmed flower. CHUM-FM became Toronto's first free-form, progressive, underground music station.

Father Tom Donahue would have approved of CHUM's switch from César Franck to freaky-feely music as CHUM-FM moved PDQ into AOR (album-oriented rock). CHUM-FM had made the jump from long-hair to long hair. Music was one thing, but what about the people?

The CHUM-FM personality-to-be was already making its presence felt in the form of Peter Griffin. In his mind, Pete was a walking arsenal. He imagined himself decked out in explosives like a fanatic prepared for martyrdom. Except that Griffin didn't blow himself up — it was *you* he hungered to splatter on the ceiling.

Commando-like, Pete would sneak down the main hall, alert for enemies. He'd open every office door and toss in hand grenades. He'd wait for his own *ka-boom* before he closed the door and moved on. If he met you, he'd shove a stick of dynamite down your pants or in your blouse, light it, and duck into the nearest doorway until you ka-boomed. When his backpack of explosives ran out, he'd fire his machine guns, throw his knives, and head towards his studios where he lost his serious mien and got silly on air.

Another host of Christmas Future was David Haydu, better known as Geets Romo. This terrible twosome personified CHUM-FM in the double-handed guise of Pete 'n' Geets.

David was, if possible, even further out than Pete. He took shifts on weekends as disc jockey Phil Inn. He told audiences his father's name was Ramada.

Terrific with dialects, he balanced the lunacy of Griffin as Hungarian Beans Rontosh, McTavish McRono, Sean O'Rono, and gave traffic reports as Warren Down. Pete and David were joined by fellow free-formers, including Walter Soles, David Pritchard, and Tim Thomas.

CHUM-FM was soon to be a dog's breakfast of quirky commentary, undisciplined disc choices, devil-may-care quips, personal prejudices, we-know-better-than-you attitudes, and listener-catch-up challenges.

And that was the music. The jocks . . . ! CHUM-FM (Freaky Music) was just learning to say "Zappa" without exhaling all the good smoke.

As for CHUM-AM's continuing powerhouse performance, that is another story. Why, it might even end up as an all-sports station. Ah, ha! Ah, hoo! Let's get serious. An all-sports station? Roll me another one.

WAY TO GO, T.O.: GROWTH, GIRTH, AND MIRTH

CHUM and Toronto journeyed hand-in-hand through the late '40s, '50s, and '60s. Growth matched growth. Maturity matched maturity. Now they could let go and seek separate destinies.

Toronto, a city that had doted on dull and made pursed-mouth conservatism an art form, always had fiery, red-eyed factions that fought change or innovation. They fought against the subway in the fifties, fought crosswalks, fought chlorination, fought the design of the new City Hall, and made a stand worthy of the Greeks at Thermopylae against the Moore sculpture in Nathan Phillips Square. However, heads — saner or not — usually prevailed. (One might wish Torontonians had railed with equal zeal against the early parking meters in '54 or the opening of the first phase of the Gardiner Expressway in '58.)

As Toronto tested forbidden waters by enjoying a full weekend, service stations tested the Sunday closing laws and Sunday sports became legal. Sunday became fun-day in Toronto. Some declared it a miracle. With the O'Keefe Centre opening its doors in 1959 to a glittering *Camelot*, Torontonians began to go out more. And Honest Ed Mirvish bestowed yet one more gift to Toronto with a refurbished Royal Alexandra Theatre in 1963. Two tickets, front and centre, please.

Toronto had begun to develop a palate. Shopping baskets shouted out colours and odours — deep-green and devil-red peppers, eager herbs, orange or pale pungent cheeses, and the mother smell of fresh-baked baguettes. Toronto went to market. Restaurants sprang up like mushrooms for tonight's sauce. Menus spoke French, Italian, and oriental tongues. And it became quite all right to ask, "What's in this?" or "What does that mean?" The city pulled a chair up to the groaning board and tucked in with gusto.

CHUM, in 1967, was standing on its hind legs, pawing the air, and eager to charge. The city had taken down its weather-beaten "Toronto the Good" sign and replaced it with a modern, electronic beauty that read, "Toronto, the *Damn* Good." Way to go, T.O.

AFTERWORD

TIES THAT BIND: COMING HOME TO CHUM

Today, when I visit CHUM, I check with reception like every other guest and wait to be ushered in for my appointment. Recently, as I sat waiting, my eyelids drooped, and I slipped into a delicious reverie.

In my dream-like state, I thought I could hear Boliska, gleefully hitting Just Plain George with the punchline of a World's Worst Joke. Or was it Jungle Jay on "Hello Toronto," conniving to convince a four-star hotel chef to prepare chicken cacciatore with the feathers on?

Johnson's infectious laugh seemed to echo in the halls as Deschamps kidded him unmercifully. Duff's baritone contrasted with ghostly moaning from Skinner's *Grooveyard*. A kaleidoscope of blurred images included noses pressed against the glass on Yonge Street, peering into the newsroom, much to the discomfort of Kirck. A whistling sound and a splat! Dickens had just fired a sandwich across the newsroom, as Drylie barked and Woollings got off a zinger. In the studio, Solway's snorts meant he'd blown off yet another listener on *Speak Your Mind*.

Was that Millie's rich laugh? Ferrier had gone into a comedy bit as Scoob gave McAdorey the gears. And I could swear I heard Moose announcing that Eddy's was open. In the night, Laine introduced himself to the world. The world reciprocated.

An audible sigh escaped the lips of Allan Waters as he learned of yet another dodgy promotion being unleashed on an unsuspecting public. Slaight could be heard clearly exhorting the jocks to "Sock in the hits!"

At the back of the Satellite Station, Spragge was concocting a potent Honey Dew Driver as Darow warmed up his talented tonsils and led the Chummingbirds in a drum-thumping folk song. J.J. Richards covered the event, growling his commentary while checking out the pulchritude of the CHUM Chicks at the same time.

All the while, the FM gang was doing something totally indescribable. Griffin's "Pows!" suggested he'd just blown up the traffic department.

Listener sounds pulsed in this mist of memory. Calls and shouts and cheers as record stars passed in glittering array — everyone from Elvis to the Beatles — and their sweet salute swept across a panorama of nostalgia.

A voice roused me from my daydreaming. "Excuse me, sir." The woman waiting beside me was speaking.

"What's that?" I mumbled, struggling to focus my eyes.

"I didn't want to disturb you," she said, "but you were smiling and humming some sort of CHUM jingle."

"I was?" Amazed.

"You certainly were." A pause. "Tell me, are you connected with CHUM?"

I hesitated only a heartbeat. "Connected?"

I said. "Yes, you can say I'm connected to CHUM. Indeed I am."

TWO WORTHIES HAVE THE LAST WORD

ALLAN WATERS: Many people have said to me over the years that I've been lucky. I don't believe in luck. You make your own breaks.

I concentrate on getting into the right place at the right time — and then going after the opportunity.

Incidentally, I also believe the whole process should be fun.

GARRY FERRIER: You know, although I wrote some pretty demanding shows in Hollywood, I never worked as damned hard as I did earlier at CHUM.

But — looking back — it sure was a lot of laughs, wasn't it, man?

ACKNOWLEDGEMENTS

Perhaps my most vivid memory of writing this book is the willing, often eager, assistance I received from so many people. (Apologies in advance to those I miss.)

Thanks to Duff Roman at CHUM, who set a high and ongoing standard of support, opened doors, and found a distinguished publisher; to old friend Bob Laine who contributed a bushel basketful of missing bits and helped keep me on track while he razzed me mercilessly about my days at CHUM; to the committed, professional Stoddart editorial staff, Don Bastian, Sue Sumeraj, and Elizabeth d'Anjou, who gave the book structure and miraculously created the impression that I can form cogent sentences and even spell; to book designer Bill Douglas at The Bang, whose design caught and reflected the spirit of CHUM; to the photographers — with a special click of the shutter to Neil Newton who created art out of our antics; to a very pleasant Marjorie Waters, and to Sheryl, Ron, and Jim, all of whom talked about Allan with such respect and affection; to (Honest) Ed Mirvish, Sam (The Record Man) Sniderman, and Frank ("it tastes awful") Buckley for their matchless marketing savvy and input — please stay young forever; to Moses Znaimer, who has the disconcerting habit of listening intently to a question, reflecting, and conjuring a unique (and quotable) insight; to Doug Thompson and David Haydu, who returned to CHUM to help The Team score; to Brad Jones, who acted as a cheerleader for the project from the first day I met him at CHUM; to Richard Maxwell and Shirley Hart; and to the CHUM listeners I encountered across Ontario. Hey, we did it!

Special thanks for interviews, stories, and information from ex-CHUMmies: Wes Armstrong, Warren Cosford, Claude Deschamps, Peter Dickens, Garry Ferrier, Bob Hall, Peggy Keenan Hodgins (my West Coast pal), George Jones, Harvey Kirck, Johnny Lombardi, Bob Magee, Bob McAdorey, Wilf McIlveen, Mary McInnes, Millie Moriak, Peter Nordheimer, J.J. Richards, Fred Sherratt, Brian Skinner, Allan Slaight, Fred Snyder, Larry Solway, John Spragge, Barb Sterino, Phil Stone, Madeline Thompson, and Denis Woollings.

I also owe a debt to CHUM associates and friends for their contributions: Lorna Anderson, Pierre Berton, Sheila Boliska, Don Buckley, Terry Cox, Gary Dickens, Celeste Fairchild, Mike Filey, Ron Hall, Catherine Myhowich, Kevin Nelson, Kal Raudoja, Harold Shields, Kori Skinner, Ellen Wheatley, Bill Williams, and, yes, Dave Marsden.

Most of all, love and gratitude to my wife Caroline Luce. She badgered me into writing this book and saw me through my black-dog days. Now she wants me to write another book. Yikes!

And thanks to you, Allan Waters. And CHUM. And radio. Bless ya.

INDEX

PHOTO SOURCES

Every reasonable effort has been made to obtain reprint permissions. The publisher will gladly receive any information that will help rectify, in subsequent editions, any inadvertent errors or omissions.

Alex Gray Photo Services: 32, 85, 138, 169, 236
Anderson and Cole: 80, 155
Bic Photography: 238
Camera 35 Prod. Ltd.: 38, 48, 111, 120, 126, 133, 208
Christopher D. O'Brian Photography: 91
CHUM archives: 21, 58, 64, 68, 84, 89, 92, 106, 114, 141, 178, 181, 182, 184, 202, 220, 229, 249
Farrell family archives: 55, 70, 217
Federal Newsphotos of Canada: 26, 72
Gerald Campbell: 150
Gilbert A. Milne & Co. Limited: 162
Hall family archives: 16

Herb Nott & Co. Ltd.: 71, 168
John Beecher: 170
John McGinnis: 53
Jones & Morris: 13
Michael Burns Photography Ltd.: 22, 60, 63
Neil Newton Photography: x–xi, 2, 18, 20, 37, 42, 45, 52, 56, 66, 74, 77, 79, 81, 82, 86, 94, 96, 108, 116, 119, 123, 129, 134, 137, 140, 143, 144, 147, 151, 156, 159, 173, 180, 183, 188, 198, 200, 222, 228, 233, 242, 244
Nordheimer family archives: 122, 135
Plum Studios Inc.: 245
Rick Shaban Promotions: 165
Roman family archives: 235
Turofsky (Alexander Studio): 232
Waters family archives: 11, 14, 35, 177, 190, 204
William Dunn: 148
Wim Vander Kooy: 224